14th & 2nd

Charlie Cifarelli

Copyright © 2021 Charlie Cifarelli

All rights reserved.

ISBN: 9798753791825

Parts of this manuscript have been left in colloquial or informal language in order to preserve the humanity and authenticity of the author's voice. Some names have been changed to protect privacy and identity.

DEDICATION

To Jenn. This journey could not have been possible without you. Thank you for always believing in me and thank you for your tireless efforts and for your encouragement and support.

14th & 2nd

ACKNOWLEDGMENT

I couldn't possibly acknowledge everyone by name who helped save my life. Thank you for believing in me when I could not believe in myself. To my guardian angel at the Jamaica Train Station platform – you arrived at the right time.

1. VIRAL

"August 13, 2012 is a perfect Manhattan Day. The weather is 84 degrees with 44% humidity—practically a miracle for August in New York. In the East Village, taxis, buses and cars grind back and forth along Houston Street filled with people, while plenty of others take advantage of the weather to walk to Alphabet City instead of taking the subway. People walk their dogs through Stuyvesant Park or sit on the long row of benches under the trees and eat hot dogs and pizza slices. 14th Street has been clearing off some of its former grime, and new restaurants are popping up every month. Still, old holdouts like KFC on the corner of 14th & 2nd see plenty of people who haven't fallen prey to the ongoing gentrification.

In Lincoln, Nebraska, a guy is still thinking about a recent phone call with his business consultant.

"Charlie," the consultant says, "One day, you better care about something more than you care about making money, or it'll kill ya."

What does this consultant know about him anyway? He sees the cushy seat on the board of a company that bought his start-up trash hauling business. He sees the gold Rolex that could make a down payment on a nice house. He sees the new Mercedes Benz sedan. He sees what he thinks is a guy with all the freedom in the world, a guy with no attachments. Someone who can come and go as he pleases.

But appearances can be deceiving. This guy is not your average Cornhusker. He's from New York. He's worked for the Department of Corrections. He's been around the block, a couple of times, even been knocked around the block. Now, though, he's got his days locked into a smooth routine. The company does most of its work in the morning, and with the help of multiple pots of coffee, he navigates the challenges of managing one hundred twenty employees and thousands of customers, but those demands dwindle by the afternoon.

The trucks make it back from their routes and are safely parked in the shop. By three in the afternoon in Lincoln on August 13, 2012, he has made it through another day without any accidents or injuries or breakdowns in the fleet. He switches to going through the recycling and trash bids and answering related correspondence. When that's finished, he, like the other company heads, spends the afternoon staying busy by trying to look busy. Because this man with the nice car and the gold Rolex is from New York, (even though he left the city in his twenties, and even though New York knocked him for a loop) New York has never, ever, left his soul and so, every day, part of his afternoon routine includes reading all the news he can from New York.

In the East Village, just after four in the afternoon, a man has a seizure. Lech Stankiewicz is hanging out in front of the KFC on the corner of 14th & 2nd, sitting cross-legged with his backpack in front of him, looking for a few extra bucks from passersby. He is a twenty-nine-year-old émigré from Poland but has been in New York long enough—about six years—to see his American story dreams crumble a few times over. He is now homeless. He's hung around the area enough to be known by locals as *Polack*, and he's never without his trusty companion, Star, a Pit Bull mix barely a year old.

With his legs still folded in front of him, Lech lies on his back, with his head, still in its newsboy cap, leaned back over the edge of the city curb. Star, his faithful companion, is panicking. Star's barks are short alarms—not guttural threats of impending attack. She was dumped in a high-kill shelter when she was a puppy, but in one of those feel-good-for-a-minute stories, she'd been rescued by Collide, a group pairing shelter dogs with homeless people. Star was paired with Lech, and for almost a year, she and Lech roved together through the East Village, getting care from Collide's home base at a nearby church. Now, Star's person is down on the ground, and people are beginning to circle him. People are trying to assist the man with the seizure, but they are worried about traffic hitting him, especially if his body convulses enough to throw him into the street.

Within minutes, the first two police officers arrive to cordon off traffic. Traffic has come to a standstill, and a stopped bus marks the perimeter of the scene on the street. The two police officers stand beside the bus, facing Star and Lech, their postures twitchy and uncertain. Star is now barking at anyone who comes close, trying to maintain a perimeter around her person. She's barking, but her tail is wagging. She's not trying to attack anyone, but when her back is turned, a woman tries to help Lech, and Star senses the intrusion. She runs back toward the woman, nips at her, but then immediately returns to Lech's side.

While Star's back was turned, one of the two police officers approached Lech. His gun is drawn. A man shouts, "The dog is growling! Be careful!"

Star reacts to the incursion by running at the officer to chase him back, just like she did the woman. This time is different though: The cop shoots Star, once in the face. She screeches—the way a dog might briefly screech when her paw or tail gets stepped on or caught, only worse. Star's body is distorted, her head turned back toward her tail. She's shaking and whimpering. She flips back, and the officer steps backward, though his gun is stowed in its holster. The second officer sprays Star with mace.

Bystanders scream various comments and questions at the officers:

"Why?"

"He killed the doggie!"

"Why are you shooting him? Why are you shooting a dog?"

An older woman steps toward the cops to admonish them, and they try to push her away. Another woman takes a photo from the sidelines and yells at the officer. The second cop radioed something in, but neither officer moves toward Lech. Nearly twenty-five officers are soon on the scene, and one detective ropes off the area. While onlookers take notes, not one of the officers comes to the aid of Lech or checks on Star. Bystanders are in shock, crying and shouting.

A Bay Ridge resident named Johnny, who is visiting the New York Eye and Ear Infirmary across the street, captures ten minutes of the scene on his phone camera. Chef and author Eddie Huang, who owns the famous Baohaus two doors down, takes still photographs and posts them to his Instagram and Twitter feeds. At 5:25 Eastern Time, *HuffPost* tweets to Huang to ask permission to include his photo in their coverage of the shooting. By 6:22 they reply with another tweet saying the post is up on their website. By 7:45, outlets such as *Gothamist* are reporting on the shooting as well.

Star's story goes viral.

The former New Yorker in Nebraska has done a good job cleaning himself up. On some days, he barely registers the gnawing ache inside him. The ache has been there so long he doesn't think about its source. He marks the pain, then buries it further into his subconscious, an automatic reflex as natural as breathing and deeply imbedded into his behaviors. He turns on his computer and clicks on the first of his New York news outlets and comes across the first headline:

Police Shoot and Kill Homeless Man's Dog. Warning: Graphic video.

I watch that video I don't know how many times. I can't get over it. It is clear Star is protecting her person. I play back and watch in slow motion the moment she gets shot—she hasn't jumped up to bite the officer. She's close to him, but she seems to be solely attempting to chase him away, not bite him. I find myself yelling along with the bystanders in the video as I shout at my computer screen in a white knuckled, bubbling rage, "What the fuck are these cops thinking? How could they do this?" I ask just quiet enough to keep my employees outside my office door from hearing.

I'm not looking at some sick underground horror video. This is a video for public viewing, and it depicts a dog getting shot in the face on a busy New York City Street on a summer day.

14th & 2nd

I find another article in the *New York Daily News*. There is a photo of Lech being lifted onto a gurney by two EMTs. He looks like a sheep about to be sheered. No, I take that back – the medics carry him like he is trash – human garbage to be avoided at all costs and quickly removed from sight.

Lech and the shooting officer were both taken to Bellevue Hospital for what were described as minor injuries. Really? The shooting officer suffered minor injuries? Two eyewitnesses report to the media that one of the officers kicked Lech. Possibly they didn't believe he was having a seizure and were trying to rouse him out of what they thought to be a drunken or drug-induced stupor. If they did kick him, no wonder Star lunged. Still, she wasn't trying to attack, only chase.

Now, this dog, still a pup, is dead. Is this what I'm missing in New York? This is the New York so deeply embedded into my identity? A strange thought flashes through me: How the fuck have I gotten myself into this? There's nothing I can do, even if the distance from Nebraska to Manhattan's Lower East Side was a non-issue. This poor man probably has no idea his companion is now dead, or perhaps he is just waking up to that fact now.

My head hurts.

I watch the video again. Star is barely knee-high to the officer who shoots her. She appears to weigh under fifty pounds. I see the second officer who cowardly maces Star in the face well after she's down, and it makes me shake my head in total disgust. New York's finest. Behavior like this was not my experience with them, and believe me, I encountered the NYPD in my time.

That gnawing ache resurfaces. I look at my Rolex, my nice desk, my great clothes and my hi-tech Mercedes car key. For the first time, the gnawing is no longer some nebulous, shadowy form. My internal strife, instead, begins to take shape and materialize into something much larger than myself.

2 THE FIRST BARK

Ringo. I don't mean the drummer for the Beatles; I mean the gigantic black and light tan German Shepherd puppy my parents let me pick out at the pet store in 1968. I was three years old—not really in a position to name such a big dog all myself, but I chose him over his all-white sister. Ringo, it turned out, was an apt name. He marked the rhythms of our life and kept me steady through my childhood.

We took Ringo and headed, in my dad's cool convertible Chevy Impala SS, back to our apartment in Queens. He'd installed a custom exhaust so people could hear his car coming from over a block away. Feeling the wind blowing in our hair as we drove through the city while looking at my parents in the front seat and having Ringo with me in the back, I imagined all of life would be as great a ride.

Ringo was at my side nearly every moment of my childhood. He cuddled next to me as we watched *Lassie* and *Rin Tin Tin* as well as *The Adventures of Superman* and *The Abbott & Costello Show*—all shows were about sidekicks. Then we watched a brand-new show called *Mister Rogers' Neighborhood*, while my head filled with big questions about the world. I wondered how the world ticked, how things worked and even what it meant to be President of the United States. Don't all three- and four-year-old children wonder about such things?

I sat with Ringo and ran my fingers through his double coat, which set loose a snowstorm-flurry of shed fur. Ringo also watched every day from our second-floor window as I played with my friend Kenny, who lived down the hall with his mom and his uncle. If Kenny and I moved out of sight from Ringo in that sentry window, he would bark, which alerted my mother, who would then yell out the window for us to stay close. He never missed a beat.

My world consisted of that apartment, that stoop, my parents, Ringo, and Kenny. When the weather was bad, Kenny and I played games in the hallway, running up and down the length of the hallway. We made a lot of noise, and we were all sweaty and filled the hall with our boy sweat and heat.

My mother was one of those paranoid mothers who insisted I not eat or drink anything from anyone else's apartment. When Kenny went to our neighbor's apartment to get some Kool-Aid, I went along with him and quenched my thirst. Later, when I got home, my mother asked if I'd drank anything. "No, nothing," I said. This denial was exactly the first time in my life I lied. Clearly, I was not cut out to be a master liar, because the telltale evidence was stained in red all around my mouth. My mother smacked my face the second the lie was spoken.

"Never, ever drink anything outside our home again," she demanded.

"Never?" I asked. I couldn't believe what a big deal she was making of this. Kenny drank whatever he wanted, wherever he was.

"Never! You got that, Charles?"

"Yes, Mom."

She was unfair and irrational as far as I was concerned, though I didn't know the word for irrational back then. Still, she didn't deprive me. After Kenny and I exhausted ourselves from what seemed like hours of running, I'd go back to our apartment where my mom was ready with a cheese sandwich and a glass of iced tea, my favorite. Kenny's favorite was juice. He would drink juice from neighbors, with no warnings from his own mother about the world. Someone might have easily judged my mother for being paranoid, one day, after playing, I went back to my apartment for my food and drink, and Kenny returned to his. He drank juice in his refrigerator and then felt tired. His mother said later he announced he was going to go take a nap because he was so tired. He never woke up.

Kenny's uncle was a heroin addict. He was allowed to self-administer his daily dose of methadone, and he frequently put his dose into juice. The uncle pre-mixed the juice and then left it in the refrigerator. Kenny found the juice and became the first child in New York City to die of a methadone overdose.

Afterward, I would see his mother in the hallway and not know what to do. She was a wreck. She was barely able to function. I never saw Kenny's uncle again, and within a few months, my mom told me Kenny's mother died from a broken heart. I missed my friend. I retreated into the apartment with Ringo thinking my mom must be right not to let me drink anything she didn't monitor. "The world must be a dangerous place," I thought, "if you could die in your own apartment because of something you drank." Many years later I would come to understand the intricacies of what happened, but the terrible fear and early loss left an indelible imprint on me.

Shortly after Kenny died, my dad thought we should move out to Long Island. We would go look at houses, and my dad would tell us how great our lives would be once Ringo and I roved and roamed our *own yard* as we embarked on great explorations together. Looking for houses involved taking day trips, where we would hop in the car, Ringo included, and escape the city. I thought I had the best parents a kid could ask for.

On August 16, 1969, my dad heard about a music festival upstate in Bethel, NY. The music event was a *big thing* on the news.

"Let's get as close as we can, and maybe we'll hear some of the music," my father declared.

We packed the car for a picnic, including our squeaky Styrofoam ice chest, put down the roof on the convertible, and off we went. I had never been on a car ride that long, and the prospect of seeing a festival, with famous musicians and all kinds of performers made it seem like an adventure on par with captains like Shackleton…or Kirk. We were going boldly in the *USS Impala* where no man had gone before. But we weren't going to get there at the speed of light. Not anywhere close. Not long out of the city, we were suddenly on country roads surrounded by miles of grass. I had never seen anything like these wide-open spaces.

"Why don't we live here?" I asked.

My dad laughed and said, "That's the goal, Charles. I'd like for us to be in a place just like this."

My dad spotted a man wearing an Army backpack with a pot and pan hanging from it. He was walking along the side of the road. The man stuck out his thumb and my dad slowed down.

"Are you sure picking this guy up is a good idea?" my mom asked my dad.

"It'll be fine—he's probably headed up to the festival."

"Are we just going to put him in the back seat with Charles?"

"We are just giving him a ride."

My mom conceded, as long as Ringo sat between the hitchhiker and me.

"Hey, thanks, man. I'm Gary," the hitchhiker said, as he slid into the back seat of the Impala, his pot and pan clunking as he set his backpack down between his feet.

I was glad for the open car roof. I never met someone who didn't bathe regularly, and I could tell Gary didn't. And, as bad as he smelled, his backpack smelled even worse. Ringo sat at attention, not in an aggressive way, but he was clearly on alert at this stranger and his strange smells.

"Howdy, there," the hitchhiker said, "are you headed to the festival?"

"Just to check it out, see how close we can get," my dad said.

My mom didn't say much, but I'm pretty sure she greeted him with a quiet hello.

"Where you from?" my dad asked.

"All over," Gary said.

I wasn't entirely sure what Gary meant, but I understood from watching the news that Gary was the kind of person known as a hippie. What kind of person lived "all over," and wasn't there ever a home? Was he living on the streets? He didn't seem bothered at all by his condition, so he must have been doing what he wanted. I'd heard about people in the desert in another country, living as nomads. Maybe Gary was a nomad.

"Ah, man, Woodstock, man, I'm finally going to get there!" Gary said excitedly. He explained how it was going to be so cool because The Dead were playing in a few hours, and then The Who. They weren't bands I recognized, but my dad knew the names and asked about all the other bands set to perform. He asked if Gary knew which performers played the day before. I had never seen my dad so full of energy and enthusiasm. He had an excitement, and I couldn't help but feel we were headed somewhere bigger than any of us. We were, it seemed, about to witness the most significant thing in our lifetimes – and we'd just witnessed the moon landing.

Soon, the empty country roads were filled with cars in a line so long we couldn't see the end. It became apparent we were not going to see much except bumpers and pedestrians. Gary fell asleep in the back, his head resting against the window track. His face was deep brown and also sunburned red. It looked like a burn on top of a tan. "He must spend a lot of time outside," I thought. No wonder he didn't seem bothered by the open convertible top, the hot sun or the breeze blowing his hair into a tangled mat.

"You know," my dad said to my mom in a quiet voice, "it's a shame we can't go. But you know, with Charles and Ringo, there's no way."

"No, there isn't," mom replied.

"If we didn't have to worry about them, we could check it out," he reiterated.

"Well," my mom said, "I think it's nice we're out of the city, and I'm going to enjoy relaxing here in the sun in the middle of the country. That's what I'm glad about."

We drove in quiet, increasingly slower with the traffic, until, eventually, the traffic came to a standstill.

"Sitting in bumper-to-bumper traffic is ridiculous," my mom said, after about ten minutes. She didn't have much tolerance for inconveniences. The drive in the country was fine, but being stopped in the sun with no breeze, hot, hazy and muggy on the road with the heat reflecting off all the cars, was truly inconvenient.

"And if we get stuck here and it rains again? Look at those clouds over there," she said, pointing in the distance. "We are not going to get anywhere near close enough to hear those bands," she added.

"Let's just see," my father said.

My mother wasn't having it.

Gary woke up and said, "Hey, I can just hop out here—it's close enough, and I got some good rest. Thanks for the lift!"

"You sure?" my dad asked, hanging onto his last lifeline at getting closer to the venue by car.

"Absolutely, thanks, man, outta sight!" with that, Gary clunked his way with his stinky backpack out of the car and set off. Ringo sniffed the seat and then spread out, relaxing for the first time in an hour.

My dad sat there for a few more minutes, tapping the steering wheel.

"We are not going to get anywhere near close enough," my mom said, "look at the traffic! We won't be hearing anything except car engines."

My dad sighed, waiting a couple minutes more, then, in a huff, as soon as the car in front of us crept forward enough, my dad swung the car left into a great U-turn and stomped on the gas pedal, to at least leave Woodstock with the impression that he might not hear its music, but he drove the coolest car.

By the end of the month, we found an old Cape Cod house in Westbury, in the epicenter of suburbia. My dad got his workers from his union to help us with the move, and I played with the lift gate of the moving truck while watching the group of men pull out boxes and furniture while they laughed and smoked and swore. I was excited—Ringo was not.

Was it a sixth sense? Who can say? Albeit Queens wasn't the city, but we moved from a place where Ringo could stare out the window and watch the goings on of a thousand people all day long to the Boring Suburbs, in capitals. When we all drove up for the final move in my dad's Impala, Ringo didn't want to get out of the car. For weeks after we moved in, Ringo would stare at the Impala, waiting for someone to say, "Okay, it's time to head back to our real home in Queens now!"

The move was something new, and at first, my parents seemed very happy about the house. The house was a fixer-upper, having the original interior from 1929, including trunks full of ladies' clothes left behind by the previous owner. The closets were full of antique but stylish hats, purses, and gloves and shoes, and my mom kept saying how they were like new, in almost perfect condition. My dad found a trove of letters from the turn-of-the-century, in their original envelopes and stored in trunks in the attic. Beyond these treasures, my parents were committed to converting the house into a style suitable for the approaching decade. They wanted all the modern conveniences, done to their specifications. Room after room would be gutted to the studs and built anew. It's no secret that a large-scale remodel can put a strain on a marriage. My parents were no exception.

In fact, that new house marked the end of us as a happy family forever.

3. A NEW REPORT

I click on my computer.

[UPDATE] An NYPD spokesman confirmed officers shot and killed a dog at the location at approximately 4:25 p.m. The spokesman could not comment on why officers opened fire. **However,** *Animal Care & Control records show the dog, which is named Star, was taken there and is clinging to life.*[1]

So, Star is clinging to life?

Ringo was the start but not the reason for Star's story reaching into my torso and latching onto my guts. There was also Kane—but I can't think of Kane right now. It's all too much. But I was with Kane when New York's finest busted me—and those guys went out of their way to protect a guy's dog. That's why I can't fathom the reaction of these two officers: The shooting and the subsequent mace spraying. What good could that have possibly served?

But Star is clinging to life all the way up in East Harlem. She has to make it through this horrible ordeal. A sense of helplessness slides over me and feels like an old suit that used to fit but is now too tight. I can't cope with not being able to debug the problem and find a solution. Repairing and solving has been my job since 1999.

---

[1] Robbins, Christopher. "NYPD Officers Shoot Dog After It Allegedly Tries to Protect Owner." *Gothamist*, posted August 13, 2012, 4:41 p.m. www.gothamist.com.

"No," I thought, "of course Star will live. I must make sure she does. Why, though, do I feel so certain?"

I need another opinion, on what, I'm not entirely sure. I can't quite explain what I need, but I can't be alone. "Hey, Mike, Micah," I say as I walk over to the offices of my CEO and VP, "can you come take a look at something for a minute?"

Mike and Micah are practical Midwesterners, rational, with a prudent sense of themselves. They would tell me—what? What do I need to hear?

Could a dog survive being shot in the face?

Suddenly, I'm like a little boy asking if things will be okay.

They huddle over my computer in my office, and I click the mouse to play the video of the police shooting Star.

Two minutes in, and Mike has had enough. "I'm sorry, Charlie. I can't watch anymore," he says, as he walks out, hands behind his back, not looking back. He has seen plenty in his life but seeing the travesty on screen is too much for him.

Micah stays with me, though, unable to take his eyes from the video. As soon as the video ends, without a pause, he says, "Poor dog died a painful death."

"Are you sure?" I ask, stunned. "The report says she survived."

"Yes, Charlie," he says, "there is no way the dog survived. She went through too much and lost too much blood."

Crushed, I repeat what the report says and ask him again if he is convinced the dog is dead.

"I am," he replies quietly.

I can't accept this conclusion for whatever inexplicable reason. Why do I have such a connection to this story – to this dog? Why is this hitting me so hard? This dog simply cannot die, I know this in my very bones.

The news of the day, however, contradicts my feeling. Both CBS New York and an NYPD spokesperson report the dog has died. News of the dog's death is flatly unacceptable. I won't jump to conclusions until I find out all the particulars about what happened to Star. Instead, being a logistics guy, I Google, discovering New York City Animal Care and Control has a contract for New York City animal shelter needs and is, ostensibly, the "dog police" of New York. Aha, there's the phone number. So many people are probably making calls around the city, trying to trace Star's whereabouts, and if there is a spokesperson involved, real information might be in lockdown. My strategy will have to be to come in laterally.

"Yes, hello," I say to the woman who answers at Animal Care and Control after following a long series of voicemail prompts and after my gut leading me to try the administrative office instead of the shelter departments. "I'm Charlie Cifarelli," I say, "and I am the Chief Operations Officer of Midlands Recycling Inc. of Lincoln, Nebraska. Just making a courtesy call to see if your office is doing its part and recycling."

She is only too happy to tell me they are. Does she know about the latest in green disposal? She knows some but not all of the details, and so we chitchat on environmental waste disposal for a while.

Finally, I ask the question I have been wanting to ask all along: "Oh, hey, by the way, do you know if the dog shot in the East Village is still alive?"

"Oh honey," the woman, named Renee, says, "we have a lot of dogs. That doesn't narrow it down for me."

"Right—her name is Star. I saw the story on the news. I would just like to know if she survived."

There's a pause, and I wait for a comment along the lines of *how did we get from recycling to talking about a dog?* Instead, I hear her typing into her keyboard. Finally, she says, "What do you want to know?"

I hold my breath. With great anxiety but hopeful anticipation I ask, "Is she alive?"

"Yes," she replies flatly.

"Are you sure?" I ask, needing clarification.

"Yes, I am. She's at the Fifth Avenue Veterinary Hospital being treated."

I have to remind myself to breathe again. Though I was convinced she was alive, I still couldn't believe she actually *was* alive. "Thank you so much, Renee," I enthusiastically say, "I guess that's all for today, but I might follow up with you, if I may."

"Sure thing, Charlie, you have a good day now."

Star is alive. The fact she is alive just made my entire year.

Next up is researching the spokesperson for the NYC Animal Care and Control, and once I find him, I connect with him on LinkedIn as a lateral approach. I then call the Fifth Avenue Veterinary Hospital. "I've spoken with Renee from the NYC Animal Care and Control," I say, "and I am calling to inquire about Star. I was told she was stable."

"Well…yes," says the somewhat perplexed assistant on the other end. That's all I need to know before reaching out to the spokesperson for NYC Animal Care and Control on LinkedIn.

"Star is alive," I write on a note to myself, "and in stable condition."

For Star to have a fighting chance, get the best care and survive the next steps, she needs as many people to know about her case and her condition as possible. People cannot give up on her.

It takes two days before multiple media outlets report with the headlines *Miracle Dog Survives Police Shooting*. I check in with Renee again and then the Fifth Avenue Veterinary Hospital. Not only is Star surviving, but she is making a lightning-speed recovery.

The facts seem impossible, but the impossible has become irrefutable reality.

4. DROWNING IN RAGE

I understood my parents' financial situation changed because of the room by room remodeling in their new house. My dad was moving up in the union now. He walked around like he was a big deal. Life at five years old was suddenly different than life at four years old. Ringo and I lived in a suburban neighborhood now with a yard, and a world to ourselves. Still, I was sad about the loss of my friend, Kenny. Before long, I was also grieving the loss of the idyllic childhood lived in the cramped Queens apartment.

We didn't venture far from home at all. Suburban smells and sounds were too tame for Ringo, and most of the neighborhood kids were a little older. Instead, I made a makeshift clubhouse for just Ringo and me—two best buds.

I never understand the phrase "as mad as a dog" or even "mad dog." The dogs I've known have all been the stable ones in relationships. Ringo was the steadying force in my life. He was the only respite from the chaos inflicted by my parents. I don't remember the exact start, but the fights between my parents turned to screaming matches and the screaming matches turned into my dad destroying pictures, glasses, furniture—breaking whatever he could get his hands on—including at times my mom. Both my parents would be drunk, and then the next day, they often would act as if nothing happened. My mom would go out the next week and replace all the broken items, which would last for the next week or two before being sacrificed once more to rage rubble.

Usually, the fights would ensue after a Saturday night bender, and then, Sunday mornings, my dad, all sweetness and innocence, was awake early cooking breakfast for my mom and me. Ringo took to hiding in the mud room, where he slept as soon as the voices raised—it was the safest place for him to hide from flying glass. Ringo and I tiptoed around the house. We willed ourselves into disappearing like phantoms as we slunk along the walls and wondered what would set off the next attack, not wanting to be in the crossfire.

I was just five years old when I woke up to my parents fighting one evening. It was another Saturday night, and my parents came home from a party in the neighborhood. My dad was accusing my mother of doing something at the party, and my mother was making her counter-accusations. Both were jealous of something, and both blamed the other. They screamed at each other at the top of their lungs, as if their voices were ammunition. My father yelled he was leaving, and his voice hung for a moment in the air like a ghost haunting the old house.

I crept down the hallway and peeked downstairs just in time to see my dad wrestling my mother to get at the door. I recognized the bank book in my father's hand. I watched them write down information every time a contractor came to the house. I knew the bank book was important. My mother stood with her back to the door, blocking my father's exit and trying to push him away while also trying to grab the bank book without giving up her position in the blockade. Then, my mother spotted me.

"Charles!" she said, and my own name suddenly terrified me. "Give Charles the bank book! That way, neither of us has it!"

My heart beat so hard my head hurt. The tears were already burning my eyes.

My father turned around and studied me for a minute, the anger and hatred in his body almost visible as steam. It was a toss-up which one scared me more.

"Fine," my father said, "Charles, come down and get the book."

I nodded and slinked down the steps, feeling like they were the longest flight of steps in the world, and then the bank book was in my hand.

"Now go to bed, Charles," my father commanded. He didn't have to tell me twice. I ran back up to my room, placed the bank book under my pillow, then buried my face into the top of my pillow, trying to muffle my sobs. I wasn't sure what it all meant but was aware of keeping the book as a responsibility. I was learning all about what responsibilities were: picking up after Ringo. Making sure Ringo was fed. Making sure I washed behind my ears. This bank book, though, was different. My ear grew hot, as if the book were burning through my pillow. My parents' rage at each other was burning into me and soon would set us all ablaze.

I wasn't sure how long I'd been asleep, but the house was quiet when my father woke me up. His hunched figure formed a formidable shadow looming over me.

"Charles, give me the bank book," he demanded.

"But I'm supposed to keep it," I said.

"Give me the book, now."

I slid my hand under my pillow, feeling the leather sleeve between my sheets, and then handed the book to him.

"Good," my father said, "go back to sleep now."

He left my room, and moments later, I heard the front door slam and his Impala peel out of the driveway. My father and the bank book sped quickly into the darkness of the night.

"Charles!" my mother shouted. Her steps were heavy on the stairs. "Where is it?" she demanded, and then said, "You let him take the bank book?"

I nodded, tears streaming down my eyes, and said, "He made me give it to him."

"How could you? He's taken all our money! Do you realize we have nothing now, thanks to you?"

I shook, and we both sobbed. My mother stormed out of the room leaving me to replay my father's visit to my room and to grapple with any possible strategy I might have employed to stop him. Would it have helped if I begged my dad not to take the bank book? What if I begged him not to leave? Should I have pretended to stay asleep?

All week, my mother reminded me of what I allowed to happen. "We have no money. We're going to lose the house. I don't know what we'll do for food, but maybe a neighbor will take you in," she lamented, leaving the weight of my father's departure and our recent destitution squarely on my shoulders.

Ringo and I were playing fetch in the front yard when Ringo stopped, his ears perked. Then, I heard something as well: That damn custom exhaust on my dad's Impala. He came around the corner, and Ringo barked. My mom was at the front door, watching. She turned back into the house when my father pulled to a stop and turned off the engine.

"Hello, Charles," he said, offering Ringo a rub behind the ears before heading into the house.

"Where were you?" I asked, but my dad ignored me, or maybe he didn't hear me. As I followed him into the house, my mom said, "There isn't much for dinner, but I can find something in the fridge to throw together."

"Sure, sounds good," he said.

I couldn't believe what I was hearing. There was no apology, either to each other or from either of them to me. As far as they were concerned, everything was perfectly normal, and they were back to the old routine. Ignoring the past bad behavior was not okay with me. I was angry at both of them. If they were getting into such bad fights, how could they act normal now? If they were able to be normal now because the fights weren't so bad, why couldn't they control themselves when they were drinking?

If my dad were home from work, he would inevitably get violent and my mom would stoke his anger, which didn't need much stoking.

After my dad's sudden return after the night of the bank book, I came downstairs one weekday afternoon to my mother sobbing on the couch. I noticed the open bottle of liquor, way more gone than the last time I saw the bottle. My mother's eyes were red-rimmed and puffy. Her whole face changed with her eyes like that. She was some alien from outer space who shape-shifted into something resembling my mother. The person I saw could not be her.

Except…

"What's wrong, Mommy?"

"Oh. Nothing."

"But you're crying."

Finally, she bellowed out, "I miss my parents," looking more like a lost five-year-old than I did. She was looking at old black and white photos of her parents, who she hardly knew.

Her father died when she wasn't much older than I was then. He spent years consistently sick, and no one could give a diagnosis matching his symptoms. After he died and the medical examiner did an autopsy and only then did they discover a nail, an old nail, that must have been in my grandfather's body since he was young. They figured he swallowed the nail, and it moved through his body, cutting through tissue, and eventually lodged in his lung, causing internal bleeding. He dripped blood like a leaky faucet toward the end of his life. How he didn't die sooner is possibly the most miraculous part of the story.

There was certainly nothing miraculous for my mother, however, because just two years after her father died, her mother died from a massive heart attack. She was shoveling snow from their entry walk and came into the house and dropped dead in front of my mother. There was no place for my mother to go, no family to take her in, so she moved in and out of a series of foster homes for the better part of the late 1940s and 1950s.

Only later as an adult would I be able to recognize the feral anger bottled up and allowed to grow molten hot within her. With such a molten core, no one could get near her emotionally. She would not have allowed me to get close even if I dared, despite my desire just to hug her. I was confused, though, because her coldness was not a side of her, I saw when we all lived in the apartment. That anger and resentment, thought, must have always been there, which meant there was never a time my mother was not angry.

I missed the mother from the apartment, even if I never saw the real her. If my father had not been so openly violent, I'm sure my mother would have continued silently angry in her own way. She would have simply seethed on the sidelines far removed from me. My father, though, brought her incredible rage and fury to the surface.

Just after her mother's death, while my mother was living in her first foster home, she was at school, sitting at her desk by the window, when a rock, shattered the glass and soared into the classroom. The flying glass directly hit her small, eight-year-old hand. Shards of glass sliced her hand and almost completely severed her thumb. The school officials who rushed her to the hospital asked how they should get in contact with her mom.

"She's dead."

"Oh," the school official said, rather surprised. She paused for a moment and then said, "Dear, I'm so sorry. Well, how about we call your father?"

"He's dead, too."

The school didn't even know that both of her parents were dead. Maybe her file was never updated.

It was obvious this story held deep significance for my mother, because she repeated it many times over the years. We all knew what happened to her. My dad certainly knew. But when he was drunk and in one of his rages, he would never consider my mother's history, or consider what might trigger (a word my parents' generation would never have used, but trigger is the only valid term) my mother's very real post-traumatic stress.

On yet another warm summer Saturday night, my dad became angry after a party and threw a heavy push broom at the large back window of our home. I don't know why he chose a push broom. Perhaps it was handy. The broom was sturdy, heavy and probably satisfying to throw. My mother stood next to the window as the push broom pushed its way through the glass, sending shards of broken glass in all directions.

14th & 2nd

My dad swore he hadn't thrown the broom with the intention of showering my mother with broken glass. To this day, I don't believe him, but his intentions, whatever they were, don't make the story any better. The flying glass lacerated my mother's hands, arms and face. The incident made my mother remember the trauma of her nearly severed thumb just after her mother died.

To say she had a breakdown would be putting it mildly. My father, after waiting until she composed herself, drove my mother to the emergency room. I have no idea what either of them said to the medical staff, but I do know my father was never questioned by the police. When they returned, they were back to their routine of gaslighting me, each other and undoubtedly themselves.

I could never wrap my head around the fact that my mother lost both her parents and no one in her school knew about their deaths. Apparently, they failed to read in her school file about her life in foster homes. Suddenly I realize my mother was a deeply secretive person. She was reticent and guarded her whole life, apparently. She did not want people seeing her up close, seeing how she lived, or seeing what was going on in her house. I stopped asking if friends could come over because she always said no. When my father tried to invite people over, she always found a way to thwart the plan. If she wasn't successful in preventing my father's visitors, she made him pay for her unsuccess in ways leading to the inevitable break-up-the-house fights.

I never fully understood her techniques or tactics.

There are other examples of my mother's secrecy jarring and vexing me. For example, when going out to the shops to replace goods broken in a fight, if something needed to be ordered for pick up, she never left her real name. She always used an alias.

I saw her crying, I knew of her past, and I certainly saw her vulnerabilities, but I could never fully get to her. I could never penetrate her cloak of secrecy or her presumed safety she so stoutly maintained. Much of her remained a secret to me.

I don't think, by the way, my mother's predilections were the reason for my father's destructive side. His behavior was not metaphorical; he was not breaking household objects as a surrogate for breaking through to my mother. Nothing so tragically poetic.

Though my mother was cold and distant, we were both hostages to my father's mood swings. He was never diagnosed with anything like bi-polar disorder or borderline personality disorder, but then again, not many people were getting such diagnoses in those days. My father *never* would have visited a shrink let alone acknowledge *anything wrong* with his behavior.

My mother learned to avoid my father due to a convenient (for her) turn of events—as I was nearing the age of seven and instead of destroying the house, or hitting my mother, my father turned his physical rage onto me. My mother simply locked herself in the bathroom and focused on her hair and makeup. She was relieved to finally be out of the line of fire.

I don't remember the first time my father struck me, but it was probably when I touched the glass on the sliding doors to the backyard. I was seven and my hands were on everything, as is the way with kids. My father, on the other hand, would go on weekly epic cleaning sprees—he always said it was time to "GI the house," giving the place a thorough power-washing, followed by turning the windows streak-free and spotless.

"Charles!"

I hated the sound of my name in his voice. At seven years old, my own name gave me a sinking fear.

"Charles, come look at this!" He was at the sliding glass door, pointing to a small handprint near the handle. "Did you know I just cleaned this yesterday? Yesterday!" He grabbed me by my wrists, crossed them, and then banged the bones of my hands together. Repeatedly. And hard. "Do." Bang. "Not." Bang. "Touch." Bang. "The." Bang. "Glass." Bang. "Do." Bang. "You." Bang. "Think." Bang. "You." Bang. "Can." Bang. "Remember." Bang. "That?" Bang.

I was stunned, but as soon as the shock wore off, I felt the pain in my wrists and hands and ran outside to my clubhouse to hide my tears. Ringo followed me.

The next time he went after me was a week later, when I left a small splotch of water on the bathroom sink when twisting off the faucet handles. Could I not keep anything tidy, he wondered as he clenched my wrists and banged my hands together, this time, more forcefully, so I would remember. But seven-year-olds can be in a rush, which makes them occasionally absentminded.

So often, his mood swings and abusive temperament flared when he didn't get his way about something, and when he wanted something, his desire was couched in something seemingly innocent. In the early summer of 1972, I was seven years old. My father asked me, "Hey, would you like a pool in the backyard?"

I never thought about a pool. I wasn't much of a swimmer, and I took a look out in our yard, noting the small space between the two-car garage, which was old, and the big oak tree casting almost the entire backyard in shade.

"Don't worry, I can take down the garage to make room for the new pool."

I shrugged. Sure, whatever.

"I want you to tell your mother you want a pool."

"Why?"

"Just tell her and keep reminding her." I didn't quite realize yet that everything my father did was motivated by self-interest, but I was learning. Still, he was in a good mood, and I didn't want to be responsible for things turning south from there.

My father had two moods: the complete raving lunatic in tornado mode, and then sweet husband, custodian of my mother's feelings and boundaries. There was no middle ground between these two extremes. Looking back, it's possible their mutual and individual secrets held my parents together. Those shared secrets, and my father's ability to make money and give funds to my mother kept their marriage together.

That night, I mentioned to my mom I wanted a pool and then thought nothing else of my request.

In a few days, my dad came to me and said I should ask her again. "Don't forget," he said, "tell your mother you want a pool."

With such prodding, I repeated to my mother my need for a pool, noting how pleased my dad seemed to be with me after each time. I would ask my mother, almost to annoyance, if we could have a pool, and then she in turn would talk to my father about the possibility of getting a pool. "What do you think?" she'd ask.

"Sure, I'm all for it!" he said.

"Really? I'm not so sure. Charles doesn't seem into swimming."

"He is probably not into swimming because he doesn't have a pool."

After a couple more go arounds in my father's charade, my mother said a pool sounded like a project worth doing, and my father began almost immediately dismantling the old garage. On his days off, he worked from sunup until sundown, pulling apart the roof, then the walls, hauling the wood away. Then, he began the breakup of the concrete floor, and after that, he graded the area, by hand, with a steel rake. Then he methodically spread sand over the space. I watched him every day from different windows in the house, and it struck me as odd that he never once asked me to come help him. Other boys in the neighborhood would help their fathers with household projects. Maybe not all the time, but enough to the point that it seemed strange that my father was undertaking this solitary and time-consuming endeavor.

Perhaps my father suffered from some form of mania. Maybe he just liked the idea of hard work. He was happier doing manual labor than he ever seemed when he came home from work at the trucking union. Maybe he hated people in general and wanted an excuse to be alone, though there were probably easier methods to pursue solitude. Of course, I knew none of this project was about me. The pool wasn't for me, even though my father felt like he needed me as a pretense. I knew my father wanted a place to invite his friends over after work, where they could hang out and drink, and it perplexed me that my mother hadn't yet figured that out.

When all the prep work was completed, my father drove to Harrow's Pool Store to pick up the above-ground pool he ordered. He arrived back at the house with several large boxes, which he laid out in the backyard, unpacking them now like an archaeologist unearthing a pharaoh's tomb.

"Here is the boxcutter," my mother said, and suddenly, my mother and I were both helping my dad set out the pieces, organizing them by size and use. Working on the pool was the first time the three of us did anything together that did not involve sitting in the car. Though I knew the pool wasn't for me, this time with my parents was the first joy I felt with them since we moved to Long Island. Perhaps one day, I would invite my friends over to swim in the pool with me, and in that way, I could think of it as my pool. The pool would be there for me if I ever wanted to use it.

When the pool was set up, we stood back, marveling at the work. Well, my dad marveled, my mom reflected, and I shrugged. It was taller than I anticipated. A couple of houses had above-ground pools, but the ones I thought of were built-in, so you could walk straight in from ground level. The top of the pool came up past my eyeballs. "It was the tallest one available," my father said, full of pride. The pool came with a metal ladder a person could climb up and over the sides, which would then drop straight into the pool. It couldn't have been more than four-and-a-half feet deep, but the layout, the whole style of it, irked me as more of an eyesore and it limited the space I had to play with Ringo.

We spent the next two days just filling the pool up with water using only one skinny garden hose.

There was nothing for me to do but sit and watch the water level rise. My dad, meanwhile, spent several hours coordinating with his friends from work to come over the following weekend and check out the new pool, have some drinks. He raced around, possibly on a manic high, buzzing through the kitchen, pouring himself another scotch, making a list of booze and food he wanted to get.

Suddenly, my mother's alarm bells were triggered. I watched her stew in silence as my father's plan grew more elaborate, then she began to seethe. A crowd of people in her house? Especially men, drinking and dragging their wet bodies into her house to use the bathroom or grab food, half-naked and on her furniture? She poured herself a drink, slammed a cabinet, folded the laundry with added urgency.

Finally, during dinner, while my father was discussing what my mother could make for appetizers, my mother abruptly interrupted him and said, "You know, this *is* Charles's pool. We put it up for him, and that's who it's for." Taking a long drink she added, "Let the kid enjoy his pool before you bring a bunch of people over to use it. We put it up for *him, right?*"

My father's jaw tensed, and he squeezed the glass of scotch in his hand—his third of the day. It would not be his last. "Fine," he said, knowing there was no way out without admitting the ruse of getting the pool to begin with. "Fine. Charles gets to use the pool first. I'll call my friends and we will postpone the pool party."

He got up from the table leaving his food on the plate, and went outside into the evening air. My mother barely hid a satisfied smile as she took another drink from her glass before going to the freezer and diving into the half gallon of ice cream. She spooned the ice cream into her mouth non-stop, though I knew in a few minutes, she would rush to the bathroom to vomit it all up. I forked meatloaf into my mouth and cleared my plate to get out of dodge before any fallout, but when my dad came back inside an hour later, there was no fight, and things went on as usual.

Each day for the next week, my father came home from work and asked what I had done throughout my day.

"Oh, I rode my bike, and then Ringo and I played fetch…"

"Did you go in the pool?"

That would be a no. That water was ice-cold, under that giant oak. No sun was getting through the canopy, and the air wasn't hot enough to get the hose water warmer than about fifty-five degrees. No and no.

"Well, you have to go swimming sometime," my father said.

My mother was more pragmatic, and in keeping up the appearances that she cared anything about the stupid pool, she came home with an inflatable boat to compel me to go into the water. No dice. I did not want to touch that cold water.

"You know," my mother said to me one day, "I bet if your dad cut down the oak tree, the water would warm up."

Again, this suggestion was in no way related to my wishes or to me in any way. Nor did my mother have any interest in going in the frigid waters. No, my mother loved to sunbathe. If the oak tree was down, she would have a yard full of sun and could brown herself to her heart's content.

I humored her and said, "I guess so."

That was it. As soon as my father got home, my mother told him, "That tree has to go. The pool is just too cold because the tree is blocking the sun. I bet Charles would get in the pool if you cut down that tree."

My father sighed in exasperation, but that very weekend, he began the process of cutting down that huge oak tree, by himself. He took out a rickety forty-foot ladder that reached only part way into the tree. To get to the upper limbs, he climbed higher in the tree, attaching ropes to the limbs.

A few of the older neighborhood kids took interest and offered to help him with the tree, waiting at the top of the ladder for him to cut the limbs with the handsaw—yes, a handsaw—and then lower the limbs down to the kids, who would pass them down to the ground. Then, the rest of the kids, all with handsaws, would cut the limbs into manageable pieces and make piles. All the larger pieces were seized on by the neighbors for firewood, and the smaller bits and branches were set on the curb for special pickup.

The movements were orchestrated fairly efficiently for a group of kids with no experience following a semi-sober man with limited experience. I was impressed with how much patience and restraint he showed around the neighborhood boys. Maybe they should come over every weekend to do chores. Maybe my father was good with people as long as they weren't his family.

But just as I was marveling at the smooth success of the whole endeavor, a rope that was slowly lowering a limb to the ground slipped out of one of the neighborhood kid's hands, careening through the upper branches, and landing square on the ladder, snapping it in half as it ricocheted off the trunk of the tree and to the ground.

The boys on the ground all screamed and scattered out of the way, but the bigger problem was that my dad and the other kid were stuck up in the tree with no way to get down.

"Mikey," my father shouted to one of the boys, "go see if you can get your dad's ladder."

After ten minutes, Mikey came back and said that his dad only owned a twenty-footer, and it wouldn't reach. The next kid said his dad wasn't home so he couldn't ask, and two others didn't have anything more than an six-foot stepladder at home. I don't know whose ladder was finally dragged by three kids into our yard, but it took almost an hour to produce. Despite the setback, my father was undeterred. The boys worked through their dinner and were back at work on it all the next day.

During the week, my father was up in that tree pumping away with that flimsy saw from the time he got home from work until past dusk. By Thursday, he cut down to all but the tree's massive stump. The branches took several pickups over a two-week period before they were all cleared from the front of the house. My father's hands were blistered, his shoulders ached, and our yard was strewn with sawdust, but the tree was gone.

"There, now," my father said to me, "happy now, Charles?"

No, but I wasn't going to say so. I liked the tree. My mother, on the other hand, was delighted. The next afternoon, she was out on a lawn chair with an ice-filled drink and a pulpy romance novel.

"What, you haven't gone in the pool yet?" my father asked every few days. The water was still cold, but I really had no—and I mean zero—desire to go into that stupid pool. Perhaps the height of the pool intimidated me. At least, that may have been part of the reason.

"That's alright, Charles," my mother said, staring out the window, "I rather like the look of the pool there."

The sunlight reflected off the water and into the window, casting my mother in a rippling light. She looked beautiful and otherworldly in that light—as if, in that light, there was finally my real mother, happy and full of peace and love for her family.

A few days later, a Saturday, because my dad only worked half days at the union then and was home by lunchtime, I was playing with Ringo in the yard when my father finally reached the end of his patience with the pool situation. I was throwing a ball to Ringo, who was fetching it, though still attached to his long chain to keep him from bolting through the yet unfenced yard.

"Hey," my father shouted, "Why aren't you in the pool?"

I stiffened as he came closer, and I could see the wild animal anger building in him. I could feel anger building in me as well.

"I don't want to swim!" I yelled back.

"You don't want to swim." He ran his hand through his hair. "Do you even know how much work it was putting in the pool? Have you been in the pool at all since I cut down the tree?"

I looked at him and said, "No."

This was it. The last few weeks built up to whatever was coming next. There was about to be a reckoning, and I was ready for the worst, just as long as the worst would finally be over. Anger flashed through my father's face as if he'd been hooked up to electricity, as if a circuit was suddenly thrown on. He was screaming, words I didn't know, except I knew they were bad. He ran to the walls of the pool and grabbed on, pushing back and forth as if to buckle the walls. They held firm. He looked around, and then we both saw it: the lawn edger. It was the old-fashioned kind, with a long, rectangular blade at the end.

He grabbed the lawn edger then tore around the pool, poking the sharp blade at the pool liner like a madman. The first leak was a trickle, but the third flowed from a deeper gash, and another flowing even faster. My dad lifted the edger overhead and thrust downward, and I suddenly thought of the movie *Moby Dick* I'd once seen, whalers harpooning into a whale with violent, repetitive blows. All at once, the side of the pool split open, and fifteen thousand gallons of water erupted from below the metal pool sides, knocking over my father. It was a tsunami. And Ringo, chained to a cinder block, was right in its path.

All of this destruction happened in a flash. Ringo yelped, and I turned to see fur and limbs in a rush of water, washed down the driveway.

The side of the wave hit the basement window of the house, shattering it with its force. My mother screamed—she must have been doing laundry down there. Water poured into the window, thousands of gallons, flooding the basement. Within seconds, my mother was out of the basement and out the back door. By then, the damage was done. Ringo tentatively walked back toward me, coughing and shaking, still chained to the cinder block dragging behind him.

"What the hell happened?!?" my mother shouted, looking at the twisted heap of plastic and metal. Looking at the dog, she said, "What happened to Ringo? The Pool? I can't believe this; this could have killed me! The washer and dryer were plugged into the wall! I could have been electrocuted!"

She went on, but my father didn't respond to her.

"Are you okay?" he asked me. His calmness spooked me, and I started to cry. What could I say? Physically, I may have been fine, aside from the shock and adrenaline charging through my body.

"Wow," my dad said, as if he was bewildered, looking at the aftermath of some natural disaster. He acted as if he had nothing to do with the destruction. He walked to the pool and pulled up pieces of the metal, hauling them to the side of the yard. Without a word, he started to clean up the self-made disaster.

I ran to Ringo, holding him tightly. He licked my head and then tried to shake himself dry a couple of times. He was on alert, watching my dad get the pump, then lower the hoses through the broken basement window, then start to pump out the water.

I buried my face in Ringo's wet fur and said, "It's going to be okay, buddy," trying to reassure him. Maybe if I said it enough, it would come true. "It's going to be okay. It's okay. It'll all be over soon."

And like magic, my father's tirade was over without a word. As soon as he cleaned up the yard, he went inside and took a shower.

"Why don't we go to dinner? Then a movie. The new Barbra Streisand comedy *What's Up, Doc?* —I'm in the mood for a laugh."

He was as polite as could be, and we even went to the historic movie house on Post Avenue in Westbury. Had it been any other family, I would have called it a wonderful Saturday night. A family with a mother who wasn't sad her entire life, who hadn't picked a violent man to with which to share her life. My father, the natural disaster, the earthquake ready to split open the earth and crumble buildings, the volcano ready to burst its top and smother us in ash or burn us with lava, the storm cloud spinning with a tornado, ready to drop. If he ever really paid attention to the carnage, it was never more than a cursory glance, a quick look back before saying, "What, who me?" before moving on. He was as ambivalent and unfeeling as the asteroid on a direct course for earth.

It took a month's worth of weekends to put the yard back together. Doing so involved picking up the twisted metal pool parts, repairing the ruts from the patio bricks that tsunamied across the yard and calling the trash pickup to carry away hopper loads of our family's flotsam.

5. SEARCHING

I like the pace of life in Nebraska, I like the people. When I was in grade school, looking at the map tacked up to the front of my classroom, I was intrigued with a place smack-dab in the center of the country. New York might be the center of the world for millions of people, but there was something mysterious about the middle of the country—the wilderness of wheat and corn and small towns. Nebraska seemed like a safe place. I was primed from years of curiosity when I followed a woman and landed there. Sure, it was a rocky landing, but that was no fault of Nebraska's.

My fiancé Jenn (not the woman I followed to Nebraska) gives me a look. She knows me so well, and part of knowing me is knowing when to give me space to think and reflect.

Jenn also knows when I'm developing a new plan.

My specialty is in logistics, not media or writing, but I know Star needs a voice. The only thing I really know to do to spread the word is to create a Facebook page for her so others can get information and share her story. The Facebook page name is simple: *Star, the New York Pit Bull*. The page title is straightforward but gives enough details to get the attention of people following the story. Really, I want to name the page, *Star, The Miracle Dog*.

I post what I know so far—Star was initially said to have been killed but she is still very much alive—and I provide links to the various articles about her and Lech.

Lech. I think again of that photo of him being hauled away by the EMTs. He is the one without a voice. Nobody is speaking for him. Here is this guy who is trying to survive. He is an immigrant to the United States who is down on his luck but making sure his dog gets fed and cared for. It turns out, after Lech was treated for his seizure, he was taken to central booking because he had an open container of wine. After all he'd been through that day, the cops book him for a fucking open container.

Something flickers inside me, and I fight with everything I have to push it down. "Don't think of the past. Put those emotions away," I keep telling myself.

They don't throw away guys with nice clothes, a fancy watch, and good cologne. They don't plop those guys on a stretcher the way they did Lech. How do I help him?

At my desk, I pull up *Star, the New York Pit Bull* and type in a post that I'd like to help Lech and Star. I say I could offer Lech a job and help him get a place to live if anyone knew how I could get in touch with him.

The post catches the attention of a journalist named Penny, who then pens an article *Where is Lech Stankiewicz?* in hopes of someone connecting Lech with me.

A New York City non-profit calls me within two days to ask if I'd be willing to state what specifically I would like to do for Mr. Stankiewicz. "Could you put your offer in an email for us? That way, your offer won't be confused when we tell him about it. We can share your email with him."

I explain who I am and tell briefly about knowing how hard it is to have nothing. I say I've spent a lot of time helping people get their second chances in life, just as one was given to me. I tell him I have a waste and recycling business in Nebraska.

While I wait to hear back from Lech, I read Star is now having surgery to remove her left eye, because bullet fragments migrated from her head and destroyed the eye. The non-profit calls me back a day later and says, "Mr. Stankiewicz really appreciated your offer, but he has decided to decline." They don't tell me why Lech declined my offer.

The Mayor's Alliance for NYC's Animals, who are acting custodians of Star, give Lech a long list of requirements he must adhere to if he wants to get Star back. They include no more drinking (which can trigger his seizures) and getting a permanent residence. They act as if he could just go from being homeless to having a place to live overnight with no problems and no extra assistance. He is basically given an impossible choice. The list is long, and I'm sure too daunting, especially after all Lech and Star endured (were *still* enduring). When he surrendered Star to the City of New York because he could no longer care for her, I knew the secret heartbreak he felt. He must love her tremendously if he's willing to do what he feels is best for her. His sacrifice means he will lose the only friend he has.

I can't help Lech, but I can find a way to help Star. I have my work cut out for me, but at this point, it's not really a choice—or, rather, I made that choice the instant I found out Star was alive, though I didn't yet know it. Maybe there was a greater force at work. Maybe my entire life, I've been moving toward Star.

If I were in a jam, I sure would want a one-track-minded person who was inexhaustible coming to help me. "Wherever you're hidden, Star, you have the best person possible sniffing your trail," I whisper to myself.

With over $10,000 in donations, the Animal Care and Control of NYC provide care for Star. I track her ownership to a legal defense firm fighting for animals with no voice, but after two weeks of her story getting public attention, news of Star suddenly goes quiet. The official word is Star is on the mend and once ready, will be adopted. As sweet as this all sounds, I know the reality of how hard it is to adopt even a well-trained Pit Bull, let alone one with Star's background. People are so often all for making the donations, but it's a different story when it comes time to put in the work to support an animal with challenges, some of them known but many more unknown. The chances of her seeing a happy ending are bleak.

A new article on Star quotes the legal defense team saying, "If you want to talk to Star, you need to speak to her attorneys." What planet am I on? Star has lawyered up? Most humans can't afford this kind of representation. Right after the statement is released, Star goes into hiding. With her whereabouts unknown, I must now up my game.

The secrecy around Star and her story are incredible, and I see why. The largest police force in America shot a homeless man's dog, and the public reaction turned squarely against the police and their use of force. Star's Facebook page is getting hits from people all over the globe, saying what a horrible occurrence this is. The story sets off a chain reaction of people sharing other stories—so many stories—of police shooting dogs when out on calls. The story also details the often-monumental payouts to the dog owners. Some posts are anecdotal and from heartbreaking personal experience, while others provide links to news items that came and went as momentary blips. Many times, the police said they felt threatened after shooting dogs turning out to be Chihuahuas or Labs – dogs not typically known for being harmful. These incidents were PR nightmares made to go away.

Suddenly, the online conspiracy theories gain momentum. With the police's history of shooting dogs—and this one shot in the head and first announced to be dead—much of the public believes news of Star's survival is a lie. The news is a PR scheme designed to get people to lose interest in the story and move on while forgetting all about the shooting. The NYPD spokesperson initially reported Star died, after all.

Then, a photo emerges. The photo, released by the NYC Animal Care and Control, shows Star, looking like a healthy and normal dog, which causes a great deal of confusion.

"Police found a lookalike dog," more than one person writes, "they're trying to pass her off as Star because of the backlash."

The "lookalike dog" hypothesis is not the craziest theory I've ever heard. Meanwhile, East Villagers take notice of Star's Facebook page and recognize Star as the dog they've seen around, some even having photos on their phones of her. A few people post side-by-side shots of the Star they'd seen before the shooting and the photo released by the ACC, using arrows to point to similar markings. The dog in the released photo has the same white "socks" on her feet and white band around her neck, with the small spots in the white, like brown paint dripped on her. I don't care about the conspiracy theorists at this point—I'm convinced its Star and equally convinced that she's still alive.

As three weeks pass, *People* magazine reports they have reached out to the mayor's office and have been updated by the Mayor's Alliance communication director that Star is recovering quickly but isn't ready to be adopted, but again, no information on Star's whereabouts is revealed. I'm running into similar roadblocks, and I don't want people to forget about Star or what happened to her and Lech.

Because of Star's Facebook page, I'm contacted by a radio talk show in the UK to share her story and discuss all the details I know. Our neighbors across the pond naturally think we're crazy in the US because of our love for guns, and for them, this story is a prime example of an overzealous police officer using his weapon. I preface my interview as a concerned citizen/dog lover with the time and the means to investigate further. I tell them all I can state is my opinion on the situation—I'm by no means a representative for any party involved. My strategy works: Star's Facebook following grows, and within days, she has more followers than the *Omaha World-Herald*.

Jenn shakes her head. "I know you're not going to let this go," she says, "so what's next?"

What's next is I become one of those fringy detectives in a thriller with whiteboards and arrows pointing to clues. I have a whiteboard in my office and buy new markers and then pull all the facts, dates, and people involved in clear view. I call Star's legal team, but they are aware that I'm the guy with the growing Facebook page for Star. They remain tight-lipped, though they are polite enough to let me vent to them about what Star and her story means to me.

Summer ends, and by October, there is still no word on Star. Maybe she's been secretly adopted already. If so, great. I need to know, either way.

Each day, I come home from work and go straight to my computer, making desperate pleas for any information on Facebook, looking for clues, researching stories of police shooting dogs, pouring over stories of the dark, sometimes sadistic world of animal rescue. Not everyone is out for the animals' best interest, but then, I also see groups fighting hard with limited resources. What most upsets me are the stories of how dogs end up dumped at kill shelters. The people who share their stories are business owners, executive assistants, janitors, teachers, even a couple of CEOs, who all have some story about animal rescue. Some nights, I am so completely consumed in my search, I don't eat dinner. Showering and sleeping are optional. I might sleep a few hours a night, and the first thing I do when I wake up in the morning is check my computer before I get ready to go to work.

Then, out of the blue, I get an email from Rhonda at the legal defense team—the email contains a video of Star at an unknown location. She's in a fenced yard, but she's frolicking. *Frolicking*. She looks good, and most importantly, the video is proof of life.

They probably think they are satisfying me. They might think I would see their video and it would be enough to keep me happy. On their own Facebook page, they post they will no longer be making updates on Star. The one thing I learned during my time in corrections: Never give an inmate anything. A cigarette today will become a whole pack next week, and then a hacksaw a month later, because they will build on whatever is given to them. The legal defense team (and whoever had Star and made the video) gave me the pack, and now I was about to MacGyver my hacksaw.

As many supporters come to Star's Facebook page, so do the trolls. For some people, cruelty is a sport, and callousness comes as easily to them as breathing or eating a pack of Hostess cupcakes. These people are small, insignificant keyboard warriors with a penchant for typing and posting things they would never say in person. In direct response to the trolls, a Star follower named Sarah S, a self-proclaimed "soul coach," starts writing beautiful and articulate responses warding off the trolls. She reaches out to me, telling me she has a huge Facebook following and her supporters, including a journalist, are giving Star the online presence she deserves.

Then, a New York State court officer quietly sent me a copy of the police report of the shooting, which names the officers involved. I was asked not to share the report with the public and not to share the names, and since the person sending the report risked his or her employment to pass me this information. I honor that request.

14th & 2nd

The thing about the NYPD is they don't, in general, release officer names when they're involved in an incident. Plenty of other states release officer names when police are involved in a shooting, but New York likes its secrets. My New Yorker parents sure had their secrets, even regarding their own jobs and families. You can't let outsiders know what goes on in your house. Living in Nebraska broke me of that trait. Still, I wasn't sure what to make of the shooting officer's words: It had been the worst day, month, and year of his life. I don't know if I buy his contrition. Sure, his life is probably awful now because of the attention and pressure put on the department. And there has to be some people who recognize him from the video.

The shooting officer, it turns out, is a Long Island kid like me. I visit his personal Facebook page, and his cover photo is, conveniently, a photo of him and a smiling dog. I check the date of the post, and sure enough, the post was put up *after* the shooting. Good marketing. There aren't quite so many animal-lover posts on the rest of his page, which consists of mostly photos of partying. There is no lack of alcohol in his photos. A New York cop, one who's just shot a dog in a famous case, doesn't have these kinds of photos set to private? I pray to God he feels true remorse, but honestly, I will never know, and I have grave doubts.

I compare this cop with the woman Star chased away just moments before trying to chase away the cop who shot her. The woman was interviewed several times later and said the shooting was not Star's fault. The police were the real threat; the dog was innocent. Here was a woman who had just cause to be scared of this dog, and the opposite was the case. There was no good reason to shoot Star. There are so many dogs who meet the same fate as Star and don't survive, all because a cop's reaction is to shoot to stop the threat per their department's use of force policy, sometimes multiple times.

I stare bleary-eyed in front of the computer screen, reviewing the new video of Star in that yard, scanning for any clues. Not one can be found.

An animal advocacy podcaster based out of California, calls me for an interview/discussion on Star's condition, as does *Canine Crusade* out of the UK. Star's story is international now, and I have no qualms in calling on the audience to press New York City officials for transparency in Star's shooting. The more interviews, research, and focus on Star, the less awareness I have for my immediate surroundings. And my loved ones.

"Charlie, come on, that's enough, come to bed," Jenn says.

"Hey, you just worry about you," I say, not even turning around to look at her.

She retreats, but the next morning, she corners me as I'm getting ready for work. "Charlie, Jesus. Look at you."

"Don't worry. I'm fine."

"You're not fine, you're a wreck." She is right. Though I've skipped dinners, I generally binge on junk the rest of the day. I've been putting on weight again. I'm snapping, a lot, whenever Jenn "interrupts" my search.

"Look at us," Jenn declares, "You either need to find this dog or let it go and move on with your life. Okay?"

6. THE BARK AND THE BITE

Ringo was never the same after the pool incident. He never opened his mouth in a wide smile again. He moved cautiously through the house, especially around my father. He grew quiet and skittish. I wasn't the same, either. My dad was regularly beating the shit out of me, whether it was knocking my hands together—his favorite tactic—or knocking me in the head or arms with his hands or whatever was handy to cause blunt-force trauma.

In some fits, my father would tear up money in front of my mother. Though she spent plenty of money replacing household items broken by my father, and though she was happy to buy plenty of clothes and makeup for herself, she was otherwise miserly with money, as a result of having grown up poor.

My dad reveled in extravagance. If my mother complained, made a comment about him bringing home, say, another new convertible, he might say, "What, you telling me what to do with the money I make? Not the money you make. I make it." Then, he'd take money out of his wallet—or sometimes her wallet—and tear it up in her face.

If we were in the car, he might tear up money and throw it out the window, then toss 8-track tapes out the window—whatever was handy in his console. He had a hair trigger temper.

Then, there was the night my mom threw herself out the car.

I don't remember what the fight was about—not that it matters. I'm sure they'd find a way to fight about the weather or the existence of narwhals. But she'd had enough or wanted to make a point, so she opened the door while we were still in the shopping center parking lot and leapt out. She didn't fall—it was like something out of one of my cartoons. She kept her balance and kept running, then slowed to a stop.

My mother's unexpected escape only served to enflame and enrage my father. He circled the car around, following my mother, then hit her with the bumper of the car. Though he didn't mow her down, he hit her with enough force to knock her to the ground. As a child, all I knew was my father deliberately hit my mother with our car. I jumped out of the car to help her. She had never once come to my aid, but she was my mother, and I felt the need to protect her. As soon as I was out of the car, my father sped away, leaving the two of us on the asphalt.

My mother's leg was scraped up from the fall, and she was shaken up from both the impact and the fight, so the otherwise short walk home from the parking lot might as well have been five miles. We walked to the payphone and called a cab. While we waited, my mom called Iris, who just moved from Queens, close to our old apartment, to our block on Long Island in Westbury. Because of that, they'd gotten friendly, although our families didn't know each other well. Iris agreed to let my mom and me stay the night at her house, four houses down from our own. When the cab came, we went straight there. As we pulled onto the street, my heart raced. I wanted the cab to drop us off quickly so we could run inside Iris's house before we were seen by my father. The entire exercise was all so covert.

Iris embraced us and ran to get some iodine and bandages while my mom sat in the kitchen.

"Are you sure you don't want to call the police?" Iris asked when she returned to nurse my mother's leg. "You really should file a report."

My mother sneered and said, "Nothing would happen to him. And as soon as he found out I called, he'd only get angrier."

So instead, Iris poured my mother a drink, and we all went into the TV room, where Iris turned it on low for me while the two of them talked. After an hour, we heard the approaching Impala followed by a loud knock on the door. It was my father. Through the door, we heard his voice announcing, "It's Charlie Cifarelli from down the street. Can I talk to you?"

"Tell him you haven't seen us or heard from us, okay?" my mother pleaded.

We crouched down while Iris went to the other side of the house and opened the door just a crack.

"Yeah, uh, have you seen my wife?" my father asked.

"Your wife? No…I don't think I've seen Cathy for a couple of days. Is there something wrong?"

"Oh, nothing, no, just a misunderstanding."

"Well, I hope nothing serious." Iris was doing a good job of sounding natural.

"Yeah, you know," my dad said, "it's just that I think she was upset over this little thing, and I accidentally hit her with the car."

"What? Oh, my!"

"No, but she was fine, and it was her fault, because she jumped out of the car while it was moving—I know, I couldn't believe it."

"So, what happened to her, after she got out of the car?" Iris asked. I wondered how my dad was going to account for why he had no clue where we were after he'd run off. Iris was smooth. Looking back, it must have taken a lot to stand her ground against my dad, someone my mother was afraid of, a likely drunk and definitely violent man at her door in the middle of the night.

"Well, uh, that's the thing, uh, I tried to get her to come back to the car, but she ran off." There was no mention of me. "And I went back but then I didn't see her, and now, see, I'm worried I didn't get to talk to her because, well, I don't know if she went to the cops, and I don't really need or want any problems with the police. It was an accident. She overreacted and jumped out of the car. She might have called the police just to get back at me."

"Well, gosh," Iris said, "I surely will let you know if I see her. Do you want me to say anything or call anyone?"

"No, no, that's alright. Uh, just let me know if you hear from her."

He was gone. Even after the door bolt clicked into place, I wasn't sure if we were really safe. But then we heard the exhaust of the Impala going down the street, then back, and every ten or fifteen minutes, we could hear it come through as it crisscrossed the neighborhood street grid.

"Charles, why don't you sleep on the couch, and I'll set your mother up in the extra bedroom," Iris said, holding up a blanket for me to fall into. There was tenderness there, and security. She didn't seem capable of causing harm, and I found myself fantasizing about my mother and I moving in with Iris, or maybe even just me, though I knew it wasn't likely. But maybe, I thought, we could live with her for a week or two until we found a new place to live.

Living with Iris was another of my futile wishes. The next morning, Iris fried me an egg, and as I ate it, she kept asking, "Are you sure?" and it took me a few minutes before I realized she was asking my mother if she was sure she wanted to go back home. Overnight, my mother put up the wall that slipped as she fled from my father the night before. Now, Iris and I were on the outside of that wall.

We showed up at the house, where my father was nursing a hangover, and that was that. Nothing was said. I ran over to Ringo, and we went outside in the backyard, as far away from my parents as I could get.

All my absence served was to prolong the inevitable. It soon didn't matter what I did or didn't do. Possibly, I would leave a little water on the sink when I turned off the flow. I'd get my hands banged together. A fingerprint smudge on a window he'd just cleaned or some tiny thing I had not noticed would earn the same treatment. It wasn't long before I stopped living in color, quite literally. I didn't notice color variations. I couldn't smell things. I retreated deep into myself, away from the surface pain. I shut myself off as much as I could from emotional pain.

If home was bad, then school was worse. At the Drexel School, there were local kids from Westbury along with kids bused in from New Cassel, the neighboring town over, and this mix created a generation of little tough guys who wanted to posture and then fight, sometimes on the playground, but other times, the fights broke out in the halls. Arms got twisted, in fact, for one of them, his arm was twisted so hard it busted. I tried to stay far away—there was nothing I wanted to be a part of less than fights. Despite my upbringing, it was not in my nature to take part in fights. I received my fair share of shoves and kicks, or kids would make fun of my name, which had the Americanized pronunciation as opposed to the Italian pronunciation. *Chiff*-irelli had become *Siff*-irelli, and for the kids, it was no small leap to become Charlie Syphilis. Once one person discovered the "humor" of badgering me because of my name, the mob mentality of the kids took over.

It's hard to say if these kids were bullies—they were gangs and ruffians, future made men and wannabes having what was tantamount to a free-for-all. Even teachers weren't safe. My own teacher, Mrs. Tucker, was assaulted in class by a kid named David, who seemed like a tormented soul. For a first grader, David had an incredible amount of energy—like a nuclear rod mid-meltdown—and made frequent disruptions in class. But one day, he went further than anything I could believe a kid capable of. The beautiful Mrs. Tucker with her jet-black hair and bangled bracelets disciplined David verbally during class, and right in front of the other students, David ran up to the front of class and tried to tackle her to the floor. He couldn't get her down, but he had her by the wrists as she tried to break free. Her bracelets flew in every direction. There wasn't much I could do at home, but here? I ran to get our principal, Mr. O'Donnell. He was a strict but fair man, or so it seemed. We were all more than a little intimidated by the paddle he kept on the wall in his office. He used the paddle, too. He was the only one who could do something to stop David.

"Please, you have to help her!" I panted.

Mr. O'Donnell ran down the hall and pulled David off Mrs. Tucker, whisking him out of the room with more force than the tornado that carried Dorothy into Oz.

What surprised me was the feeling of relief I got from seeking help. Somewhere in the world, there was help if I asked for it. I could beg someone to come, and they would. If only I could get that help at home. There were no television public service announcements during cartoons. There were no alphabet agencies to protect kids like me. If help was out there, I didn't know it.

And then, on a dime, things turned. Rather than spending their energy getting physical, the students at Drexel put their Montague-Capulet feud toward arguing about who had the best sneakers: Pro Keds or Chuck Taylor All Stars, which were THE basketball sneaker. The kids at school would yell at each other, back and forth, which sneaker was better and subsequently which group of them had the better sneaker.

I wanted to be a Pro kid—those were the cool kids. Instead, I had neither, which meant I was a "sneaker skip." I was already one of the sensitive kids, and I ran to get help for Mrs. Tucker, which painted me as a snitch. If I could only persuade my mom to help make me a Pro kid, I would be set.

It took months of persuasion, but my mother understood the power of brand labels and exterior statements, and so she took me to Alexander's department store and got me my Pro Keds. Walking around the next day at school, I even got a few nods, and that was it—I had been accepted as one of the cool kids. I took a breath. Finally, things might ease up.

Except they didn't, not even with my sneakers. I was still the sensitive kid, and it didn't take much to push me over the edge.

One thing that pushed me over the edge was the issue of my hair. There wasn't much control I had over my life, including the length of my hair. My mother kept my hair very long, to the point that one day, while I was riding my bike through the neighborhood with my shirt off, a woman on her front lawn yelled at me, "A girl needs a shirt on when she's outside!" not realizing I was not a girl.

One morning before school, I determined, as a seven-year-old, I should be able to decide how to wear my hair. In this decision to reclaim my bodily autonomy, I knew there was a certain line I couldn't cross. Instead of taking it all off, I took a pair of paper scissors to my bangs. They were in my eyes and bothering me, so that would be my justification if my mother said anything. I just couldn't live that way. Had I any inclination of how to cut my bangs? Absolutely not. The endeavor went about as badly as can be expected. Still, I went off to school, relieved I now could see without the hair blocking my vision.

It wasn't my mother, or the other students, who took the first shot. It was my teacher, Mrs. Tucker, the one I'd defended. "My goodness, Charlie, who cut your hair? They did not do a good job!"

Indignant that she would criticize me, I shouted, "I did!"

In that instant, all the kids turned for a closer look. Then, the ridicule started. I couldn't contain the hurt. The comments and taunting got to be too much for my seven-year-old self. I ran out of the classroom and headed for the front door. I hopped on my bicycle and didn't look back. I pedaled as fast as my legs would go, heading straight for home. It was only a couple of blocks, but my lungs and thighs burned from going so hard. My eyes were even worse: Every attempt to stop the crying only made the tears spill harder.

As I burst through the front door of our house, I heard my mom's voice calling out, "Charles? Is that you? Why are you home early?" I didn't stop to say anything. Once I closed the door to my room, I lay on my bed, holding my pillow close to me. It was the only thing helping the physical hurt I felt throughout my entire body. It was a visceral pain, as though I had been thrown off the roof of my house with all my insides turned out. I was at an age when I should have been building emotional muscle and learning to handle the hits, but instead, I was tender flesh and raw nerve. What I wanted was for there to be an end at least in sight, a time I could point to and say, "I can hold out until then. The pain will go away, and this will all be over." But that was a future I couldn't see.

A glimmer of hope came with a knock on the door. It was my principal, Mr. O'Donnell, who'd heard from my teacher that I left school.

"Is Charles okay?" I heard him ask.

"I don't know, he won't talk to me," my mother said.

I came downstairs to face the music, feeling my shame and thinking of that paddle on the wall of his office.

"Hello, Charles," he said, "I'm just checking in and making sure you're okay."

Mr. O'Donnell cared about me? He wanted to know if I was okay? I was then thrown entirely off my rocker: My principal gave me a hug.

"What happened today, Charles?"

I sniffed and said, "Mrs. Tucker made fun of me today in class, in front of everyone."

"What? And after you helped her when that student attacked her? I will have a word with her, and it will never happen again," he promised.

Oh, Mr. O'Donnell, I wanted to say, *my father beats me while my mother does nothing—please help get me out of here.*

"What is it, Charles, is there anything else upsetting you?"

Did he know? Was his involvement my chance? But my chance at what? Who would take care of me if I left? Wouldn't I just end up in an orphanage? All the films and TV I'd seen let me know orphanages were not places a child went to willingly. My mother was unhappily shuttled among foster homes. I thought also of my mother being too afraid to call the police the night we spent at Iris's. Maybe she had a good reason for not calling them. Maybe they couldn't do anything about my father. And if the police couldn't do anything, what could my elementary school principal do?

"No, Sir," I said quietly.

"Okay," he said, "Why don't you rest. You don't have to come back to school today. Take the rest of the day off, and then come back tomorrow."

As I watched Mr. O'Donnell drive away in his green station wagon with wood side-paneling, I tried to hold onto the feeling of gratitude that there was one human being in this world who cared about me. My parents certainly didn't, and there was no one else to look out for me.

At times, I dreamed of moving in with my mom's older brother. His kids were older than I was, and they were a great family. They were the family I wished I could be in, at least when I stood on the outside looking in. I would have settled for living with my Uncle Joey and Aunt Jenny, my dad's older brother and his wife, who were great to me. They talked to me like I was a grown up, but they had a terminally-ill daughter, and besides—Uncle Joey wouldn't go against his brother. The worst outcome would be if I told on my parents, if I asked for help and my uncles and aunts didn't help me, what then? There would be hell to pay for letting our family secrets out of the house—both from my father and my mother. The risk was just too great. "Besides," I thought, "who'd believe a young kid like me?" The family would likely think I was exaggerating. At least, that's what I assumed.

The half day of reprieve from school did nothing to soften the blow of my return. "Look at the crybaby," they started in, making the fake crying sounds and rubbing their eyes. All of my classmates laughed at me, following me down the halls, and even whispering behind me while I was sitting at my desk in the classroom. They'd seen my soft underside and rather than take a step back, they were all in. These children were like my father—they loved causing pain, and they didn't have to be drunk or borderline to do it.

From the nightmare of every waking day, I started to wonder if my dad had maybe once been like me. Maybe he, too, had been made fun of by his class, and that was why he lashed out. Maybe torturous school kids made my father angry and violent. I refused to let myself get like him. I could make the conscious decision to not turn into him. I would just have to hang in there for a few years—I had no other choice.

Back at home, there was a simmering tension that didn't quite explode. We still went out as a family for dinners and drives, although I was always worried as soon as my father ordered a drink. Late in the summer of 1972, I'd been out of school and relaxing in the yard with Ringo, ever my shadow, letting my mind go deep into thought, when I was called to go on a family trip to my mother's doctor. It struck me as weird that my father would go along, and of course they wouldn't leave me home alone. I started to worry—it was the second visit to my mother's doctor within a couple of weeks, but naturally, my parents told me nothing.

My father and I waited together in the waiting room, which was the most modern waiting room I'd seen. There were toys for kids to play with while they waited for their mothers, and these were better than the toys at my doctor's office. I was focusing on the toy trucks, which I was rolling across the leather of the couch when my mother came out of the exam room. My father stepped up, and even thought they were trying to be discreet; I heard my mother tell him she was pregnant.

Neither one of them seemed happy with the news, and at the time, I did not understand why. Weren't babies the kind of news people got excited about? I was going to have a baby brother or sister. That should be great news. Although, I thought, maybe I would have to be his or her protector. Or maybe, with a baby in the house, they'd go back to being the same kind of parents they were when I was little.

The drive home was a quiet one. Neither my father nor my mother told me she was pregnant. No one said anything to me. They did not say a word about it for another month—when my mother's belly started to show more than she could hide under a blouse.

"Well, Charles," my father said, sitting me down in the kitchen, "you're going to have a baby brother, and he's going to be born in May of 1973."

I feigned surprise, and replied, "Really? That's so cool! Wow, what are we going to name him?"

"Christian," my father said.

I looked over at the bump under my mother's clothes. I wanted to touch it, cuddle with Christian, this brother was now more than just this secret I kept in my heart. I had no idea where my father got the name Christian. It wasn't the kind of name heard very much. There just weren't a lot of New England union members named Christian. A few years later, I'd see just what a heavenly gift Christian would be.

7. STAR CHASING

Jenn's ultimatum turns out to be the push I need to get on with things. I continue to make regular calls to Star's defense team, being the ultimate squeaky (annoying) wheel. By mid-October, the Mayor's Alliance posts a new photo of Star on their Facebook page. (I guess they were taking over the updates that the legal defense team stopped posting them.)

My career in corrections was based on many, many hours of watching surveillance footage and keeping an eye out for tiny details and any signs of malfeasance. While the first video of Star offered nothing in the way of details concerning her surroundings, this photo reveals the cars in the nearby parking lot. What strikes me immediately is that none of the cars have front license plates. This fact tells me that Star isn't in New York. Knowing which states don't require front license plates at least helps me narrow the search. The top of the list is Pennsylvania—only a short haul from New York City.

Penny, the journalist who wrote the article trying to find Lech, does excellent animal advocacy work, and as far as I'm concerned, is a saint, along with wielding a whip-smart intellect. I share the photo with Penny, letting her know my theory about the plates. I won't press it further, but now I'm convinced that it's got to be Pennsylvania.

Penny meanwhile continues to support me as she does her own digging while encouraging me to keep pushing until I find Star.

"I've volunteered at a kill shelter, Charlie," she says, "I've witnessed firsthand how these sad, voiceless animals were once a family pet and now are discarded like trash. I read about Star prior to Lech adopting her, Charlie, Star was an abused puppy. She has seen the inside of more than one kill shelter. She needs an advocate. She needs you."

It's clear, though, from comments on social media (and a heads-up from Penny) that I'm not in the good graces of Star's defense team or the Mayor's Alliance. Also, I see a great deal of negative comments from men on the Facebook page. They are chewing me out for blaming the cops who were faced with a vicious and ferocious dog. "What," they ask, "were they supposed to get mauled?" When I look them up, more than a few happen to work for NYPD, though they haven't let on about this during their trolling.

Sarah S. has plenty of words for them. She shames them for acting like the cops were confronted by a Tyrannosaurus Rex. She tells me I should block them. Do these cops not know that I can look them up as well? Or do they want me to know they are monitoring my page? If so, blocking a couple of officers' personal accounts isn't going to stop them. Also, I mean, come on—I have friends from school who are cops in the New York region. They must know this isn't a good look.

None of this matters. I will not rest until I can hug Star. She has no idea that her rescuer isn't giving up. I just want to make sure she is happy. She deserves that. All I have to do now is contact every animal rescue agency, shelter, and veterinary clinic in the state until I get to Star. Pennsylvania is a big state—I have my work cut out for me.

As soon as I get someone on the line, I have my script: Do you have a one-eyed Pit Bull that's brown and white? If the answer is no, my reply is: Do you know someone who might? The task at times seems endless. First, it takes the better part of two nights to find the numbers for all these places. Then I have to make the calls, making sure to call during business hours, but not lunch hours. I'm put on hold longer than I speak to actual humans. While doing all this, I never stop reaching out by phone and email to Star's legal team to see if they will give any updates. Unsurprisingly, they will not.

Suddenly, in blows Hurricane Sandy, swallowing what is left of October's news cycle. One of the people I've frequently spoken with is the wife of Star's lead attorney. I call her to make sure she's okay and ask about the storm damage. Through the course of conversation, I say, "I hope Star's okay wherever she is."

"Our friends in P-A are doing a good job with Star, so don't worry," she replies.

A-ha! Even as she says it, the A is much quieter than the P, as if she realizes she's slipped. Alright. I'm all-in on redoubling my efforts to get to Star.

"Charlie, it's November," Jenn says, "and now we're into the third month of this. I'm telling you, either find Star, or give it up. This is taking over your life, and I'm worried—it has the same hold as an addiction, and your life *is* suffering. And because—if you can't make it happen after three months, with *all* this time devoted to finding her, it's not going to happen."

It's true. I've been so single-minded that I have neglected nearly everything, except the basic functions of work. I've neglected Jenn and our life together. The fact that she hasn't given me the boot in these last three months is a testament to her patience, of which I currently deserve only a slim portion.

Maybe this is it. Should I give up now, after devoting all this time, all this obsessive, even frenzied, energy to this unknown dog?

I decide to give it a week. I decide to keep going until November 12—then it's three months to the day since Star's shooting. I'll push these ten days, and then I'll go back to my life.

I don't have to wait until November 12. My lucky break comes a few days later, when the Mayor's Alliance posts another photo of Star *outside* her rehab facility, with one of the volunteers caring for her. There's no name on the building that I can see, but there is a semi-trailer truck in the background. Somone has blurred out the company name but not the transportation numbers.

If I know anything, it's trucks. US DOT numbers are assigned to every truck in the United States, and these numbers hold the information about the trucks' owners—like a license plate on a car but with more technical information. I go straight to the online database, Safer Systems, and enter the numbers.

Holy shit. Almost instantly, I receive the name of the company and its location in Philadelphia. The truck looks a bit tired, as if it has not been on the highway in quite some time. Now, I just have to hope that the truck is parked in front of the location in the database, and if it is, that is where Star is located. I put the address into Google Maps and switch to "street view." It's an industrial complex, but there's no veterinary hospital or rehab facility shown. I'm close, I have to be—I feel it. The pieces just aren't coming together.

I talk to Jenn and tell her that I know she's in the general vicinity, and she doesn't say much.

"I need just a little more time," I say.

"Be mindful of the time," Jenn says. "And, you know, maybe not make this the only thing you do?"

I try my best. I focus my search to Philadelphia and call organizations and businesses in the area, looking for animal shelters and rescues. Thanksgiving comes. Does Star know it's a holiday? It doesn't matter—it's Thanksgiving, and Star is alone, and I cannot shake the sadness. Cold air settles over Nebraska.

December means cold winters, and my thoughts turn again to Lech. As if I'm psychically or spiritually wired into his story, when I check the New York news, a local outlet reports that Lech has gone back to Poland to live, with his mother. Life had gotten to be too much in New York and America, with the homelessness, his health problems, and, of course, with the loss of Star. His homeless advocate spoke to a journalist about his departure. The advocate said Lech was disturbed and disheartened that more people cared about his dog than about his own life.

Lech's feelings are heartbreaking, and I have my own mixed feelings about him. In my personal experience, you can offer someone help, but they can't fully accept it, or fully get out of their addictions or problems, until they are willing to accept a higher power and have a spiritual awakening, whether from God or a higher power or a deep faith in something. Something must have all the power of hope. Without hope, recovery is impossible, and no amount of outside assistance can truly help a person. My experience with this is why I did not push or preach when I offered him a job and a home in Nebraska. Sadly, he turned both down.

More than three months of my life are now invested in the search. I practice my pitch for my calls. I stay up late into the night. I get up early in the morning. I spend my time intensely scouring the internet. One night, I find the website of a large rescue organization in Philadelphia, with dogs available for adoption that don't really seem like the Pit Bull type. Instead, they have many greyhounds along with a few other sporting dogs. Then, suddenly, at three in the morning, one dog stands out: A brown and white Pit Bull, stockier than the rest. I see a slight head tilt. I recognize the smile so big you might overlook the missing eye.

I scream, "Jenn! Jenn! I've found her!"

8. THE LOST BOY

My brother Christian was born May 23, 1973. From the get-go, he was healthy and happy. I knew I wasn't going to have a new best friend all of a sudden—he was only a baby. But there was something or someone in the house to love.

My mother's focus was entirely placed on him, though she became tired and irritable the rest of the time, but it was easy enough to steer clear of her irritability. My father absolutely doted on Christian, showing a humanity I'm not sure I ever saw in him. Still, it wasn't long before my father found a new outlet for his psychological warfare.

At dinner, my father took to throwing food he didn't like. My mother had overcooked it or she'd undercooked it or it was not what he wanted, or it had no flavor, or it was too salty. Perhaps she hadn't drained enough of the water out of the spaghetti. Whatever the case, he would take a few bites, then decide something was off.

My father considered himself something of a gourmet cook. His own Italian mother was an exceptional cook, and he took it as a personal affront that my mother, an admittedly lousy cook, wasn't putting in the effort to improve. That was at least part of his disdain for her cooking.

Both of my parents were obsessed with weight and being thin. My mother hated food and would often play with it on her plate for appearances before forcing down a few bites. Then, after dinner, the inevitable sounds of her vomiting in the bathroom would permeate the house.

The awful sound of my mother forcing herself to throw up each night made me ill and gave me anxiety. My father, too, barely ate. Sitting down at the table was a drag for him, and I suspected he didn't like the closeness of us all facing each other at a table being forced to commune collectively. Dining out was less of a problem for him as there was a lack of intimacy at a public restaurant than confronted him at the home table. However, he wasn't going to let his disinterest get in the way of demanding the best food be put in front of him. He was going to use my mother's disinterest in food and his enjoyment of inspecting its quality as his contention point.

Was the destruction part of an elaborate competition to not eat? A way to show off who could go with eating less or who could go longer in between meals? I'm sure plenty of psychologists would have loved to put my parents under a microscope—I for one would love answers for their behavior. Whatever their war was must have been so deeply placed in their subconsciousness because their behaviors were entirely chaotic. There was no deliberating, no method beyond each of them in their little power struggle. Just hate—hating themselves, hating each other, needing to control and keep perfect and also destroying to hurt each other before subsequently restoring order.

It was *totally fucked up* is what it was.

Inevitably, the hostility of my school and my father's personality disorder rubbed off on me at least a little. I was quick to shoot my mouth off if someone looked at me cross-eyed. That's what happened when the next-door neighbor kids gave me a glare when I took my bike out for a ride. I stopped in front of the Stanton home, where the boys usually jawed for fun. I called out to Clark, only I repeatedly called him Clark Bar, the nickname I'd heard other kids use. Clark and his brother Joe Jr. weren't taking the usual bait, so I kept at it. Then Joe Jr. spoke up, telling me to scram.

"Stay out of it, Joe, and shut your face," I said, "let Clark Bar speak for himself." Saying this didn't feel right, but that's what people did when they wanted to gain power in a situation.

My outburst got the attention of Joe Sr., who came running after me. I took off on my bicycle, and probably out of rage and frustration, Mr. Stanton speared the rake he was holding into the spokes of my bike, and I flew over the handlebars. All at once, Mr. Stanton was on top of me, holding me down with his weight and kneeling on my wrists. He then freed his right hand quickly and struck me in the face and the side of my head with the palm of his hand, over and over.

"I'm not in the mood today to deal with this!" he yelled into my face. "You were aggravating me, arguing with my sons!" Then, he laid off me and stood up, allowing me to stand.

I acted like a jerk, sure, but was his reaction warranted?

Mr. Stanton had always been nice to me. However, things were a little dicey with my father. My father had recently put up a fence between our properties without a permit, so Joe Sr. reported it to the town. Mr. Stanton might not have minded, but my father left the side facing the Stanton property ugly and unfinished. The installation was poor, and the fence cut into the Stanton property enough that Mr. Stanton scraped the side of his new International Scout SUV on the fence. There was bad blood, but I'd never suspected Mr. Stanton would attack me in this way. He worked on computers, for one. He wore a white button-down shirt with a pocket protector every day to work, and he wore the black Buddy Holly glasses that were popular over a decade earlier. However, being next-door neighbors to my parents, I'm sure he heard enough violence go down to assume we were all that way. Maybe my dad rubbed off on him too.

In that moment, though, I wasn't thinking about what a nice guy Mr. Stanton had always been. I left my bike where it skidded on the pavement and ran to my house to tell my mother.

"Charlie!" she yelled for my father, "do you know what just happened to our son?"

My father marched outside, and upon seeing what was headed his way, Mr. Stanton beat a retreat into his own yard. That was not about to stop my father.

"Joe, did you hit my kid?" My father asked angrily.

"I'm sorry I did that," Mr. Stanton said, his face fallen, his voice heavy. I could tell he was disappointed in himself. No shit.

"What right do you have to hit my kid?"

"I don't."

My father was tensing up, and I knew that posture. I was sure Joe Stanton Sr. was about to get the beating of his life. But my father held himself back.

"Look, Charlie, I'm sorry I did that. I was wrong, and your son got on my nerves, and I snapped. I didn't mean to."

My father walked away from him, corralling my mother and me back into the house.

"Cathy, call the police. I want them here."

Great, now the police are getting involved? My mom made the call, and soon they were at our house, asking me for details. I told them everything, and they went to interview Mr. Stanton. I leaned out my window to hear them.

"What happened with your neighbor's son?"

"I got mad, and I hit him." He explained about the rake and pinning me down and striking me. Then, the police handcuffed him and put him back in the squad car to head for the police station, but first they came back to our house.

They took a look at my arms, swollen from where Mr. Stanton squeezed me, and my face with its lump from being hit by him. My arms and legs were scraped from sliding on the asphalt.

"You better take your son to the hospital to have him checked out," one of the officers told my parents.

The whole way to the hospital, I felt a sinking guilt. Mr. Stanton was not a bad man. He was not the one who should have been hauled off in the back of a squad car. My father caused me a hundred times worse pain for years. I feared my father more than anyone. But it was thoughtful, regimented Mr. Stanton who I ratted out and who got locked up. Still, I was only eight years old, and had been hit hard by a thirty-five-year-old man. Even the supposed good guys in my world seemed out to get me.

I might have blamed myself, but my mother blamed my father. She blamed him for everything, for the problems with the Stanton family, for me shooting my mouth off, and she said every bit of it came from him. That just set my father off more—which meant he started ramping up my beatings. He smacked and hit me repeatedly in the face and the ears with the heel of his hand or a hard series of slaps—but of course, God forbid someone outside the family hit me. He twisted my arms behind my back while I screamed and begged him to stop. One might think this would cause my mother to step in to block my father, since she instigated him, but no. She waited to start another fight, which would lead to my father beating me once again.

One night my parents were ramping up, set off by another discussion of the Stanton situation, which was going to trial, and my mother grabbed my denim coat and, handing it to me, said, "The weather is getting cooler, here."

"What? Where am I going?" I asked.

"You need to leave the house now."

So that was her way of protecting me—kicking me out of the house so my father couldn't wail on me?

Autumn was setting in, and my denim coat did little to keep out the cold. I was angry this was the solution—I was angry at the whole situation, frankly. She didn't have a place for me to go, but she didn't want me nearby. What was I supposed to do? *Fine*, I thought. *I'll stay out.*

I walked and I walked. The train station was at least a mile from our house, but with my short little eight-year-old legs, it seemed much farther.

Okay, I was at the train station, now what? With no money, I couldn't get a ticket. I hung around the station, looking for a few coins that may have fallen on the ground but didn't have much luck. After a while there, I decided to keep walking. A few miles away was Roosevelt Field, where Lindbergh took off forty-seven years earlier for his transcontinental flight. The field had since been turned into a huge shopping mall, though a plaque memorialized the flight. My father pointed this plaque out to me on numerous occasions, resentful that after all Charles Lindbergh did for aviation, this was the only mention of him.

But I knew the mall well enough, and it seemed like the safest place to be for a kid my age. There would be people walking around, and at least I would be indoors and out of the cold air. It took probably close to an hour to walk there, and the second I got inside, I found a drinking fountain and guzzled the water. Now what? I wandered the mall, ducked into some stores, past the Friday night crowds. The mall stayed open late on a Friday night, so I could take my time. I figured someone would come up to ask me why I was alone, but no one did. Whether I was sitting alone on the benches in the large mall atrium, or aimlessly checking out storefronts, no one even took note of me.

Being surrounded by people but having no one see me, was a strange type of isolation. At home, I wanted positive attention from my parents, but I would rather have been invisible and received no attention than what they actually gave me. At school, I wanted to remain invisible. But here, I wished someone would see me and understand I desperately needed help and guidance. Instead, some high-end stores began closing up. It was almost ten, and I couldn't stay any longer.

I walked back in the direction of my parents' house, and as I thought about it, I realized that, yes, it was their house, but it was not *my* house anymore. Being scared wore off. There was a freeing sense in understanding that what was theirs wasn't mine. This realization meant while I didn't yet know where my place was, it was certainly out there somewhere away from the two people who shared a house with me.

The train station was the only place that seemed safe at such a late hour since it was lit up and bustling with people. At least, that was the logic of an eight-year-old. The station was a very different place than it had been just a few hours earlier. It was a ghost town. The lights were dim, and the only people around were two teenagers sharing a skateboard, taking turns doing tricks against the low curb. I was sitting on one of the benches, thinking about what to do and whether my parents even cared I was gone or if they were still fighting. I also thought about what might be getting destroyed by my father that very minute.

"Hey, you okay?" It was one of the teenagers. They both walked up to me but kept their distance.

"Are you by yourself?" the other one asked.

"You know it's kind of late," the other one said, "and you being kind of young is all."

They were the first and only people to ask about me. Two kids maybe only five or six years older than I was. What could I say? I told probably the second lie of my lifetime: I said, "I only live a block away from here—I just came here to say goodbye to my friend."

Looking back now, these kids probably didn't believe me. At the time, it seemed like a reasonable story to give them. Why wouldn't a small boy be out in the middle of the night, saying goodbye at a train station, waving off a friend of probably the same age? They hung out with me for maybe ten minutes, chatting and doing tricks on the skateboard, and then one of the kids told the other he needed to get home.

"Shit, it's midnight. I was supposed to be home at eleven!" he said in a panic.

It was midnight. *Shit, indeed.* They said goodbye and left, although they hesitated, they looked at me, then shrugged and went to their homes. I pulled my jacket closer around me and curled my knees up to my chest. It didn't help much. It was futile to think anyone was coming at this point, but I wasn't willing to go home.

I had two problems: I couldn't sleep there, and I had no idea how to find something to eat. I was hungry, especially since my mother kicked me out before I ate, and I walked for miles. Maybe I would have to live on the streets? If I knew I was going to be kicked out, I could have at least packed my backpack with some provisions like that hippie my dad picked up on his way to Woodstock all those years earlier. He made it on his own, but he was prepared. An hour passed, at least by the clock at the station, but it felt like three hours. There was no good way around it—I had no business being out there. It was time to go home.

The walk back took half an hour, which I know because the police officers waiting for me said it was one-thirty in the morning. Three squad cars sat in front of the house, and about a half dozen officers were milling in the front yard or on the porch. One was standing off by himself, next to his vehicle, and he saw me approach.

"Hey, are you Charles?" he asked.

I nodded.

He walked up to me and bent down. "Where've you been?"

Another officer walked up to the two of us, and I told them both everywhere I had been that evening. I heard my mother's voice in the house calling out for me, and then another officer told her to stay calm, they had a few questions to ask me first. Somewhere else, the officers were using the term runaway, conveying that my parents reported I'd run away from home. Huh.

"You know Charles what could have happened to you?" the kneeling officer said to me. "We will tell you," he continued, "a person could come up and ask you for a dime, and if you didn't have it, they'd beat you to a pulp. If you did have it, they'd see you have money and then hit you—or do worse—to get the rest of your money out of you."

I was exhausted and didn't want to argue. I knew their hearts were in the right place. My reluctance to argue was due to the inability to imagine anyone could get me out of my situation – even the police. However, even as an eight-year-old, I couldn't help but question their astuteness. There I was, coming back with nothing on me but my sad denim jacket and my Pro Ked sneakers, and I supposedly run away like that? I wanted to tell them I was a smart kid—didn't they think if I were really aiming to run away that I would at least have packed my stash of change and taken my baseball card collection to cash in? Or taken a bag of food?

I tried to respond in the manner I'd seen Mr. Stanton address the police, or even my father, when pressured by outsiders—both were calm and steady. I would be that way too.

"I'm sorry, Sir," I said, "I didn't mean to cause such a fuss."

The officer hugged me and then motioned for my parents to come over. My parents—boy, did they put on a performance. Charles, we were so worried! Charles, how could you do that to us? No, they weren't angry, they were just so glad I was safe.

Barf.

I was hungry, though, and I let them know it.

"That's fine, Charles," my father said, "go inside and wash up. We'll take you to the diner. You can get whatever you want." I nodded, then looked back at the officers once.

So close and yet so far.

As I walked into the house, I saw Donna, the babysitter my parents hired to take care of Christian. When the police cars showed up at the house, Donna was among the neighbors who rushed over to see what happened. My parents immediately recruited her so they wouldn't have to think about Christian for the rest of the night. Donna was sixteen and lived on our block. She came right over and hugged me.

"Charles, I'm so glad to see you," she said. She gave me a look, a real look, and it was then I realized she probably saw right through my parents. "Are you okay? You must have been so scared. I'm so sorry, I—I'm glad you're okay."

"Yeah, I'm okay. Thanks, Donna," I said.

She looked at me for another few seconds, and then I told her I wanted to wash up because we were headed out to the diner, which, ironically, was across the road from the Roosevelt Field Mall. It was a 24-hour diner. If I had money on me, I could have spent the night there and eaten my fill.

Donna stayed overnight so my parents didn't have to wake up Christian for an outing. I don't remember the ride, but I remember sitting in the seat at the diner, in the actual middle of the night, watching the glow of the lights in the parking lot and staring across to the mall where I'd spent a few hours. I was so hungry I could have eaten the whole menu.

I was always hungry. With my two parents daily challenging each other to eat like birds and consume as few calories as possible, shoveling food into my mouth was, to say the least, taboo—on a normal night, anyway. To counteract what they might have been setting up back at home, I started devouring my food as fast as I could, sometimes barely chewing. I wanted to get it in me before they stopped me. I shoveled in my eggs and toast. My parents ordered buttered bagels for the optics, but they barely touched their food. They didn't say one thing to me about being gone or calling the police. Not one word. We rode home in silence, and I watched them from the backseat, stiff in their positions in the front, their silhouettes illuminated by the occasional streetlamp.

And even then, even as a young as I was, it dawned on me: They were not happy people, and nothing they did, including having my baby brother, could ever make them any happier. It wasn't in them to be able to be happy, with each other or themselves. I felt truly sorry for them both, as one might pity some sad story a friend might tell you. Who really were these locked-in, miserable people who had somehow gotten together and brought me into the world?

It was worse at the trial for Joe Stanton. My dad was pushing hard for a conviction, and the prosecutor agreed, telling my father he had a great case. Mr. Stanton was found not guilty. He used the defense that he had just been roughhousing with me.

Afterward, the prosecutor came over to me, hugged me, and with sincerity said, "Really, we can only conclude he's not innocent—we know he's not—but we just couldn't prove he was guilty."

That was that. Though I felt bad for Mr. Stanton, for me, it was proof no one was ever going to get in trouble for hitting me. *That was that.*

#

School continued to be a miserable place for everyone—I have no idea what was in the water in that town back then. I couldn't concentrate—I was hyperactive, as were so many other kids, who all seemed to transfer their extra energy into fighting or at the very least, roughhousing. Then suddenly, my mother started talking about having me attend the Catholic school across the street from my current school. Why, I had no idea. We never talked about God in the house and never went to church, yet my mother decided I was going to be a Catholic school boy.

It turned out my dad was making even more money those days, and he started to say things like, "We need a bigger house. I'm thinking one of those great places on the south shore of Long Island. Picture it—that's where we should be living."

My mother nodded, but in the meantime, the new money was going into sending me to Catholic school. Saying goodbye to the people I was used to wasn't hard, as they were not my bosom buddies. Unfortunately, as I started at St. Brigid's Catholic School, I realized at least in my old school, I somewhat blended in. Now, I stuck out like a truly sore thumb. First off, all the kids knew each other since kindergarten, and there I was, entering during the middle of the school year. I didn't know a single prayer. Then, instead of buying the official school uniform for me, my mother procured her own version, which the students immediately locked onto, launching into an endless stream of ridicule. At least by then, I was used to it. Everyone was watching my every move.

Then there was the tie. I did not know how to tie a tie. So, my father would tie it loosely around his neck, then leave it hanging on the coat rack. I'd slip it over my head each day and tighten it to my throat. At some point, the kids in school were onto me, and one day, another bully on a power trip yanked it loose and over my head, undid the knot, and threw it at me. A group of kids encircled me, demanding I show them I could tie it.

I hated every one of them, as well as the nun who was my teacher and cut through our desks like a shark sniffing out blood and waiting for the moment, she could trip us up. Then, she would take the ruler to the back of our hands. I didn't know what prison was like, but I imagined my existence there was akin to being in a prison. Every day was some kind of assault, whether the bullying was verbal or physical. Afterwards, I got to go home to more abuse.

At the time, 1975 felt like the year from hell, but it was ending, finally. Then, suddenly, my parents said that after months of stalking the realtor's office, they'd finally found the house they wanted, and we were moving. The house was a large colonial built in 1927 in Merrick, a town of about fifteen thousand residents which produced notable names including *The Godfather* author, Mario Puzo.

The house was one of only four houses on that side of the block, in a part of Merrick called Lindenmere. The owner was an old man who'd lived there since the forties and had a stash of over twenty cases of empty Sherry bottles in the crawl space under the house. He showed them off proudly, saying that when the weather was fine, he'd take his daily walk to the Rhine Skellar bar a few blocks away, but if it was raining, he'd drink his sherry at home.

"That must be twenty years' worth," my mother laughed.

The old man laughed too and said, "Oh, not quite. My nephew cleaned out that crawl space three years ago. Took all the bottles away. I guess I have another load for him to clear out before you folks take over."

In the presence of this old man, a veteran of World War I, my parents were as pleasant as any two people can be. I wasn't sure it was all an act. They were excited about the house and were happy to have the old man show them around, chatting them up. It was as if for a few moments, they were imagining a completely new life for all of us. The trouble was, they were still the same people. It struck me that this delightful old man would be headed to a nursing home which would not let him drink a bottle of sherry a day or chain smoke his pipe. My heart felt a heaviness for him with the understanding his whole world was going to change as soon as my parents bought the house.

The deal was finalized in February, and after recovering from the worst bout of flu in my life, I started at a brand-new school in our new town after having been booed by my class on my last day at St. Brigid's. I swore to myself I never wanted to hear about a Catholic anything ever again. (Little did I know that Catholic monks would save my life years later.)

Then, I stepped foot into Birch Elementary in Merrick, and the tides changed completely. My teacher, Mrs. Gamp, was like having your dearest, most kindly aunt as your teacher. The students and staff were pleasant. Though my classmates cared deeply about brand-name clothing, which I couldn't care less about, they didn't harass me. In fact, they let me be, and after a few weeks, we were all on a friendly basis. It wasn't long before I was as happy as I remembered being since right before my neighbor Kenny's death in 1969.

My parents started on all the home improvement projects right away, which meant a large-scale remodel.

"Why did you buy an old house if you just are going to redo everything?" I asked my mom.

"Oh, Charles, of course we'd want to remodel whatever house we bought. We could never find one to our liking. This way, the kitchen and the bathrooms will be new," she explained.

They wanted everything modern, and my father wanted to make sure it was clear to everyone he had money to put into his new house. I'd hear the costs quoted to my parents for tile or flooring or the finishing on the bathrooms and I tallied up the totals. (I have *always* been a numbers guy.) The upside was my dad was so preoccupied with the remodel he wasn't finding the time to use me as a punching bag.

As another show of upward mobility, my dad brought home two new Cadillacs, one for him and one for my mother. He needed to show his love in the only language he understood: Monetarily. He did this by keeping his wife as well furnished as he was. My mother's complicity made sense: She was willing to put up with a horrendous tyrant because she got nice things. Growing up with nothing, she only knew how to appreciate things of monetary value, children and husbands be damned.

With my parents otherwise occupied, I quickly made friends with our next-door neighbor, Mr. Carmichael. He was a World War II veteran and owned a boat he kept at the nearby marina. My dream was to go out on a boat to fish.

"Alright, Charles," Mr. Carmichael said one Friday after he got off work, "if there's no rain tomorrow, I will see you in my driveway at 7 a.m."

I went to sleep listening to the weather updates on my AM/FM radio, willing the skies to be clear so we could go fishing the next day. They were.

I made sure to be in his driveway at 6:55, because I didn't want to miss the chance or disappoint him by keeping him waiting (or thinking I wasn't interested and leaving without me).

"So, what do you know about fishing, Charles?" he asked.

I shrugged, not knowing much.

"Well, you have to be patient. Can you be patient?"

"Yes, sir."

Oh, could I be patient.

I fished with him almost every weekend from that point on and made a point to hang around his yard to see if he had any work for me to do.

He didn't smile much, at least not with his whole face, but he was kind. He said he'd seen a lot of death in World War II.

"War hangs over everything," he said one afternoon, "You know how you see the vets coming back now, and they don't look the same? It's because war is terrible. I saw that too, when I was born, right at the end of World War I. Many of those boys came back shell-shocked."

He looked at me closely, and I wasn't sure what he was seeing. I knew he was talking about our neighbor, Andy, a guy in his early twenties who seemed like he had lived three lifetimes. I'd made friends with Andy, and he also talked about the thousand-yard stare his friends had when they left Vietnam. He had it too, and we could sit for a couple of hours in mostly silence together, staring. For a while, I was his only friend, until the one day I went over, and he pulled a gun on me.

"I could do it; you know," Andy said flatly.

I backed out of the house and never went back. I never told anyone about what happened. But Mr. Carmichael mentioned him one morning on his boat, "You still hanging around that young man?" he asked.

"No. Not anymore."

"Probably for the best."

He spoke again about the ways people get shell-shocked, then said it could even happen to people who haven't been to war but have seen bad things happen, even at home.

As I left his yard that afternoon, my good feelings were swallowed by the dread I always carried with me. Was I also shell-shocked? What Mr. Carmichael explained felt…familiar.

My other role model was the local pharmacist, Mr. Berg, who owned his own pharmacy down the road and lived across the street from Mr. Carmichael. I came around off and on when I had some change and bought candy, the kind of things my parents would never let me have in the house. I walked in one day, he said, "You look like a kid who could use a job. Would you be willing to use my tractor to cut my lawn, earn a few bucks a week?"

Before long, he found out I went fishing with Mr. Carmichael and then asked if I'd like to go out with him sometime. He took me way out to Montauk Point, and now there was another man looking out for me, mentoring me, doing any kind of fathering that didn't cross too personal a line. Mr. Berg lost his own son, a surgeon nicknamed Buzzy, to suicide a few years earlier, and he was haunted by the loss. I was fascinated by the inscription in the concrete in front of his garage: *This house belongs to Sam, Sylvia, Buzzy, and Marcy.* Buzzy was there in the concrete and in everything Mr. Berg did. Probably that was what he got out of his time with me.

One afternoon as I did some yardwork after mowing his lawn, he came over and said, "Now, let me get you some safety glasses. See this bush here? These branches stick out, and even though you're just raking, you could easily poke your eyes. There's so much you have to think about, be aware of, but you have to make sure you protect yourself."

He taught me how to do things, whether it was the right way to prune a rose bush or how to care about other human beings, or how to feel like my life was worth something (which was still hard to grapple with while living in my parent's house).

It was Mr. Berg who looked at me one day, lanky kid I was, no fire in me, and said, "You know, why don't you try doing a few exercises each day. Some pushups and a few pullups. Nothing to hurt yourself—you want to build up slowly. I think it would be good for you, make you feel better."

He didn't outright point out my lack of confidence, but it was also obvious I was the kind of kid who would rather spend his time with a man in his late sixties than with kids his own age. He took me to a pullup bar in his garage and showed me where to put my hands, where to start, then how to build up to tougher ones once I got a little stronger. He could still do a handful in a row, and I was completely enthralled. Here was an older man, older than my father, who was quite strong—and yet he never used that strength to intimidate people or to bully people. Mr. Berg wasn't the kind of guy who needed to prove he was tough. That—that would be my role model. Once I got the strength parts, both physically and emotionally, built up a little more.

The early months in Merrick were as close to an idyllic time as I'd ever known in my life. However, the remodels on our new house were ending. This meant my dad soon found himself with no other outlet for his energies, so he resumed using me as his punching bag. Some of the confidence flickering on in me was soon extinguished. However, at least this time, I had an outlet of my own. I could escape to places where I knew people cared about me. Over the next couple of years, I even found a few good friends my own age, friends at my new school. Also, my brother was getting old enough to engage with, even though he was getting ready to start kindergarten.

When I turned twelve, a couple of pivotal moments occurred. My father stepped up his beatings of me, saying I was practically a man now and didn't need to be treated like a little boy any longer. When he hit me, his goal was to get me to fall from a punch or slap, and then he would, quite literally, kick me in the stomach or ribs while I was down. Crying and begging him to stop did no good.

Christian was now old enough to see what was going on. Fortunately, my father never laid a hand on Christian. This didn't mean there was a wedge between Christian and me—I was grateful my little brother didn't have to go through what I was going through. Christian was equally horrified by our father's abuse.

As my father trapped me on the ground, kicking me in the ribs one afternoon, Christian ran into the room and screamed for him to stop. My father didn't stop. He instead yelled at Christian to go to his room.

"No, stop it, stop it!" Christian cried, then screamed so loud it forced my mother to come down from her vanity table in her bedroom and tell my father to stop. Later, I went up into Christian's room and hugged him tightly. How could I put into words how grateful I was that it took my four-year-old brother to end the beating? How could I tell him he saved me from something neither of us should ever have seen?

Then, the next time it happened, my father had me on the ground, stomping on my leg—attempting to break it—but before the bone broke, I experienced the worst Charlie horse I ever experienced, then or since.

Suddenly, Christian stepped between my father and me, telling him, "No, stop," tears streaming down his cheeks.

My father pulled away, and I tried to stand but fell back to the floor.

"Oh shit," my father said, and in the meantime, my mother rushed into the room.

"What is going on?" she said, as if she didn't know.

"I think I might have busted his leg," my father said matter of factly.

Christian rushed to me and hugged me, wrapping himself around me—basically acting as a human shield—and then my mother lit into my father, and the two were yelling at each other, but my dad's voice turned much more defensive, then panicked, especially when my mother said she'd likely have to take me to the hospital.

I didn't understand the power hospitals had and didn't believe anyone could really save me from my father. My father likely made the connection that if the hospital suspected he broke my leg, and on purpose, and I was now old enough to tell the doctors or nurses what happened, then he might go to prison.

If only I knew these things.

After ten minutes of rubbing and stretching, the Charlie horse relaxed and I was able to get up and walk it off, and suddenly my father's whole demeanor changed. He did not hurt me that badly. He could feel good about himself again. There was no lesson that needed learning, as far as he was concerned.

It was rare for my mother to intervene, because any allyship with me meant an alliance against my dad, at least in their twisted logic. Christian, on the other hand, was my father's golden child, so even when he protected me, my father wouldn't act out against him, and my mother would quietly send him up to his room and out of the fray.

Mr. Carmichael's house was right on the property line, especially near the back. He could hear everything going on, each of my father's moods, each of the beatings. I saw him less those days, in part because his son bought the local liquor store, and Mr. Carmichael spent much of his time there, helping out. Also, he probably didn't know how to intervene, and maybe he felt guilty for not doing more.

My relationship with Mr. Berg suddenly and sadly changed when he suffered his next awful blow: After losing his son to suicide, he suddenly lost his daughter, Marcy, to suicide as well. I was devastated for him, and if he was broken at the loss of his son, there was no coming back from the loss of his second child. I'd go over to his house to ask if there was anything I could do for him. He would shrug, sometimes asking me to do a chore, but it was more to give me something to do. We rarely talked the way we had before the tragedy. Usually, he'd pivot topics and ask, "How's that father of yours doing?" We didn't talk openly about what was going on in my house, but he knew my father was the source of my problems. He knew I was suffering. Because he couldn't talk about his own suffering, he was checking in with mine.

There was so much I'd gotten from Mr. Berg, but a big part of what he provided was exercises, which not only boosted my confidence, but, as I grew older, helped me fill out from a lanky pre-teen to strong teenager. Even as I turned thirteen, it was clear I was going to be a bigger man than my father, who was small, and not just on the inside.

Christian intervened in the beatings at times, and he would sometimes get my mother on board to help. Her help was rare, however, because she would incur my father's wrath. Soon, though, when my father beat me, he wound up hurting himself almost as much as he hurt me.

My father was getting creative in his beatings, but even those attempts turned against him. One evening, my father was punching me in the back of my head while I cowered in the hall outside my bedroom, and he must have hit his hand wrong, because suddenly, he yowled, and the blows stopped. When I looked up, my father was holding his hand while we both watched it swell. I thought it might be broken, but he wouldn't seek medical attention. Of course, for the next week, he acted like the victim with his injury, and Christian, my mother, and I all did extra work around the house for him since he could barely use his hand. He *actually wanted* pity from us.

    The next time he went after me, he did it with kicks, but then again, he misjudged and whacked his shin bone against mine, writhing on the floor. I called it karma. After this incident, the beatings came and went, but my father seemed to be getting diminished rewards. When they occurred, they were achieved with less success and satisfaction.

    If I thought that meant the definitive end to my abuse, I was deluding myself. Fortunately, I knew my parents weren't quitters and the diminished beatings didn't raise my hopes.

    On the one hand, my father started finding fault with my mother's food at dinner again. Any trivial detail would rub him the wrong way. Maybe it was too much water left in the spaghetti again, or the broil on his steak was darker on one side than the other. Once he found a fault, he would throw his plate of food in the sink, often shattering the plate. If he saw I was eating (or, rather, *scarfing*) the food down, that would set him off on a further tirade, as it contradicted his determination the food was inedible. At that point, he would upend the kitchen table, while I was sitting at it, so all the food would wind up on the floor.

    My mother said absolutely nothing. She'd just stoop to the floor and scoop up pieces of plate and food and glass. She could tell the ticking time bomb of my father's moods, too, I realized when she allowed Christian, barely out of toddlerhood, to eat in his room with greater frequency. He often missed the eruptions, though why I wasn't spared, I don't know. It was all the act of a genteel, respectable family, who sat together at a table despite the fact my parents hated food, and everyone hated everyone else. As this ritual of violence at dinner became routine, I learned to eat even faster than before so I wouldn't have to go to bed with an empty stomach. My stomach had a hole in it some nights, but really it was the black hole of despair pulling any light (or calories) towards it.

The final time my dad hurt me, though, happened after he gave up on the beatings. The latest accusation he launched at me, which according to him required punishment, was my puberty was causing acne. I had oily skin that made adolescence rough. For my father, though, the fault was mine: I was not taking proper care of my skin and I was clearly not washing enough. So, one night, as he was complaining about overcooked broccoli, he looked at me, inhaling the broccoli and any other food on my plate, and stared at me in disgust.

"You expect me to eat while looking at your greasy, pimply face?" he asked incredulously.

Lowering my head, I said nothing.

"You hear me?" he asked, rhetorically. Of course, I heard him. Everyone at the table heard him.

Christian looked at me and then dropped his eyes to his plate.

"I told you to wash your face before you sit down in front of me!" The agitation increased in his voice.

"I did, Dad," I said quietly.

That did it. He stood up hard enough to knock his chair backward. He grabbed the dishtowel from the counter, then stormed to me, grabbing me by the back of my head by my hair, then scrubbed my face with the dry towel. The burning started immediately, and he scrubbed until his arm got tired—which took what seemed like an eternity. Every time I thought his cruelty must be ending, more blows came down on me. My skin turned to fire, and the pain screamed across my nerve endings, already sensitive because of the pimples.

Christian cried again for him to stop, and he pleaded with my mother, but she said nothing. I couldn't see their faces because my entire face was covered in the towel, and though I could barely breathe, that wasn't as bad as the flames across my skin. I clung to the chair as if it were the only thing keeping me alive. Finally, my father quit and threw the towel into the sink, then rushed out of the kitchen the way a natural disaster moves across a landscape.

Within a few minutes, blisters formed, like second-degree burns. I looked like a shipwreck victim rescued after weeks of salt and sun exposure. I sneaked a cold towel from the kitchen and slept with it over my face for some relief. I refused to go to school for three days, but when existing no longer caused excruciating pain, I knew it was time to go back. My friends immediately saw something happened to me, but they didn't know what to say. Part of their reluctance to say anything was my false pride—I didn't want the first real friends since moving to Merrick to know that every day I worried my father would beat the hell out of me. Kids don't know how to talk about those things, or at least we didn't in the '70s.

I learned nothing but how to keep silent. Instead, my friends and I talked about the latest KISS record we'd bought, and I finally saved up enough to buy their entire catalogue, both studio and live recordings. I'd spend hours in my room, my giant headphones on, losing myself in music, playing record after record. Other than buying food when out and about, records were the only thing I ever spent my money on. At home, music was my one escape.

After the towel incident, a month passed with my father a mere interloper in my life, and there were no hits, no attacks, no meltdowns that included him breaking up the house. Instead, he subscribed to retail therapy, buying himself (and my mother—always in twos) another new Cadillac and disappearing from the house for long stretches at a time, sometimes a day or two. I was old enough to know about women on the side and wouldn't have been shocked to learn he spent most of his free time with his secretary.

Now, though, it was my mother's turn to lead the charge of abuse. What she wanted was to exert control over every area of my life. If I were going into the shower, she would turn down the water heater to low so that I wouldn't have hot water.

"Mom, please, can you just turn it on?" I would implore.

"You're taking too long!" she said through the bathroom door.

Then, I'd come home from school, having ridden my bike, and put my clothes in the hamper before taking a shower. "Don't put your clothes in the dirty laundry. You need to wear those tomorrow."

"But Mom, I wore them today. They're dirty."

"Hang them up on the line in the yard. They will air out overnight."

I never wore my clothes two days in a row. At first, I figured she just didn't want to be bothered doing so much laundry. So, I made the mistake of washing my clothes myself.

"Charles! How fucking dare you use my washer!" She picked up a nearby box of detergent and hit me with it, several times. She grabbed the far less cumbersome dustpan and hit me with that.

I apologized, but the hitting didn't stop.

I wore my clothes four days in a row, and the kids at school noticed. Though they didn't bully me, these were kids who were into clothes and paid attention to such things.

A month later, I asked if I could use her washing machine to wash my clothes. "No." That was it, no reason. Just, "Hang your clothes outside."

My clothes by this time were rank. She was the fashionista who could have a whole wardrobe of clothes to launder at will, but I stayed dirty. My clothes were dotted with stains, and my collars were so dirty that the acne worsened on my neck. Oh, the irony.

"But Mom, it's not fair," I would say, "I can't believe my own mother won't even let me wash my clothes."

"Hey," she said, "I had no mother. You're lucky to have one."

That was it, that was her defense. What really motivated this? My father gave my mother a monthly budget to run the household and pay bills. This meant if she were miserly enough with the water and electric use, as well as with buying food or any other household necessities, she could pocket the rest of the money and use it to go shopping for herself.

Finally, I sneaked my clothes into the washer when she was running errands and I almost made it, but when she came home, she went into my room and saw my clothes were wet—I'd even skipped the dryer so she wouldn't catch me. She yelled, then got eerily quiet. She went to the top of the banister, pulled up the decorative, torpedo-shaped corbel that had never been secured with wood glue, and came back into my room.

"What, Mom?"

She went straight for my collection of records—my entire earnings, my only refuge—and torpedoed every one of my records, still in their album jackets. I begged her to hit me instead. That I could take.

"Mom, please, I'm sorry, please, don't!"

"Maybe this will teach you not to use my washing machine without permission."

My heart was broken. There was no replacing them—I'd built up my collection almost my whole life. Each one meant something to me. I was attached to them the way little kids get attached to stuffed animals—and my mother knew this.

#

It took a while to put the story together. Some of it became clear when she received a card from some random woman saying what a wonderful man my father was. It was clearly designed to make her jealous or get her to ask for a divorce, opening the way for other eager women to marry into my father's finances. My mother wasn't going to give up her stakes in the one investment she'd made, though. Instead, she put the card out on the kitchen table and drew attention to it whenever she could. My father tried to ignore her, or he seethed in silence for a while, until it was time to blow up and turn over the dinner table. Her life was miserable with my father, and with us, but she sure as hell wasn't going to be the only one stuck in misery.

9. ANSWERS

Jenn, bleary-eyed, joins me at the computer, where I have the Philadelphia adoption page open.

"It says her name is Shiloh," she says, pointing to the screen.

"Yeah, but look at her—same exact markings," I pull up the photos I've saved in a file, and Jenn leans in, "the exact brown spots, and that pattern—"

Jenn is quietly shocked. I have found Star.

"She's definitely getting fed," Jenn says, comparing the image on the adoption page to the photo of a frail Star, just after surgery in New York. "Would you look at that smile, though?" she asks, smiling slightly.

"Alright, well, I can't call them now—"

"No, Charlie, you can't."

"I know, I know."

"Nobody's going to be up."

"I know."

"Get some sleep," she says, looking at me.

"I'll be right there."

"Charlie," She shakes her head, rubbing her arms to ward off the night chill, "Good night."

The office opens at eight, and I'm chock-full of adrenaline. There's no way I'm sleeping tonight. Not after three-and-a-half months of searching and investigating. Fueled by my adrenaline and some coffee I've decided to brew, I make it until a little after daybreak, and then I can't wait any longer. "Someone could reasonably be answering phones at this time," I tell myself, "And if not, I'll call back in an hour."

Surprisingly, a friendly voice answers the phone. This is it.

"Do you have a brown and white Pit Bull missing an eye?" I ask, excitedly.

"Yes," she says, "we have a dog like that."

"Is her left eye missing?"

"I'm not exactly sure, but that does sound like our Shiloh."

"Does she have brown dots on her white fur by her neck?"

There is a brief hesitation, then the woman says, "Look, sir, I need to get my supervisor on the phone with you."

It takes a few minutes to get the supervisor, who has unquestionably been given a heads-up to the subject of this call. I repeat my questions, asking if there is a dog from New York, whose name was Star—

"I'm really not sure about her history," he says flatly, "This dog was brought to us as Shiloh."

Maybe they really didn't know.

"Is there someone else who might be able to answer my questions?" I ask politely.

"Our director, Dan Woods."

"Can I leave you my number to have him call me when he gets in? And—if I don't hear from him in a reasonable time frame, I'll come out from Nebraska to see for myself."

An eternity goes by. Thirty minutes after leaving my number, I get a call with a 215-area code. Here we go.

"Hello, this is Dan Woods, I'm returning a call," the voice on the other says.

"Yes. This is Charlie Cifarelli. I have a few questions for you," I say as calmly as I can.

He gave me the go-ahead.

"Do you have Star, the Pit Bull that was shot in New York City back in August?"

"I'm sorry," Dan Woods said, "I can't answer your question."

The adrenaline and coffee are spiking at Everest-heights in my bloodstream. "Okay, sir. I have to ask: Are you a liar?"

"I take offense to that question," he said.

"Do you, sir, have Star, the Pit Bull?" I ask again.

"I can't confirm or deny."

"You do!" I shout. The non-denial marks the confirmation. "I'm coming to see her!"

"You can't!" Woods says.

"Why?"

"Star is the property of the Mayor's Alliance of New York City, and you would need their permission."

"Huh," I think to myself, "Except isn't she up for adoption?" Turning back to the phone, I say, "Look, I'm going to the radio, news, and all her fans with this information. Everyone deserves to know."

"Don't do that," Woods says, with a new force. "She is in good hands and receiving great care. We don't want to jeopardize her care by having to move her."

As exciting as it is to finally have answers, Woods really does sound caring and, most importantly, rational. I believe he would help me get to see Star—if I don't blow it. Several days later, Woods calls again, informing me he's received permission from the Mayor's Alliance for me to visit Star.

"Really? I can?" I say enthusiastically, "Oh, thank you so much, sir."

I'm beside myself.

"There are stipulations," He says candidly, "you cannot take any photos. And you can't tell anyone of her location, or that you visited her."

"Understood."

I make my arrangements to fly out for two days the following week. When I book my flight, I don't even think about how much flying terrifies me. (Well, I only think a little bit about it, but in this case, it's worth climbing into a tiny airlocked tube and hurtling through the sky.) At the airport in Omaha, I run into a corrections officer I used to know who now works for the TSA.

"Charlie, where you headed?" He asks.

"To meet a dog!" I say, all the jubilation of a kid on Christmas morning.

My former co-worker realizes I'm not kidding. "Alright, well, you have a good time!"

I survive the flight, riding on jitters. Woods is gracious enough to send a car to pick me up at the airport in Philadelphia, which is especially helpful as I'm operating with a flip phone and a Blackberry.

"Navigating around Philadelphia is not for the faint of heart," Woods says.

By early afternoon, the driver pulls up to the complex I saw online, with a sign for the National Dog Sanctuary. Woods greets me warmly. He's a Philly native and all business, but also very caring, under the surface.

"This place wasn't listed on Google Maps," I say.

"The hospital and rehab actually just moved into the complex not long ago. Google must not have updated with the new info."

Well, isn't that something. Here I am, acting satisfied with my flip phone while being foiled by technology that hasn't updated at lightning speed.

Woods explains that when Star arrived back in September, she was in such bad shape it would have been an entirely humane choice to have her quickly euthanized.

"Okay, now remember the agreement: no photos or videos," Woods reminds me. He then adds, "However, the staff can take photos for you. Also—my staff only knows Star as Shiloh, and they have no knowledge of who she really is or what she's been through."

"But her name is Star," I say.

"Yes, but here, she is referred to as Shiloh."

The image conjured is of Star in a canine witness protection program, new name, new location. The old New York secrecy at work again.

As Woods leads me into the complex, it's clear for the first time how massive this facility is. And about as secure as the Nebraska Department of Corrections. We pass through a set of gates on arrival that would make any county jailer proud, and then a series of long corridors. Woods explains not only is this a veterinary hospital and a rescue and adoption center, but it is also a facility for dogs who are unable to return home for whatever reason.

"Their family can come here to see them," he says.

He doesn't elaborate, but Woods nods to two Airedales, saying, "Sometimes they get into big trouble. Now they make this place their home." It is an alternative to them being destroyed against their owners' wishes.

My hands tremble, and I realize I'm shaking from my very core. I'm walking toward the dog I've been tracking down for now four months. The dog from the video, lying lifeless in the street, blood pooling around her head. The dog I've written about, spoken about, dedicated my life to finding. Just a few moments more. I try to make conversation in order to calm my nerves. "I like the music," I say, referring to the classical music piped in on low volume. None of the dogs were barking—you could hear a pin drop.

"We put it on for nap time. As soon as the music comes on, the dogs quiet down, on cue," Woods says, gesturing with his hands.

We walk through a heavy door labeled *Supervisor Only*, and a small entourage of staff join us inside the twenty-by-twenty room, with a smaller section fenced off. Woods opens the gate for me.

It's her. She's right there. The words pour out of me as I kneel down. I quietly whisper, "Star girl, it's me, Charlie." She sits and gives me what I'll learn to be her signature wide smile with her tongue hanging out the side of her mouth. I hug her and hug her again for what feels like forever. I hug her for me and for Jenn and those sleepless nights and for the entire world wondering where she is. I am so lucky to have this time with her. Her coat is so smooth. And…she's so small. Even for a Pit Bull she's barely knee-high to me. She is absolutely not the Tyrannosaurus Rex the police chose to see.

As I sit with her while she plays with the toys the staff have put in with us, I can't even fathom using a bullet to hurt her. Sure, it was terrible of the cop to mace her (and unforgivable to do it after she was shot), but IF they were going to use force, they clearly had alternatives. The problem was not with Star.

I talk more with the staff, and they take photos of the two of us. I ask if I can give her a treat, but then I see Star has already found my coat I had set aside when I got into the room, the pockets of which had the treats inside, and she is tearing into the pocket, her nose detecting said treats. Remarkable girl. We all laugh.

It's hard when I say goodbye to her, but my time is up. I'm allowed to come back the next day to play with her again, and as I leave the second time, overjoyed I've gotten to see her, I worry this will be the last time we meet. Where will she go from here? What will her life be like? Woods has discussed with me that this isn't a long-term solution for her, and also, he says, it's not cheap to house her. The way Woods talks to me, he doesn't see me as a potential adopter of Star, only a troublemaker getting appeased.

Maybe it is time for the story to go away. For me to go away and put it all to rest, Facebook page and all. We should all go back to our lives, at least until the next story. I can look at this time and feel a sense of accomplishment, knowing Star made it through the worst and I succeeded in exactly what I set out to do—finding her and meeting her. I call Jenn to let her know how things go, then head for my flight home.

Jenn picks me up at the airport, and I tell her all about my visit with Star, the dog consuming my life since August. "She'll be okay," I say. "Certain people gravitate toward taking care of mistreated or suffering dogs. If the Facebook page has taught me anything, it's that a lot of people care."

Jenn listens to me for three days, talking about my visit, about Star's smile, her antics with the treats, how I hope there is somebody out there who deserves her and will give her the best life.

Finally, Jenn says, more than a little sternly, "This is all great, but now you have to get the dog."

"What?" I ask.

"Charlie. Come on. No one else would be able to give Star a better home. And really—how would you sleep at night *not* knowing whether she was well cared for?"

I have to hand it to Jenn. Nobody in my life knows me better or has been more patient and understanding.

"Okay," I say, and it's as if this nebulous idea is suddenly crystallizing into something real.

Now, if they'll *allow* me to adopt Star.

10. FERAL

My mother was in another fight with my father—what else was new? There wasn't necessarily a particular reason for the fight but something at the core, some hatred or resentment never articulated to me was the underlying cause. Perhaps the fights were because of me, which would make the most sense. I don't know what happened during those first four years in Queens that made things so peaceful or why my parents' dispositions or moods suddenly changed so dramatically. There it was, though, another fight.

Finally, my mother came up to my room. "Charles, you need to leave. Now." The hurt hit like a rock—my mother hadn't told me how long, or to wait until my father calmed down and then sneak back inside. There was no offer of comfort, only the order to get out. She held open the door, and I walked out with nothing.

1978, summer—I was thirteen years old. Other kids were spending their summers going to camp. Meanwhile, I walked the streets during the day like a zombie, looking for any discarded morsels of food.

There was no going back home that night. I would have died before pleading with her to let me back in the house. Begging just to do laundry resulted in the destruction of my record collection. Instead of sleeping in my bed, I went to the Lakeside schoolyard, where they had cement tunnels on the playground. It was a familiar place, and the tunnels kept me protected from the nighttime rain. Also, no one could see me sleeping in there—they would have to be right next to the tunnel to see me. I figured out, too, that if someone was going to try to come at me, I could escape through the other end of the tunnel—I had my out. Plus, the tunnels were noisy as hell if there was any movement on or near them. If I fell asleep and someone were to climb in, the echoes would surely wake me up. Even at that young age I was already thinking in terms of survival strategies.

As the evening wore on, a cop car parked in the schoolyard, about fifty yards away. At first, I thought they might inspect the park, but they were there just to look out for drug dealers or vandals. I soon discovered they were mainly there to eat their takeout dinners. Another patrol car pulled up next to the other car, positioning driver window next to driver window to chat. For me, a kid from the neighborhood, I felt safe knowing they were there, in case I needed them.

Every sound rattled me, despite my precautions and the police cars.

My sleep was fitful, and by first light, my back was stiff from the hard surface. The police cars were gone, so I climbed out and started walking back through town. There was no objective—the night was cold, so staying in motion seemed like the right thing to do. As I passed the local supermarket, I watched the bread delivery truck drive away. The store wasn't yet open, but the fresh baked loaves were set neatly outside in cardboard boxes. I swiped a loaf and ran off to the park. I broke off chunks by the handful, shoveling them into my mouth, devouring two-thirds of the loaf in maybe a minute or two. I decided to save the rest for later just in case I found nothing else to eat.

I naively hoped I'd be in my bed that night. But when I made the mile-long walk back to my house later, the door was locked, and my mother wouldn't answer, so I left.

14th & 2nd

I wasn't sure what it meant to be thrown out of one's house. My cousin Josh, who lived several towns away, had several times caused trouble for his family due to his drug and alcohol use. I'd seen his drug use firsthand.

I went back to the tunnels in the playground, and at around 10:00 p.m., the police rolled up and parked in the same spot. "Okay," I thought, "a routine." This time a third police car parked with them. He couldn't get his driver's side window next to the windows of the other two, so he parked as close as he could and shouted his part of the conversation. I passed the time trying to listen in and was amused by what they had to say.

After about ten minutes, the police got a call and tossed out what remained of their dinners. As soon as I saw them clear the corner, I ran over to retrieve what was left of their food in foil packages. I left no crumb behind on those packages. Sleep came and went, and at daybreak, I walked straight to the grocery store to pick up another loaf of bread. I had to hang back a few minutes because the delivery truck was still unloading boxes of bread and rolls, but as soon as they split, I grabbed a loaf and ran.

For two weeks, I lived this way. I was thirteen years old and living on the streets with no clue as to why I was thrown out of my house.

Suddenly, I was back home, the door was unlocked and nothing and no one barred my reentry. All that suffering for no reason: Little had changed, including my parents' inability to discuss anything in between blow-out fights.

My absence went unnoticed in part because I wasn't in school due to it being summer recess. In the autumn, I started 8th grade, and things changed once again. I was growing, and the girls were taking notice. They took to calling me Charlie.

"Charlie Cifarelli, it almost rhymes, how wonderful!" they exclaimed.

No one was making fun of my name anymore. I couldn't have friends over at my house, but I'd go over to their houses, listen to their records with them, and avoid being home as much as possible. My friends all talked about what they would do once they were in high school. They dreamed of playing football, basketball, or baseball for the varsity team. They wanted that all-important letter emblazoned on a letterman's jacket. I fantasized for all of thirty seconds before realizing my parents would never pay for my jacket if I were to make a team. There was still a possibility of playing sports, but even those daydreams disintegrated as, once again, I found myself one morning hearing the words, "Charles, I want you out of my house, now."

    My mother again, arbitrarily threw me out to appease my father. I packed my backpack, grabbed the few bucks out of my stash, filled my pockets with change, and hopped on my 10-speed bicycle.

    Being a year away from high school, I no longer felt like a kid anymore, not the way I had the summer before when I hid in the playground tunnels. If I wasn't going to be home, then I didn't want to be anywhere my parents could find me. I rode to the public library, where I figured I could kill some time, and saw the payphone out front. I called the one person who would understand my situation—my cousin Paul, Josh's older brother. He happened to be the only person to *really* know something was up with the way my parents treated me.

    "My parents kicked me out," I said.

    "Shit, man," Paul said empathetically.

    "I don't know what to do. Can you help me?"

    "Hey, look, I can talk to some people. I got a buddy who might let you stay with him. Can you get to my house? My parents won't be home until late—we got some time."

    After a failed relationship, he was back living with his parents, my aunt and uncle in Floral Park, nearly twenty miles away. I'd never ridden that far in one go, but it was my only solution. Besides, focusing on biking to his house would help keep my mind from completely succumbing to the despair of knowing I wasn't wanted by my family. Though I came close a couple of times, I didn't break down and cry once that whole ride.

Two things happened: I figured out on my own how to navigate a very nonlinear path on my bike to a place I'd only been by car. I only had a vague notion of how to get to my cousin's house. Also, I stopped off along the way at a corner deli to get something to eat. I discovered over my two-week homeless summer the year before that the starches in bread could sustain me. With this in mind, I bought a buttered roll and two packages of cupcakes, then wolfed them down with a chocolate milk chaser—all cheap junk food purchased for under three bucks. The sugar rush was immediate and emotionally numbing but the energy carried me the rest of the three-hour ride to Paul's. There was no more emptiness in my stomach. I'd just hit the lottery, and the jackpot was called emotional eating.

Paul's dad was my mom's older brother. My cousin Paul was a big, strapping guy who'd set records in high school as a shot-putter. He was an avid surfer who was into martial arts, and he had a fondness for barbiturates, pep pills, and other types of drugs. He certainly wouldn't turn down weed either. Josh, his younger brother, was even less discerning and did every drug in the book. He was responsible for me trying drugs in the first place. When I was ten years old and left at his house while my parents went out to dinner with his parents, I'd gone to look for Paul and Josh, and found Josh in the basement with some friends, snorting something on the bar. Josh saw me watching and freaked out.

"Charles, come down here," he demanded, "you can't say anything."

I shook my head.

"Here," he said, and he shoved the rolled-up dollar bill into my hand. "Use it like a straw for your nose. You have to *sniff* cocaine."

I didn't even question him—here was someone paying attention to me and being nice. Afterward, I was bouncing off the walls—it was easy to see the appeal, even as a ten-year-old: Cocaine was like exceptionally powerful sugar. The ever-present pit in my stomach was also gone.

It wasn't long before Paul returned home and immediately recognized something was off. "Charles, are you drinking gasoline?" he asked pointedly.

I knew he was playing with me, trying to find out what I did do.

"No—it's cocaine!" I blurted out frankly.

"Josh—what the fuck?" Paul said angrily. "Get your friends out of here now!"

"All of you," Paul said, pointing to Josh's friends, "Get the fuck out of my mother's house and never come back!"

For all his own interest in drugs, Paul was trying to protect me.

That was the household I was riding toward at fourteen. I had a belly full of sugar and a voracious appetite for more. My only thought was Paul was my savior.

He hugged me when I got there and said, "So they just threw you out?"

"Yeah," I said quietly.

"Did they say why?"

"No."

"Why do you think?"

"I don't know. I think my dad hates me."

Paul sighed and asked, "He gives you a lot of hell, doesn't he? Hits you, right?"

I nodded and sniffled.

"Hey, look. I got a good friend, Cut, known him since grade school. He's agreed to keep a roof over your head."

Cut was a hard-working local truck driver who lived five miles away. Paul loaded my bike into his van and drove me there. "One thing, though," Paul said, "We have to be careful the neighbors don't see you."

"Why?" I asked quizzically.

"What we want is for your parents to have to report you as a missing child. You really need the police to be called in to actively look for you. That way, the school will also know you're missing. That is the only way the school will get involved. They will have to make sure you get put into a safer home or a foster home. At the very least, it would keep your parents from throwing you out in the future," Paul explained seriously.

My brain reeled. Here was Paul with this methodical, well-conceived plan, advocating for me and explaining how my current situation should play out, despite the fact he'd been having his own run-ins with the police.

"Oh brother," I thought just then, "my savior needs a savior of his own." Wasn't this the ironic mess?

We arrived at Cut's, and Paul had a key to let us in.

"How'd you get the key?" I asked.

"I crash here every once in a while," he said without elaboration. I was just grateful for his and Cut's help. It was good to know I would have a roof over my head for however long this would last. When Cut arrived, I was relieved Paul was with me. Cut was a big guy with a short haircut, and he was wearing his driver's uniform. It didn't take long before I saw I didn't need to worry. He had a heart of gold.

"So sorry to hear about your problems, Charles," he said kindly.

"You can call me Charlie," I said.

"Alright, Charlie. You are family here," he said as he waved his arm around the place. "I got a girlfriend, and I spend most nights there, so you'll have the place basically to yourself. Come see the pantry."

Both the pantry and the fridge were completely stocked. I'd never seen so much food inside a home before.

"I told my girlfriend you were on your way, so she came by and stocked it up for you," Cut said.

I couldn't help but cry at his generosity. He was a complete stranger to me, but already he was treating me better than my parents ever had. He took me into the next room. It was full of weights and a bench press.

"Go ahead and use any of the equipment you want," he said invitingly, "just don't overdo it and hurt yourself! Also, there's the TV, and here's the shower, so really, make yourself at home."

Years' worth of pressure escaped from my body. How lucky I was to have Paul understand me, and for Paul to have such a great friend to help me.

"Alright, Charles—Charlie," Cut said, "don't answer the phone, except when either Paul or I call to check up on you. You'll know it's one of us because we'll have a code: I'll let the phone ring three times, hang up, and then call back. That's when you know it will be safe to answer. Got it?"

I nodded.

"Alright, I got to go," he said as he patted my shoulder and added reassuringly, "you'll be okay. I'll be back in a couple of hours, though, just for a shower. Then I'll be heading to my girlfriend's place for the night. If you think of anything you will need in the meantime, you can let me know."

"Thank you so much, Cut," I said appreciatively.

"Like I said, you are family," he said again.

The first thing I did when he left was take a shower. The water was hot. No one turned down the water heater. No one timed me. I must have stayed in there for twenty minutes, which was the longest and most decadent shower I'd ever taken. I got out, then turned on the TV, but my mind was racing. I was safe, but I still couldn't grapple with what happened. I couldn't believe I was here.

I wished Paul hadn't just dropped me off. He could have stayed a bit and helped me unwind. I needed to talk to someone. The place was strange, and I was confined—but I'd sworn not to go outside. Worry suddenly crept in – an undefinable worry. This was a real plan, and I was really in hiding. I didn't know what to do, and I couldn't focus on the TV.

"Alright," I thought, "I'll try the weights."

Despite my meager pushups and pullups, I was mostly still a weakling with noodle arms. Mr. Berg had encouraged me to work out, and he was the best mentor I had, and now that I had access to weights it seemed like the best time to try. I laid on the bench press, not sure of how much weight to put on. I tried twenty-five pounds on each side and even that was a lot. I gasped and pushed, but I got through three reps. I had nothing to do but practice. With practice, I would have to get better. That's all there was to it.

Cut came back to shower and get ready for his girlfriend. He was a straightforward guy. "Have you heard anything from Paul?" he asked.

"No," I said.

"He probably figures you're settling in for the night. You'll hear from him tomorrow, or soon."

In under an hour, Cut was back out the door. This became our routine. "Has Paul stopped by or called?" he would ask.

"No," I would say.

"Oh well, he must have gotten busy. Do you have everything you need?"

"Yes."

"Okay, great. Have a good night. See you in the morning."

That first night he left, and I heard the door lock behind him, I suddenly remembered all the food in the pantry and fridge. I was so used to not having food around that I'd forgotten all about it. I scarfed the food down. I shoveled it. I Inhaled it. It was a complete gorging. The food had the same effect as the cupcakes and buttered roll and chocolate milk, I suddenly, as if miraculously, felt okay again. Food abruptly equaled happiness. Food helped me believe everything was better.

It was strange and lonely being in an unfamiliar place, but at least I was safe. I slept the sleep of the dead, not even waking when Cut came home in the morning to get ready for work. The days passed with no word from Paul. His mother, June, was someone my mom regularly talked to. I figured my mother must have had some contact with June, or my uncle Pauly. I thought there must be some word my cousin could pass on to me. He was my only source for updates.

Cut was so busy with his long days at work, and his time spent with his girlfriend, that we didn't speak for more than five minutes at a time. All I did to pass the time was lift weights and eat. I overate, really. Food might as well have been cocaine, because in no time, I was addicted to stuffing the hole inside of me with a whole bunch of calories.

After a week of holing up at Cut's, I heard the three rings on the phone, the hang-up, and then the second call.

"Paul?" I asked, in hope. This had been the only time the phone rang, and no other person had been to the house except Cut.

"Alright, buddy, I got you some updates. Both your parents have been over to the house a few times. They're now getting worried that something may have happened to you, especially since no one's seen you anywhere. This is good, this is what we hoped would happen," he said reassuringly.

"Okay," I said.

"School officials were notified, and they asked the student body if anyone knew where you were."

"So, my whole school knows?"

"Sounds like it."

Wow. They knew. My story was out there. Someone had to do something now. Still, it all felt so…nebulous. Do what? Protect me, that was what. Help me. Save me.

"The police are involved, and they've extended the missing person report to thirteen states. Listen, Charles, I'm enjoying the fact your parents are worried, and also the fact they lied to the police and made a false report. Hopefully, when the truth comes out, there will be legal ramifications for them."

The police. The police were worried about me. It didn't feel right to lie to the police, and we were all lying to them.

"I know they threw me out like trash, but Paul, I feel bad the police think something bad may have happened to me. Can we let them know I am okay?" I asked.

He sighed. "Yes, of course. But give it a couple of more days. Otherwise, your parents will do it again."

After all this there was so much to think about. I was a lost boy. Do I just go back to things being normal?

"How will I re-enter my life?" I asked.

My trust was in Paul, and I knew he was looking out for my best interests, but I also knew he was a con man and didn't do much that was legitimate. This was the person I was entrusting with my life. Really, I'd gone to him to find a place to be safe while my parents threw me out. It wasn't my intention to go and purposely hide my whereabouts. I'd have no problem telling the searching police what had happened.

After a long pause in the conversation, Paul finally broke his silence. "I was thinking about that part, too," he said, "It's not like the police are out there combing the streets for you. They have you in their system, along with a description."

Always slippery with his words, Paul could explain anything away. He was in his twenties, and I was fourteen, not a kid, not really, but all I knew was this felt wrong in some way.

"How do I go back to Merrick? Back to school?" I asked.

Now that my stomach was full and I'd had a good run of solid sleep, I figured I could go back to the schoolyard and sleep in the tunnels at night, as I'd done the year before. Already, I was feeling like I was overstaying my welcome with food. After hanging up with Paul, I depleted the last food stock. All of it was gone. Along with the disappearing food, though, the pain I'd been feeling, the fear, all of it, was numbed down with the insulin boost.

That evening, after the call with Paul, I psyched myself up to talk with Cut about possibly leaving.

When Cut came home, he said, "I don't mind you staying, but the next round of food is on Paul."

He and I both knew that would never happen.

"Thanks, Cut, for everything. Hey, if you talk to Paul, have him call me or stop over."

"I will. And if you're gone before I see you again, I really enjoyed meeting you, Charlie. I'm so glad I was able to help you, even a little bit."

"You helped me a lot, Cut," I said gratefully, "and when I grow up, I hope I can help you, if you ever need anything."

He chuckled and said, "Just worry about yourself right now."

Cut must have had a way to contact Paul, because within the hour, Paul was letting himself into the apartment. "So, how've you been? What have you been doing to pass the time?"

I shrugged and said, "I've been using Cut's weights. Other than that, I have been eating and sleeping a lot."

"Yeah, I heard all about your eating. Cut said he'd never seen anyone with an appetite like yours."

If I hadn't already numbed myself, I might have felt a little shame. If I was eating like I'd never see food again, it is because I probably wouldn't, at least not much of it. I just hoped the same grocery store I got bread from in the past, had the same bread delivery hours.

"Hey, look," Paul said, sitting on the couch. "I think I've got a plan. I'll call your parents and tell them you contacted me for food and money. I'll tell them you've been living on a boat in drydock down by the marina. Then, I'll say that while I was on the phone with you, I convinced you to let me pick you up and bring you back to the house for a shower and a meal. Then, while you were at my house, we can say I convinced you to call your parents to let them know you're okay. All you have to say is I told you they were worried about you, despite the fact they threw you out, and you don't want them to worry about you."

I hate lies. I didn't like any of this, and *all of it was a lie*. Maybe it was a family trait, this ability to lie with a straight face. I sighed and said, "What I really want to do is to tell them, along with the police, the full truth and to see where that takes me."

"Uh, I don't know," Paul said hesitantly, "In fact, no, man, that's a bad idea. Here's the thing, with my record, if the police hear I've been aiding and abetting a minor, it could get me in big trouble, you know?"

Great, so once again, it all falls back on a fourteen-year-old kid to carry the burden and make everyone else feel better. I saw how it was. Really, the whole ordeal was incredibly exhausting. Maybe it was better to go back to whatever life I had because at least life was predictable, as opposed to being sequestered in limbo.

"Fine," I said, "let's go back to your house."

Once I was at Paul's house, Paul gave me a couple of minutes to settle down and then went over with me what I was going to say to my parents.

"Okay, you gotta call her now," he said, pointing to the phone.

The phone felt like it weighed two hundred pounds. It was an old rotary phone, and each clicking revolution was as slow as molasses. My finger trembled a bit as I inserted it into first one numbered hole and then another. Finally, with the number dialed, there was the familiar ringing on the other end. My mother picked up on the second ring. I got right to the point the second she said hello.

"I'm at Paul's house, he picked me up because I needed money and food."

"Charles—oh Charles, are you okay? We have been so worried about you."

"I'm calling you because Paul said you were worried about me, and I didn't want you to worry."

"Charles, we love you."

My stomach knotted in an instant. She loved me but this was how she treated me? The hypocrisy. Here she was, having the sweetest conversation with me—I'd never heard her be so sweet to me, ever. "There must be an outsider at the house," I thought, "either that or she figured Paul was listening." I reminded myself her geniality was all an act; it was all part of her denial and coverup. She needed to appear to the outside world like she was a great mother. Wasn't I the lucky one for even having a mother?

Indeed.

"Charles, your father is going to be home from work by 6 p.m. Once he gets here, we'll ride out to Uncle Pauly and Aunt June's house and pick you up."

She did not mention the police. She did not ask where I'd been. What was the truth? Were the police ever called?

We hung up and I told Paul my parents were coming. I had a few hours. "Can we go to Umberto's for pizza?" It was my favorite pizzeria, just a town over, and when I was lucky, we'd go there when visiting Uncle Pauly and Aunt June.

"There's that appetite again," Paul said. "Sure, buddy."

We got there, and I ordered two large slices of the Sicilian. When the server brought them to me on a paper plate already pooling with delicious grease, I started devouring them. Paul went to the counter to grab red pepper flakes and garlic, and when he turned back, I was starting my second slice, not caring the cheese was burning the roof of my mouth.

"Geez, kid!" Paul said, "Chew before you swallow."

I chugged the fountain Coca-Cola in the big cup, which I'd gotten without ice because it was easier to gulp, in a rush to fill my stomach as quickly as possible. It's probably a good thing there weren't any All-You-Can-Eat buffets around when I was young, or I might have ended up in the ER on a regular basis.

Paul finished his slice, and then we went back to his house to wait for our parents' arrival. He called his mom.

"Hey, Mom, good news. Charles is here. He is standing in our living room now. Yeah. Yeah, he's okay. Yeah. He's been sleeping on a boat in drydock. Yeah. This whole time. Okay."

My Aunt June was one of the smarter people I knew. She worked customs at JFK Airport. She was also trained to sniff out bullshit. I couldn't imagine her falling for that business about the boat, but there it was.

Aunt June was the first one at the house, just before 6 p.m. I was glad to see her, and in reality, I wished I could stay with her and my Uncle Pauly, one of the nicest and most rational people I knew. If they really knew what was going on at home, I'm sure they would have let me stay.

"Would they go against my parents?" I asked myself, "or had they fallen for the 'happy family' lie my parents tried to sell?"

Aunt June hugged me. "Wow, you look good, Charles. You haven't lost any weight while on the boat."

Ugh. I knew she was much too smart to fall for Paul's story.

"I'm going to pour a glass of wine and put on the TV. Want to join me? The TV, that is—not the wine. Are you hungry?"

"We just ate," I said.

"Oh, good."

We didn't say much—she was waiting for me to speak, but I didn't know what to say. The only thing I knew was my whole body was wrestling between the insulin high from the pizza and coke and dread as the clock ticked toward 7 p.m. It was a little after the hour when I heard the familiar Cadillac engine pull into the driveway. I'd hoped my Uncle Pauly would be there as well because maybe if he were, I'd have the guts to say something. He was not there though because he was in the motion picture business and was working late on a film shoot.

My parents brought Christian, and when Paul let them into the house, Christian ran up to me and wrapped his five-year-old arms around my legs, crying at how much he'd missed me. His reaction to seeing me damn near broke my heart.

"Hi, Charles!" my parents jingled in unison.

Dear God. They seemed so happy and not the least bit upset.

"Hi," I said, cautiously.

"Let's go to the kitchen table," Aunt June offered, "anyone want anything to drink?"

She poured drinks for my parents, and they asked her how her day was at the airport.

Paul stood up and said, "Hey, Uncle Charlie, come outside, I want to show you my new van."

Paul's request was a ruse, of course. Christian and I sat listening to my mother chat with my aunt over mundane talk. Not one word was brought up about my disappearance. My name didn't even come up until Aunt June got up to get Christian some ice cream.

"Charles, would you like some ice cream, too?" she asked.

"Yes, I sure would." It took four swipes of my spoon to finish the bowl. Aunt June filled the bowl again. Then, there it was, the beautiful sugar rush on its way.

Paul came back inside with my father—they'd been out there for twenty minutes. Then, in a not-at-all subtle way, Paul said, "Hey, Charles, I have to take Wimpy for a walk. Let's both go." (Wimpy was the name of their Doberman, who, despite the aggressive reputation, especially in the '70s, lived up to every bit of his name and completely disappointed Paul in the process.)

It wasn't much of a walk—Paul just let Wimpy do his business in the fenced-in side yard. Turning to me, Paul said, "I have to tell you this: I am blown away. First off, your father is not buying the boat story, so I would suggest you not use it and instead avoid any conversation about where you've been."

"Great," I said ironically, "The story I never wanted in the first place you're now saying is unbelievable."

"I made a mistake. I should have thought it out better," Paul admitted.

Hmm. Maybe the upstate police he'd had problems with had his number, after all, and weren't just "out to get him" like he told anyone who'd listen.

"Anyway, your father said he and your mom want to move past this ordeal and get you back into school."

I nodded. The ice cream wasn't working as well as I'd hoped.

"I did ask your father what the problem was with you at home. Let me tell you, I'm blown away by what he told me. Absolutely. He told me, and I quote: 'Paul, the kid washes his hands and drips water all over the vanity, and no matter how many times I say something, he doesn't get it! He brushes his teeth with his head up and gets toothpaste splatter all over the mirror. His approach to everything is unorthodox—he just does everything ass-backwards. He eats everything and causes me and his mother to fight. I wish he were older and on his own. Damn, Charles, I was waiting for half a good reason as to why they were upset with you. This? I can't believe this."

Coming from an actual troublemaker, that said a lot.

Paul shook his head and said, "Your mother doesn't have a word to say, but your father says he is upset, and it causes problems between them."

I couldn't believe it. My father articulated his bullshit position and actually thought he'd get a sympathetic response.

"Look, Paul, those two couldn't get along with each other on a free cruise," I said.

"I believe it."

"They drink, and then all hell breaks loose. Seriously, I've seen my mother drinking straight out of the J&B scotch bottle, clear as day."

"It's a sad situation. You have to hang in there. Just don't say much, go home, get back to school, and stay out of the house as much as possible."

"What do you think I've been doing?" I asked exasperatedly.

But all Paul did was shrug and lead us back into the house.

As soon as we were inside, my mom said, "Well, we haven't eaten dinner, so your father and I want to go get something before heading home."

"I'm sure you wouldn't mind, Charles," my father said. If I'd been older or a different kid, I might have decked him. I wasn't that kid, though.

Just like that, suddenly, I was in the back of their car, next to Christian, my bike in the trunk, and the four of us headed to Sizzler. It wasn't my parents' first choice in a restaurant because it was not nearly formal enough and it had no real service, but it was on the way home. They wouldn't be eating much of their food anyway.

We ate in silence. Well, my mom pushed a few small piles of food around her plate. Then we left. The whole ride home nothing was said, except, five minutes away from home, my mother said, "We have an appointment with your guidance counselor tomorrow. He wants to see you and me, and unfortunately, your father can't make it."

"What time?" I asked.

"9 a.m."

That should be an interesting meeting, I thought. As soon as I was back in the house, Ringo hesitantly limped up to me and licked my hand. That was the one good thing I had at the house: Poor Ringo. His hip dysplasia had gotten bad, and he'd had a series of skin ailments, probably brought on by stress from living with my parents. After saying hello to my friend, I ran and took a quick, nearly cold shower lasting three minutes, max. Then I went to bed.

The next morning, I understood what I was in for when we went to the counselor—my mother was already in performance mode, complete with large sunglasses, which she kept on during the meeting. The counselor asked what the source of my disappearance was, and completely on cue, as if rehearsed, my mother said I caused disturbances in the house, and I was impulsive when I didn't get my way, creating more problems for her and my father. Her role wasn't as weepy mother; no, she was full of indifference, as if it was a great inconvenience having to be there. Inside, I thought of all the door handles and inanimate objects she was having to touch, knowing her hands were in for a scouring as soon as she got home.

The counselor's indifference matched my mother's. He seemed to be running through a checklist based solely on formalities in order for me to resume my studies.

I shuffled out of the office and into my classroom, just in time for the break. My friends immediately rushed me and peppered me with questions like, "Charlie, are you okay? We were so worried!" Everyone I knew told me how upset they'd been and how glad they were I was okay, and I was back. But when they asked what had happened, I didn't know what to say, only that my parents had thrown me out in a fit. "You, Charlie?" the girls said, incredulous.

Though I was shy of girls, they had no problem rallying around me, completely protective. They thought I was cute with my long hair and skinny body and made sure I knew their anger and the injustice of the whole situation. The reaction was the complete opposite of my parents. "Alright," I thought, "I may not matter to my parents, but my life does matter." My friends taught me that. They cared about what happened to me.

I did what I could to bury my pain by focusing my attention on my friends and the good things. One of those good things? I'd caught the iron bug. After lifting weights at Cut's and feeling myself get just the tiniest bit stronger, I loved the feeling of exertion especially when it was mixed with overeating. This was my new high. Fortunately, a few of my friends had weights at their house, so I spent my time at their houses. At school, I used the pullup bar as much as possible, and then I would do pushups and sit-ups in my room at home. There was my refuge.

And, slowly, life got a little better—as long as I bracketed out my home life.

After my two-week disappearance, I had attracted not just the sympathy but the interest of Teresa. She was the prettiest girl in Merrick Avenue Junior High School. She was tall, athletic, blonde, and on the kick line team. Her family had money (her father owned a bunch of diners), and pretty much everybody wanted to be her friend or go out with her. So, in Mr. Goldstein's math class (a man, by the way, who looked and acted exactly like Gabe Cotter from *Welcome Back, Cotter*), I was racing to catch up with the two weeks I'd missed when I heard a pen fall near me. It was right under my desk.

"Oh," a voice said, "can you pass me that, Charlie? I dropped it."

Teresa.

I smiled and said, "Here you go," I said, handing the pen to her. I didn't look directly at her.

The pen fell again just before the end of class, and I retrieved it for her. The next three classes in Mr. Goldstein's classroom, the pen kept coming. There was no way I thought Teresa could be interested in me. Even though I did not know what to do with a girl interested in me, I kept retrieving the pen, and each time, my insides hummed with electrical current.

It took a few more days of pen retrieval before her friend came up to me and said, "Hey, Teresa really likes you—why don't you ask her out?"

This was a revelation to me. Okay, I had some new clothes and my mom let me have a barber cut my hair. I was almost fifteen now. I was terrified. Terr-i-fied.

It was a Friday. Tonight? Could she go out tonight? I propelled myself forward, toward her locker, and was able to formulate the sentence, "Teresa, will you go out with me?"

She lit up and cheerily said, "Of course! I'd like to go out with you tonight, but my parents are having a big party, and relatives are coming over."

Petrified and relieved, I practically shouted, "Teresa, that's fine, we can go out another night!" I might have taken a breath at that point.

"Are you sure?" she asked.

"Oh yeah, I'm definitely sure."

So, I didn't go out with her that night, but I went out with my friends to our regular pizzeria, Violetta's, in a local strip mall, and while the pizza wasn't as good as my favorite Umberto's, Violetta's had a juke box with Led Zeppelin and Black Sabbath and Lynyrd Skynyrd, all tunes a couple of years old but still THE tunes of the day. Over pizza and unlimited Coca-Cola refills, the guys kept razzing me, saying, "You're dating Teresa, and you didn't try to get her to go out?"

"She had a party," I said.

"And you're not going by her house tonight, so she can sneak out with you?"

"No, no, no, it's fine."

That's when my friend Scott said, "You got the best-looking girl," and I reached a new level of terrified. She was the best-looking girl. Did I "have" her? We had a twenty-second conversation and a rain check date. She *had* thrown her pen under my desk all week, though. That counted for something.

I had all Saturday and all Sunday to think about the next step, making the actual plan to go out with Teresa. On Monday, I was all nerves waiting to see her. As soon as I did, in the hallway before class, she grabbed my hand and held onto it. My sweaty hand. She held my hand and stood right against my side at every break, and then at lunch, as our arms touched while we ate, I fumbled with my plastic fork, breaking it.

"Are you okay?" she asked.

"Oh, yeah, I'm fine."

I smiled and wiped my palm off on my pant leg, removing the sweat before she took it in hers again. I had no idea what I was supposed to do, with any girl, let alone Teresa. It didn't seem real that someone could want to give me affection. This was an alien encounter.

I botched it.

After a few days of this awkward handholding, after school, right in the hallway, Teresa came up to me and kissed me. And—she stuck her tongue in my mouth. I was mortified. I had no idea about French kissing, and it felt like something was coming inside of me, and there was no capacity to process or deal with it. I pushed her away, horrified. She looked at me with the strangest expression. Had I known what to do, had I been ready to accept affection, had I been able to give her my affection more than just from afar, had things gone *really* slowly, we might have worked out.

After the kiss, Teresa cooled off (because we didn't communicate about any of our feelings). The next week, one of her girlfriends came up to me and said, "Teresa's going to break up with you, Charlie."

Well, that lit something in me. I raised my courage to walk right up to her and say, "Teresa, I need to speak with you."

"Yes?"

I said courage, but if that's really what I had, I could have walked up to her like The Fonz and resurrected the relationship. Sadly, I did not have the Fonz's courage. My courage was more like facing up to misery, at which I was an expert.

"Teresa," I said quietly, "I'm breaking up with you. It's just not working."

"*You're* breaking up with *me*?" she asked, in a curious tone.

"Yes, I am," I said, matter of factly.

She didn't say anything. She just took it.

I felt miserable.

Over the school year and through summer, I continued to work out, spend time with my guy friends, and when the next girl was interested, I was better prepared to deal with physical contact. Having missed the opportunity with Teresa, I gained just enough confidence to ask out other girls (eventually). I found I could relate to them. Around my guy friends, I was compelled to act like this strong, tough, sports guy, but I could be vulnerable with girls. Of course, I was a victim of what's referred to as toxic masculinity, though nobody talked about it in those days. Fortunately, I wasn't as toxic as many guys could be, but my life would have been so much easier had I been able to be open about everything I was going through rather than hiding all my pain behind lifting weights and eating.

One might think my parents were impressed when I started to date girls, but as soon as my mother found out there were girls involved, she did whatever she could to put them down in front of me. So, I stopped telling my parents, especially my mother, about which girl I was seeing, but parents still talk, and so at dinner, I'd hear plenty of derisive attacks on any girl who was interested in me. Sometimes, she'd cut girls down who were just platonic friends. To her, it didn't matter. My mother was deeply insecure and was always competing with other women and simultaneously finding ways to punish me and put me down.

"Oh, Carla?" she'd say, raising an eyebrow or rolling her eyes, "Did you see the size of that girl's *snoze*?" She said nose like that: *snoze*, not even *schnoz*. Or she might say, "Ha, Michelle? She's got thick thighs like her mom," or she'd make fun of Sarah's complexion. She was hyper-astute to the physical features of women and girls and had an endless supply of cuts ready to go. Being a young teenager, it was hard for me to recognize how much of it came from her own insecurities and her obsession with her own appearance. It got to me, but I treated it as just one more attack I could push inside and then eat away.

Beginning in 9th grade, I briefly tried track and wrestling but couldn't do either because I needed to work to survive. While I still had no emotional muscle to speak of, on the outside, I was a strong, athletic kid. On top of my school activities, I also got a job at the gas station down the block from my house, working four hours a night for three weeknights, then half of Saturday and from eight in the morning to eight at night on Sunday. A job would offer me freedom to buy my own food, to take girls on dates and to have an actual life. Making $4 an hour, I was taking home $80-$90 a week, which felt like a small fortune. Apparently, my mother thought it was a small fortune as well.

"Look at you, making all this money," she said, when she found out what I was making. She firmly said, "I think it's time you can start paying room and board, considering how much it's costing us to feed you, not to mention the cost of the water and electric bills. You're going to start paying your way. I think forty dollars a week is fair."

What was room and board anyway? It sounded to me like a term straight out of the 1890s, without getting the charm or any of the food.

So, when I turned fifteen in 1980, I paid $160 a month for my room and board, such as it was. I was never allowed to have a key to the house, though, because my mother didn't want me home when she wasn't around. My mother still turned down the hot water heater whenever I took a shower (but naturally, it was up when she took a shower, which often made her laugh, much like a cartoon villain). She continued to tear me down at any chance. My acne, that had disgusted my father, repulsed her, and though she didn't scrub my face raw, she commented daily on how awful I was—without providing me with any cleansers or medications to treat it. Her teeth were perfectly straight, so she found endless horror at my crooked teeth, yelling at me, "I don't know where you came from; me and my family all have beautiful teeth!" Certainly, she might have taken me to an orthodontist to get braces if I was so hideous, but braces would have deeply cut into her budget. Meanwhile, she self-medicated with alcohol and shopping binges and controlled her world via eating as little as possible to try to drop another pound in weight she didn't have to spare. Beyond *all that*, the money mostly kept her off my back, because I was rarely ever at home.

Though I thought my father was done with his abuse, he had one final trick. He set up a sawhorse in the basement and was cutting oak strips to repair an antique table. He had these strips of oak. They were lightweight 2x2s and shaped like a square-edged billy club. One evening, he said, "Charles, where's my 9/16 wrench I know you use?"

"Oh, I used it on my bike and then put it away," I said, with my stomach clenched.

"Had it been put away when you found it?" he asked shrewdly.

Had it? Where did I get it? "I—"

"No, no it hadn't, I had it sitting out because I was using it, and now I needed to search for it."

As soon as the sentence was out of his mouth, it was like a chemical reaction in which the exercise of speaking his annoyance mixed with air and became rage. His face turned red. He picked up one of the oak 2x2s and launched toward me in a flash. I turned and ran, but he was on my heels, up the stairs, and then billy-clubbed me in the back of the thighs. I fell. He kept hitting. He wouldn't hurt his hand or his shin this time. The piece of oak wouldn't break. What broke was my skin. I felt the split, the excruciating pain, but he didn't stop. Suddenly, my body let out a stench, an animal, skunk-like stench.

"Did you shit yourself?" my father said, striking me again.

"No! I didn't!"

"You," strike, "are," strike, "disgusting!" Strike. "You," strike, "are," strike, "a menace." I could hear the heaviness in his breath. He was wearing himself out. Eventually, he stopped—but only because he was tired.

That was it—I was going to redouble my time lifting weights and working out. I would take care of myself physically. It didn't solve the emotional problems, but I would control what I could. I was delighted when my friend got a punching bag. We spent hours working out hitting the bag. If my friends ever asked if I wanted a snack, I would inhale whatever they offered me. There was a diner next to the gas station, so during my breaks from work, or the second I got a tip for changing or checking oil or washing windows, I'd go next door to buy a slice of cheesecake, then on the next break, I would get a strawberry shortcake.

Because I was a teenager who worked out compulsively, the eating didn't put an ounce of fat on me, and I could continue to numb my feelings with the sugar/carb rush.

While my eating problems and food addiction escalated, so did Ringo's. He regularly raided Mr. Carmichael's garden next door, and he even got in trouble after snatching Mr. Carmichael's fresh-caught fish he was getting ready to gut and clean. Part of his behavior was the result of the steroids he was on for his hip, which made him swell up. One day, I caught him eating roadkill in front of our house and my dad heard me admonishing Ringo, telling him to get away from the dead animal.

"That's it!" my dad shouted. "Charles, get him into the car. We're going to the vet."

"Why?"

"Look at this dog! It's time, Charles."

"No." I looked at Ringo. Ringo looked up at me with his milky eyes and dry nose. Was he suffering? Was it really his time?

My mom said nothing as my dad changed his shirt and got his wallet.

The vet was only a few blocks away—a minute's drive. Hardly time to say goodbye. I remembered the drive home back in Queens, Ringo was a new puppy enjoying the rush of the breeze in the back of my dad's convertible. It was a different lifetime. In that instant, there was only puppy Ringo and old sick Ringo. His life had no middle. My brain blocked out those years completely. Where did the time go between the puppy and the old, sick dog? What happened to the time? The agonizingly drawn years out now seemed to no longer exist. Every minute I spent away from Ringo was a minute of his life I lost forever.

Maybe the vet would be crowded, and my father wouldn't want to wait. I prayed for it. We entered an empty waiting room. We were taken to a back room, and I lifted Ringo onto the table. I pet his fur as they put a needle into his front leg. Then, much too quickly, Ringo's breathing stopped. Ringo was gone. The vet technician picked up Ringo's body and took him out.

"Alright," my father said, "we have to go."

As we headed to the front so my father could pay the bill, I watched the tech put Ringo's body into the freezer. My father paid, then we left. No words were spoken. When we got home, I noticed my mother had secluded herself in the bedroom for a day, and for once, I realized there must have been some fondness in her heart for something other than herself. When she finally emerged, though, it was as if nothing had happened, and Ringo wasn't mentioned. The last glimmer of my childhood left with Ringo's last, fleeting breath. There was nothing, absolutely nothing, left of the child I had once been.

11. THE DOGHOUSE

Throughout my adult life, I've enjoyed leasing homes rather than owning them. I like the feeling of being unencumbered. I watched my parents obsessively rebuild their houses and collect a ton of objects and antiques and be beholden to these objects, hoarding them like jealous dragons. Homeownership to me has always seemed restrictive. Even when I did have my own house, I went overboard with my own renovations and improvements and updating. Whether my behavior proves nature or nurture, I'm not sure. Either way, being a homeowner is too exhausting.

However, I know if I have any chance of adopting Star, I will need to have a home able to accommodate her and pass vetting by all the relevant agencies. So before even discussing adoption with Woods or the Mayor's Alliance, Jenn and I go in search of a home in Lincoln. The home must have a nice yard, but not have a lot of stairs, since Star's vision is diminished by half. Our search goes on for most of January 2013 before we finally find the perfect place in a quiet, established neighborhood. The house sits on tree-lined streets with manicured lawns. There are long-term residents with homes mostly built in the late 1950s, now on their second, maybe third owners. These people take pride in their homes and in the neighborhood. We take possession without any certainty Star will ever be able to live here.

There are dogs in the neighborhood, but almost no fences. Star will need a fence, and a tall one for both privacy and security.

The neighborhood is tightly knit with very respectable residents, including a well-respected retired judge, an engineer married to a nurse, a retired sheriff, a successful real estate agent and a university professor. I fit in, at least by appearances with my white-collar job and Mercedes Benz.

Then I build the fence.

Contractors descend to update the inside while landscapers work on the outside. Crabapple trees are removed, concrete is poured, new sod is put down, and an area of pea-sized gravel is laid in case Star doesn't want to go to the bathroom on the grass in the rain.

The fence will go around the entire perimeter of the backyard, and I tell the contractor it needs to be at least eight feet high.

As the fence goes in, the neighbors react. A retired professor who walks the neighborhood daily while shouting, "You're destroying the neighborhood!"

Other neighbors walk by slowly, staring at the fence. Some cars turn the corner and slow down, scanning the fence. My engineer neighbor calls Lincoln's department of Building & Safety only to be told I've secured the proper permit, and all is okay.

I'm not an amateur.

"Hey, look," I explain to each of them, "I'm getting a dog—a big Great Dane, and having a six-foot fence just won't suffice." The Great Dane is made up, but since I have no idea if I'll get Star, who knows—I may go out and adopt a Great Dane just to get use out of my $20,000 fence!

Once the fence is in place and the cedar turns a nice dark brown, the neighbors quiet down. My neighbor behind me likes the fence, so much he puts a similar one up around his own yard.

Not one of them knows what I'm preparing for.

Next, I put in a surveillance system so Star can be monitored from anywhere.

While all this is going on, I haven't stopped negotiations around adopting Star. We are entering the next level of our strategy. Woods has been alerted to our wishes. Now, it's Jenn's turn.

She's the official negotiator of our camp, which she volunteered to do, wisely, as I'm not everyone's favorite concerned citizen. Jenn is the great communicator, on top of being a professional recruiter. I've done the recon, but I don't have the right diplomacy skills to get Dan Woods rooting for me to be Star's adopter. Jenn makes multiple calls and emails laying out why the two of us are best suited to be Star's parents.

Finally, in late February, we get somewhere.

Woods agrees that we would be a suitable family for Star. "The fact you live so far from New York City will be good for her and it should help her story disappear."

The next step involves the legal defense team vetting us and our new house to see whether it's acceptable living quarters for Star. They request photos of the yard and fence, as well as veterinary references. Since I've talked to Rhonda at the legal defense team many times, I call her to coordinate what she needs. For the first time, her voice is stern and cool as she asks for all our house details.

"We have people in your area, too, who can stop by and do a home visit," she says.

Hey, I'm ready. I'm a guy who likes challenges, and there cannot possibly be a more secure home for Star filled with all the love she needs to get on with her life. I send the packet of info back, with detailed photographs. I never hear another word from Rhonda about a home visit, and there are no further requests or requirements.

"Alright," Dan Woods tells Jenn, "There is only one final hurdle. That's Jill Harrison, the president of the NYC Mayor's Alliance. I believe this will be a tough one."

With Jenn's nuanced help, Woods is now fully in our corner and wants to make sure we succeed in getting Star. And, frankly, the Mayor's Alliance is tired of my bullshit (I'm projecting, though of course I don't believe any of what I've done so far to get Star is bullshit). What I didn't realize until the adoption process started is how interwoven all these NYC officials are, in their various departments, with the collective desire for this story to vanish. And in every story done on Star, when the NYPD has been contacted by the journalists for a comment, each request has been declined.

Jill Harrison will be calling me, and the prospect looms overhead like a dark cloud. As fate has it, though my last six months have been spent in a single-minded hyper focus to everything Star-related, I miss the very call I've been waiting for from Jill Harrison while I'm on a work project. She leaves a voicemail, and, surprisingly, it's pleasant. This is turning out to be a best-case scenario. Though I've been prepping myself for battle, the tone of her voicemail is anything but.

"I'd like to talk with you about the details of Star's adoption," she says kindly.

The details of the adoption. Okay. I'm not preparing for battle. It will be a conversation. I return her call, and we begin with genuine pleasantries before the getting into the details Jill had foreshadowed.

"Charlie, if you want to adopt Star, I have some contingencies I would like you to abide by," she says emphatically.

"Such as what?" I ask.

She inhales slightly and says, "I don't want you to post any updates on her Facebook page or put up any current photos of her. And you can't reveal you adopted her to the public."

I listen and take a breath. Her demands are more of the New York secrecy shit. It is like this dog is in the witness protection program. If this incident with the dog is really this detrimental to NYPD, maybe the force needs to take a closer look at themselves as an institution. Jill doesn't seem to mind that I don't respond, as most New Yorkers are really great at talking and less so at listening. (The Midwest helped me become a much better listener—the old me might have had plenty of choice words back at her, which would be of no help to anybody.)

Then, she concludes, "Okay, then I'll call Dan Woods to set up a date for you to head out to Philadelphia to pick up Star."

Just like that—it's real. My date to head to Philadelphia to pick up Star. This is going to happen. It's all I can do to stay calm.

"Sounds good," I say, and then add, "I have one request as well. I'd like to get a copy of Star's medical records."

There's a pause, and then she asks, "Why would you need those?"

"Secret dog or not, Star will have to be seen by my Nebraska veterinarian as a new patient, and I will have none of her health history."

"Well, I'm just not sure—"

"This is about Star's health. If there is something ongoing, I need to be able to communicate her potential health issues to her vet."

Jill will see what she can do, but eventually, I receive those records. Most shocking: The x-ray of Star's skull with dozens upon dozens of small metal fragments in her head. The note reads that these fragments are indeed a concern. This seems like a pretty essential piece of medical information Star's future vet will likely need. But yeah, I'm sure New York is worried about a vet seeing a dog with over thirty *bullet fragments* in her head.

At the end of our call, I thank Jill for her time and hang up before I explode.

"We're getting Star! We're getting Star! We're getting Star!" I announce over and over again.

Dan Wood's one demand is, when I come to Philadelphia, I rent a minivan, because it would offer Star the most comfort while making the long trip from Philadelphia to Lincoln, Nebraska. I believe *I'm* the one on *Star's* leash, buying her a house and even driving a minivan for her. If I needed to, I'd ride a shopping cart to the moon for her.

12. BAD DAYS AHEAD

At school, there was one kid who wasn't concerned with my wellbeing after I'd been missing for two weeks. Joey didn't like the attention the girls were giving me. He was small, the way my father was small. Some people might call him "a terrier of a kid," but my impression of terriers has always been more positive than it has of bullies. *Joey was a bully.* Like the kids at St. Brigid's, he started in with the "Charlie Syphilis" bit. He'd say it over and over again, following me around school. In the locker room during gym, he'd shove me. I didn't want the fight, so I stopped showing up for gym class, which only got me in more trouble. The teachers probably were buying into the portrait my mother painted of me. To them, I was the problem child, the truant-runaway.

I'd be walking the halls to class, and Joey would come up behind me, knock my books out of my arms then call me a pussy. This harassment was the last thing I needed. I was still trying to navigate my mother's insidious psychological warfare.

The thing was Joey was itching for a real fight. He didn't want it to be just talk. I let it go and let it go until finally, I gave in.

"Fine, let's do it," I said.

"Alright, Syphilis," Joey said, "after school, at the gate."

Any news of a fight will always bring a crowd, and news of the strange spectacle of me fighting Joey sparked a good deal of curiosity. I was skinny but tall. I was lanky, but most of the kids didn't know I'd been working out. My close friends did.

"You can take him," they told me.

I wasn't sure. What I thought was, "Who the hell did this kid think he was? It was bad enough my father hit me, no one else was going to lay a hand on me."

I had to put up with it with my father, but I sure as hell wasn't going to let anybody else knock me around. I psyched myself up with that mental refrain: Only my father can hit me! Warped and morbid, sure. But it worked.

We met at the gate; a sizeable crowd was waiting for me by the time I got there. It wasn't long before he swung at me, and then I swung at him, and then he swung again. Most of these were stupid, harmless swings, but then I lunged at him, grabbed him, lifted him up and then came crashing down on him, right onto the pavement. I really could have given it to him, but I didn't want to hurt him. I wasn't going to be the bully my father was, or that stupid Joey was. He was pinned under me and the crowed jeered at me to punch him, but I wouldn't.

Finally, when someone said, "Just knock his lights out," I said, "I'm hurt." Joey was only too happy for me to stand up, and he tried to push me off of him, though I was already up and off him. He gave a quick glare around before pushing through the crowd and leaving the school grounds.

The next day, he was spreading it around the halls that he'd kicked my ass, though the people who'd seen it knew better. I didn't care about the stupid fight. What I cared about was the fact that he never said a single word to me ever again. He didn't even look in my direction. My victory was in nullifying the bully.

I now understood the full power of having physical strength, and I threw myself into weightlifting. Weightlifting and eating. I had no desire to flex my strength on other kids. Really, it felt like it was for my own survival, not because I wanted the power to wield over anybody else. Lifting really was another way for me to be independent of anyone else and, of course, my emotions. I could deaden any emotional pain with the burning in my body and fill the gaping holes of my emotional life with food. The starch converting to sugars, the endorphins after the workouts all worked to distance me from anything else.

My father was gone most of the time, and I was learning how to navigate the minefield of my mother's emotional abuse. I would shut down in her presence, thinking only of the next meal or the next workout.

By senior year of high school, I was a two hundred pounds of solid muscle. The year was 1983, and the legal drinking age in New York was eighteen (although plenty of kids would sneak into bars with a fake i.d. as early as sixteen or seventeen—anyone could fabricate one of the state-issued paper licenses). I could be a bouncer in a bar at age eighteen. I was hired slightly before my eighteenth birthday and because of my size, no one questioned me. Malibu was the name of the nightclub, and it was the biggest nightclub in the area. I worked Thursday nights, Friday nights, and Saturday nights (while still keeping my job at the gas station). I was seen as *someone*, because here I was, working at the hottest spot in town, and it was another form of power and prestige. Suddenly, my father wasn't the only big shot in the house (he cared nothing about my job or what the other kids thought of me).

The only problem was I was working so much, so late, that I frequently missed my gym class, which was my first period class. Because of this, they didn't pass me, despite the weightlifting and wrestling I did, and because I didn't pass, I wasn't going to graduate with my class in 1983. For the first time ever, my mother advocated for me. She drove up to the gas station and told me, "Get in the car," then drove me straight to a meeting with the principal.

The principal and my mother arranged for me to go back January 1984 and do one more semester including two periods of gym and one academic class, which was English. As ridiculously bureaucratic as this was, that semester was the time of my life. I worked all my jobs but had few school responsibilities, and all the kids knew I was working at the club. My job became a conversation starter, which led to me having a ton of friends.

Girls befriended me as the sensitive older guy, rugged on the outside, but Jell-O on the inside. I realized I was connecting way more with the girls than with the guys. The guys always fought with their girlfriends, giving them grief, and when one of them would complain about his girlfriend to me, I frequently found myself taking the girlfriend's side. From that point on, though I always had male friends, my closer relationships were with women.

#

When I did finally graduate, the next question was what to do with my life. My father had already dissuaded me from my lifelong dream of becoming a cop. After doing well on the NYPD written exam and receiving the call to come take the physical exam, I had only the medical and psychological tests left to take. My father caught wind of what I was up to, going to the police academy for the tests, and said, "You do not want to be a cop. Some are honest, and plenty of them are crooks. There are a bunch of dirty cops on the payroll in New York City." I let him destroy the dream of me becoming a cop.

Next, I went to the US Army recruiting station and got as far as Fort Hamilton for my physical, only to discover I had a pilonidal cyst flaring up. The doctor said I would need to get it lanced, otherwise it would become infected during basic training. I never saw my doctor, having a change of heart. I ignored the recruiter's calls as he stalked me for months to come back and give it another try.

Life at home grew worse again. My mother increased her controlling behavior, staying out with my father until 1:30 in the morning and leaving me coming home from work stuck outside because I still didn't have a key to the house. By this time, she'd moved me down to the basement, which was a musty, depressing place. After one particularly awful bout of her screaming at me for some unreasonable reason, I packed a bag and left. A friend from the nightclub had a brand-new house in Oceanside, a couple of towns over from Merrick, with a couple of roommates, and he was more than happy to have me come stay with them.

While I was there, my cousin Paul, the cousin who had helped me out years earlier when my mom kicked me out for two weeks, resurfaced amid his own drug-fueled descent into mayhem. He showed up with beer and Quaaludes and pressured me to try a pill. (Paul was the one who'd chastised his brother for getting me to do a line of coke when I was a kid). Being drug-free, I refused. However, after drinking one beer, then two, then some more, I relented, taking a Quaalude.

Within minutes, a tidal wave of anger and resentment toward Paul broke through, and I started shouting at him that my life had been going well, and now he was coming back to ruin things because he was selfish. The argument grew heated, then physical, and of course being on Quaaludes and out of control, we moved to the street in front of the house, shouting at each other. Paul was a big guy, and had practiced martial arts, but he didn't want to tangle with me. The rage in me only swelled again, and it probably wasn't just rage at Paul, but rather a long-standing rage at the entire world and my life. I resented my parents and resented the recent fight leading to me leaving home.

I wound up bashing my hand into the nearby storefront window, breaking the window and slicing open my hand. Paul ran away from me and into my house, locking the door behind him. There I was, stuck on the street, banging on the door, unable to get in, and then came the police sirens. Realizing I was not getting into the house, I tried to jump over the fence as the police drove up, and one tried to grab me. I fought back until they sprayed mace into my face and tackled me to the ground. However, my fight wasn't over. While on the ground, I managed to dislocate one of the officer's shoulders, eventually winding up in cuffs and down at the station.

The whole scene was ugly, and even at the police station. I fought with the officers until a detective picked the typewriter off his desk and threw it at me while I was handcuffed to the desk.

After a few days in county jail, my mother came to bail me out for $5,500. There were multiple charges against me. I called my roommates, who told me I couldn't go back to their home.

"Charlie, you're crazy," one of them said, "where did this come from?"

Where indeed? Just one Quaalude? Had all that rage been locked in there? Was I becoming like my father? I was miserable, ashamed, and back in my parents' basement, where I was even more miserable.

"If you're back here," my mother said, "I don't want you costing me any money."

Fortunately, I had my jobs and intended to work full time. Unfortunately, the Malibu nightclub found out I had gotten in trouble and didn't want a bouncer who had trouble with the law, so they let me go.

What's a poor nineteen-year-old kid in trouble with the law and miserable at home and heartsick about his life to do?

In my case, let myself be mothered and nurtured by Erin.

I knew Erin from around town, and I had seen her at the club. She had black hair cut like Joan Jett, the same kind of makeup, and my mother despised how much we liked each other, so she proceeded to try to talk me out of the relationship.

"She's so pale," my mother said.

"She's fair-skinned. What's wrong with that? She has fair skin, dark hair, green eyes. What's not to like? Besides, she's got a great personality."

"She's fat," my mother added.

"Mom, jeez, how is she fat? She weighs no more than a hundred twenty-five pounds."

Once again, my anorexic-bulimic mother in competition with the girls my age, was utterly caught up in her own body dysmorphia. It didn't matter, though because Erin's family brought me into their home. Though I didn't fully move into their house, I was there more than I was at my own home (or, rather, in the musty basement of my parents' home). Her parents became my surrogate parents for the next three years.

The high school I ended up attending wasn't the one typically sending students off to college and fancy careers. I could have attended the high school that did because we were right on the district border and my father could have petitioned to send me, but he didn't. I was fine with this because I pictured myself doing blue collar work. While many of my friends were venturing out of the city or state or had family businesses to follow my father was not about to welcome me into his field. I was okay with staying far away from his work.

By 1986, I fell into driving a cab for the local taxi station—work I loved. I got to meet new people every day and talk about whatever topic was on their mind or on mine. I was sort of like being a mobile therapist, sometimes getting therapy from my fares and other times giving it. There was no shortage of people willing to talk about themselves, which was good, as it gave me an opportunity to learn about anything I could. I was never returning to a classroom again. Being a cab driver provided an early lesson in listening to people (which primed me for becoming a true listener once I got to Nebraska). It helped, too, that I had a look the businessmen I drove to and from the airport liked. I was clean cut and muscular. They sometimes gave me advice, but they always tipped well.

The taxi company was primarily owned by John Albers, who ran the other family taxi business in Charlotte, North Carolina, while his two sons, John Jr. and Mark, ran the day-to-day operations on Long Island. Though they were doing business the same way for decades, I convinced them to let me buy my own cab and to lease me one of their medallions. By doing this, they were guaranteed the same money every month, and if a I wanted to workday and night, seven days a week, to get ahead financially, there was nothing stopping me.

Both brothers liked me, though John Jr. was all business. Mark wanted a friend, and I was happy to be his friend. Both brothers were, like me, addicted to food. The brothers also had gambling addictions. John mostly bet on horses. On the weekends, Mark would take me to Atlantic City in a limo, and he would bet thousands at blackjack and craps. Sometimes he'd win, but other times, he'd lose the five or ten thousand he'd brought. Sometimes he would win big because he had no fear in wagering the table limits, and the casino was more than happy to give him markers if he lost all his money.

I learned to play craps, though sometimes I'd lose a weeks' pay in a weekend. Other times, I'd win a month's pay in a matter of a few hours. I was done with gambling forever the night I was up $35,000 and then lost it all back to the casino. I had enough struggles with addiction, and I didn't need to add another one to the mix. I was so crushed by the loss of so much money that I never wanted to go back. Still, I was starting to think of myself as a big shot. My ego was getting the better of me. The money and feeling healthy and good about life left me feeling conceited.

Though I was still seeing Erin and spending many nights at her house, things were chilling between us. It didn't help that I was away for so long, but the three years were running their course. Rather than break up with her, I wound up hooking up with her friend Linda.

The timing seemed like some kind of sign: Erin and I were clearly at our end, and here Linda and I were. We even shared the same birthday. Maybe we were meant to be. Linda was a beautiful girl, so much so that when I got with Erin, my mother had asked why I wasn't dating Linda instead. What my mother didn't know was Linda was a closet drug user. She was chronic pot smoker, but she also sniffed heroin and snorted crushed up pain pills. But she was fun.

It was easy, when surrounded by a person who liked to party and still seemed to function, to slide down along with them. My slide didn't exactly start with Linda.

There were other guys I liked at the taxi company, including a podiatrist who'd had his license suspended while being investigated for Medicare fraud. A few years later, he had his license reinstated, which meant he could write prescriptions for pain meds, which was good. After all the weightlifting, then all the sitting in cabs, and all the many other tolls on my body, my back was wrecked. Sure, I needed to see a doctor, but I was busy with work, and hey, my buddy was a doctor. He knew what he was doing. The pain pills weren't strong but if you took enough of them, they worked well.

I took the pain pills from my cabby-podiatrist, and then took a menu of other drugs with Linda. Soon, I was as hooked on her as I was the drugs. She knew how to calm me, and she went that extra level to really know me and understand me. She had no fear—which was probably due to the drugs she took. We connected and we did drugs. We connected on increasingly deeper levels and, of course, did more drugs. The drugs picked up the slack where my food addiction left off; the more drugs I did, the more numbed the pain and emptiness. The guilt might bubble up—guilt from the way my life was going from doing so many drugs when I knew I shouldn't—but the great thing about drugs is you can just do more, and then all those feelings get pushed into some internal abyss.

Another taxi driver was a guy named Doug, and he partied as much as I did. We both hit the scene hard for a while, thanks to the podiatrist's help and thanks to plenty of other sources for the stuff without a prescription. Doug wasn't one for deep conversation. He was a junkie for sports more than drugs, and suddenly, he met a girl from Poland and told me one day, "Look, the writing is on the wall. I can't keep up this lifestyle." He got clean from drugs and settled down. He bought a house and married the Polish girl. If only I'd had his head on my shoulders. I wasn't about to slow my pace.

Sure, there were times when I felt the buildup of the drugs in my system, or when I recognized I needed too many pills to feel the same effect. A buddy of mine recommended I try a detox center, where I could check in for a couple of days, have a controlled environment to get the drugs out of my system, and then be functional again. The detox center was like hitting a fabulous reset button. What the center didn't solve was the pain, but now I only needed couple pills here and there. After a while, the need for pills escalated and I could see the situation was getting bad again, so I checked myself back into the detox center, for maybe seven days.

The centers were either free or required only a small co-pay under my insurance. I thought of myself as refueling my tank: One full tank of gas could go about three hundred miles; one seven-day detox could get me back out on the streets for about three months. This pattern became a new cycle in my life. The sequence was simple: detox, start the pills anew, increase my pill usage to an unsustainable amount, detox, rinse, repeat. It didn't take long, though, for the detoxes to lose efficacy. It didn't take long for me to lose my cab business.

People hooked on that many drugs can't keep it hidden, and even the affection Mark and John Jr. held for me couldn't cover for my bad business practices. I was losing money for their medallion, and potentially hurting their reputation. I went from having enough money to blow on gambling weekends to having only enough money to buy drugs. Here is the truth: Addicts can always find money for drugs. I knew I was going downhill, and I was embarrassed about losing my business, so I broke things off with Linda. If I didn't have money, she wasn't going to be sticking around anyway. I needed to spiral downward in my own space.

I blew through everything I had to buy drugs and continued to refill my prescriptions for pain pills. The only footwear I could afford were the flip flips at discount dollar stores, the kind often used when getting pedicures. I packed on a lot of weight over the year or so, but I was losing it while chugging pills and frantically looking for more. Such was my state in 1989 as I exited the train at the Jamaica Station, a neighborhood I had no business visiting. I was drunk and on the hunt for more pills, more drugs and more food, all while merrily chugging the bottle of pills in my pocket, with my sedation ever increasing.

#

I don't know when I actually lost consciousness.

It was a hospital. I knew that. But I had no idea who the two people were in front of me.

"Charles? Charles, are you awake? It's your father."

"What?" I asked groggily.

Nothing made sense. What did he mean, father? Who was that woman? Why was there an elephant sitting on my chest?

My slow overdose on drugs filled my lungs with fluid until one of my lungs collapsed. My father marched out of the room looking for a fight with the hospital staff and asked, "What'd they do to my son out there? What happened to him?"

One member of the staff looked directly at my father and asked, "What was your son doing in that neighborhood?"

The question shut him up.

It took me a while to put all the pieces together—that's how slowly I regained consciousness and my faculties. My mother grew emotional and left the room. My father reached out to me by trying to connect with my love of history, one of the few interests of mine he knew.

"Hey, Charles, when you get out of here, this documentary filmmaker, Ken Burns, he and Shelby Foote are putting on a really, really good show on the Civil War. It's a series, and I watched them all."

This was a nice gesture, though in hindsight, I have even more trouble processing his compassion when contrasted with his years of abuse and neglect, than I did while I was still out of my mind.

The hospital staff and my parents told me, little by little and on repeat until my brain registered what they were saying, what happened. A Haitian immigrant found me. He was a cab driver going through his beat and he saw me collapsed on the ground. I was too heavy for him to lift alone, so he summoned other people to help load me into the back of his car to take me to the hospital.

At the hospital, the staff looked for my ID, but I didn't carry mine most of the time. What they had was the empty prescription bottle with my name on it. That was how they found my parents. The damn bottle of pills that nearly killed me helped the hospital staff find my next of kin.

The doctors resuscitated me, intubated me, and then inserted a chest tube to re-inflate my lung. They told me I also had something called pleurisy of the lungs, subcutaneous water, and they would bring in specialists and push their index fingers into my chest, which was squishy to the touch. They worried my lung might be destroyed.

I was an exhibit. Several days later, when they pulled out the chest tube, my lung collapsed again, so I was rushed into surgery. Because they were trying not to medicate me, they either under anesthetized me or I had a tolerance built up, either way, I woke up during surgery, not fully aware of what was going on but seeing the finger loops of scissors and clamps sticking out of my chest. Once I realized my chest was open, I started screaming for the doctors to do something. I begged them to put me under.

"Oh, don't worry, pal, we'll get you drugged up again, you won't feel any pain," one doctor said.

It was only later that their comments and the tone of their voices, was less trying to calm me down and more like they were mocking me for being an addict. They saw me as someone only out for more pills. I was a loser looking for the next high. Sure, this was true to an extent, but it wasn't who I *was*. I knew that, but I couldn't escape. Waking up, unable to move, and seeing instruments in my chest was sure as hell like a metaphor for my addiction.

Afterward, I was in the most severe pain I had ever known, but because I was an addict, the hospital was not going to put me on a bunch of painkillers.

I begged them for pain medication; they gave me antibiotics.

"Charles, the antibiotics are building you back up. You don't need pain medicine. We need to know if you're not feeling okay, but we don't need to load you up only to collapse your lung again," one of the doctors explained.

I see the point now, especially since the drugs would have only exacerbated my illness. But there was so little compassion. In the hospital, as was elsewhere, there was the assumption that I'd asked for my medical condition by being an addict. I was a white kid from the Long Island suburbs—I knew full well that if I'd actually come from Jamaica, Queens, or if I'd been a Haitian immigrant, I might not have gotten the treatment needed to survive.

Out the window, life was happening everywhere, even on the floors below me. Life was going on without me. There in that room, for the first time, I understood life would go on without me. Never once had that fact crossed my mind. Never once had I seen outside my own life. I was good looking, and many girls told me how handsome I was. I also had a great physique from working out, a full head of fantastic hair, and an ego through the roof. Of course, I thought, what happened to me mattered to everyone—look at how people kept coming to my aid? The world wouldn't let me fall out of existence. I was a key player in the world's mechanisms, and without me, people would be lost…right? No. What happened to me didn't matter, not in the long run, not to all those people out my window.

That might have been a most sobering moment.

Might have been.

It was all hell. Twenty-one days in the ICU. After my stay in the ICU, I was sent to the ward, a long rectangular room lined with beds on either side with no curtains and no privacy. It looked like a World War II army hospital with hardly any room between the beds, and the beds filled with sick people in all stages of life, with all types of injuries, many of them homeless. They screamed and yelled. And the smell—even the memory of it makes my eyes water to this day. There were noxious fumes from every bed and from under every bed. The hospital ward was the worst thing I had ever seen in my life.

There was no way I was staying in there. I told the nurse I wanted to discharge myself, and she called the doctor.

"You are very, very ill," he said, "you can't leave."

"Then why am I not in the ICU?"

"The ICU is for people who are going to leave this planet *right now* unless we give them emergency care *right now*. You're past that condition, but you're not out of the woods. You need to be on an IV, you need breathing treatments, and you need nursing care around the clock to make sure your vitals are still normal."

The expert (me), who was resentful of everything and unreasonably full of himself, but worse, was scared stiff of being in that ward, said, "Look, what would you have done a hundred years ago?"

The doctor sighed. "Well, if you got injured like this a hundred years ago, you might have lived through it. Probably not though. You would most likely be dead."

"Look," I said, "I'll take my chances on the streets. I can't stay here another day, another hour, another minute. I've got to get out of here."

They made me talk to a psychologist to see if I was in my right state of mind, especially since I was signing myself out and not my father. I was over eighteen, they couldn't legally stop me from leaving. Perhaps it was out of guilt, but what was most remarkable was my parents agreed to let me come back home. I was back to staying in their basement. It was several steps up from the ward, but the bar was set so low a person had to dig for it. Being in the unfinished basement with its damp, gray walls was miserable, but there were no other options.

The next month was spent in total misery. I couldn't lift my arms. One condition of my resumed residence under my parents' roof (or rather, under my parents' house) was my attendance at Narcotics Anonymous meetings. The problem was the group of girls in the NA meetings who were natural cheerleaders. I was still relatively fit guy (despite the toll the drugs had taken, I didn't look like a skinny junky), and I drew these girls around me. "Oh, you're injured," they'd compliment me, practically in unison. Rather than focus on healing myself by getting over my addiction, I rushed into the attention the girls provided. We talked before meetings and after meetings to the point where my focus was no longer on the meetings.

As I slowly got back into an exercise routine, the girls were all impressed because I didn't *look* sick. I even had a woman as a drug counselor who laughed with me and took everything lightly because I didn't look like a typical addict. Also, as soon as I was in a room with a woman who liked me and could help me emotionally, (any woman who wasn't my mother, that is), I would know exactly how to make her laugh, how to lay on the charm, and how to get her to not take my addiction seriously. *I was the life of the fucking party.*

Not one of them understood me. They'd look at me and say, "Well, Charles, you used up all your 'get highs' and now you got to do this life with no drugs, just you, the program, and the higher power." They'd smile and giggle a little.

In my mind, I thought, "Yeah, sure."

As far as I was concerned, I was only taking a breather from the drugs. I wasn't stopping for real.

The Intensive Care Unit and the ward were not rock bottom for me. Even if they were rock bottom, I wasn't ready to recover. There was no awakening, no true awareness. I was suppressing too much and was much too far away from any type of spiritual awakening.

No, instead, I'd limit how many pills I'd keep in a bottle to make sure I didn't accidentally overdose and to make sure I wasn't tempted to keep taking them. I'd get smart. I'd do X, Y, and Z to be more cautious. With this mentality, and with a group of addicts who were not all rigorous about kicking their addiction, it didn't take much for me to fall back into old patterns. Trying to manage addiction, they say, is like switching seats on the Titanic.

It took me a year to heal to the point where I could do a single pullup at the gym. I couldn't do a pushup to save my life, not for a long while. I had no job and no money. I had no girlfriends. My skin was gray, and I looked trashed. I was a shadow at the edge of the River Styx, although I wasn't sure which side of the river I was on.

#

Though the details are unimportant, I found myself out of my parents' house again. I had a run-down truck, and I was surviving off drugs and the shared interests of other addicts. There were plenty of woman problems, but I'd move from one to the next, always charming enough (at the beginning) to get someone to take care of my emotional emptiness. One night, a year or so after my hospitalization, I stopped by my parents' house to ask if I could borrow my mom's car because the heat in my truck was not working.

My relationship with my girlfriend wasn't working either, but I was not about to talk to my mother about my relationships, and I was delusional to expect my mom to help me with the car (but drugs do tend to mess with one's judgment). She asked me inside and I sat down, still wearing my winter coat over my sweater and long-sleeved thermal shirt. My mother was talkative, which was odd, and I wasn't in the mood to have a conversation.

"Charles are you okay?" she asked.

"I'm fine," I said quickly.

"Oh, well, did you know—?" and she moved on to another conversation before circling back to ask if I was okay, a little louder this time. "Charles, really, what's wrong?"

Telling my mother about trouble with a woman was the surest way to open me up to criticism, as well as invite my mother's eager bashing of any other woman, which I didn't want to instigate. The only reason I didn't leave was I had nowhere to be, and the house was warm. The old numbness set in as I buried any feeling inside, away from my mother, and let the shell of my body take the force of whatever it was she said, her voice gaining in volume and pitch. Then, the doorbell rang. Followed by a pronounced knock. An official knock.

My mother sprang up and opened the door, revealing six uniformed police officers. They looked in, then called to me to join them out on the stoop.

"Mom, what are the cops doing here?" I asked, incredulously.

She stepped away and an officer ushered me out.

"Your mother was worried about you, so she called us," the officer said.

What? My mother called the cops on me? While I was sitting in her house?

"Why did six of you come?" I asked.

The officer who addressed me said, "Well, you're a strong young man. You could get upset with our presence."

What the actual fuck? "How is this a police matter?" Leave it to my mother to use police as a social service resource. Family problem? Call the police—unless, of course, your husband is beating the hell out of your son.

"Well, your mother said you might be under the influence of alcohol and medication, and she was concerned you wanted to drive and might hurt yourself or someone else. How about we take you to the hospital and have you checked out by the doctors?" the officer suggested.

Huh.

"Are you planning on taking me against my will?" I asked.

"We can't take you against your will because we haven't observed you acting as a danger to yourself or others."

"Well, then, can I leave since it's apparent I'm not a danger to anyone?"

"We would rather you did not."

What did that mean? If I wasn't a danger and didn't seem like I was going to hurt anyone, and they couldn't take me to the hospital by force, then why couldn't I leave? Here I was, in my early twenties, face-to-face with a veteran police sergeant and five officers behind him, giving me what sounded like a request. Turns out it was more of a directive, but then why couldn't they take me but also not let me leave?

"Without seeing a doctor, you cannot drive your car," the officer said.

My blood pressure had been rising, though I wasn't marking it. The calm withdrawal I'd had while sitting with my mom was now draining—and rapidly. This, now, was all I could deal with.

In a split-second, I decided to leap over the handrail of the stoop to get away from the officers on the stoop, though they came around faster than I would have expected (if I had been even thinking at that point), and they cornered me against the house. One of the officers grabbed my wrist, trying to wrestle handcuffs onto me. I tried to squeeze between them and held onto them as each one grabbed at me. A struggle ensued for several minutes.

One handcuff finally latched onto my right wrist, and suddenly I broke free. The police backed off—I now had a swinging weapon, and this break allowed me to catch my breath. In a matter of seconds, they surrounded me again, lunging for my legs. They pinned my arms together to get the second cuff around my wrist, but I used my free hand to hold onto the cuff so they couldn't get to it. Six of them against one of me plus time meant I wore out faster than they did, and I stopped fighting back.

Now I was arrested, strapped to a gurney and taken in a police ambulance to the ER, where I was wheeled inside for an evaluation. Bound to the gurney, I was no longer deemed a threat to the officers, so most of them left. Though I couldn't move my arms, I realized the bindings on my legs were loose enough so I could free one leg and then the other. Once my legs were out, I rocked the gurney from side to side until I fell over. It was an effort to get onto my feet, the gurney still being strapped to my body. I got up and made a run for it, though I didn't make it far, thanks to hospital security.

They tied two gurneys together so I couldn't flip them, and thinking I was harmless in my handcuffs, they unstrapped my shoulder straps to readjust them. I was all reaction. My body had taken over, and it was telling me to do whatever it took to get out. Holding my cuffed hands together, I swung down in a chopping motion, multiple times, sending the hospital staff running for cover. I took the opportunity of my newfound freedom to make another run for it through the ER.

The resulting struggle was ugly. I was still in my thermal, sweater, and tight-fitting winter coat, oblivious to how much I was overheating. The only thing I knew was someone had jabbed a needle into my neck. I still fought for another few minutes until I finally felt a true fatigue and I surrendered. The sedative should have knocked me out, but it had a minimal affect. I was strapped, tightly, to a gurney and wheeled into a small room of the ER, where I was left with the lights out and door shut.

I was a combatant who resisted both arrest and care. Now, I was shelved out of sight. And I was overheating. My clothes were drenched. I couldn't breathe, and despite calling for help, no one came. They probably thought it was a ruse to make another escape. Maybe they thought whatever was going wrong I had coming to me. I could die and no one would know for a long time. I was sure I had been sedated and I struggled to stay awake. I was convinced that if I fell asleep, I wouldn't wake up. I refused to die like that.

My predicament was because I wanted to borrow my mother's car. That's where it all began.

Of course, I was combative and had an addiction problem. That was on me. However, I had not been a threat to anyone until the police escalated the situation by saying they couldn't force me to come but I wasn't allowed to leave. My mother had no business using the police for family counseling.

I should not have proven my mother right. I played right into her game—maybe it was a spectacle she craved, or a deliberate need to see me get punished for something. Why couldn't I have just gone with the police and explained everything to the doctors, all the abuse, everything, and let the police once and for all deal with my parents? Now, instead, I might die.

A freight train ran through every nerve ending, pounding up to my head. My anxiety spiked. My lung hurt. I told myself to take the deepest, slowest breaths I could. I needed to oxygenate my lungs. It was just the room was so small, so hot, and because it was winter, the nearby vent spewed more hot air. My winter coat felt like a sarcophagus. It would take a miracle for me to live through this.

So, I begged for a miracle. I said, out loud, "If it's your will, God, that I live, I will live. If not, I will see you soon."

I woke up twenty-four hours later. My handcuffs and restraints were gone. An orderly was posted outside my room. I was alive.

However, I couldn't stand up on my own.

As soon as the tranquilizers wore off, I called in the orderly, and we struck up a conversation.

"The doctors will see you, but they'll want to make sure your meds have fully worn off, so they know they're talking to the real you," he said kindly.

"I don't know what happened," I said. "I'm not crazy."

"Hey," the orderly named Robert said, "I know you're not. I've been working at this hospital long enough to recognize the crazy ones. I mean, there are plenty along this very hall."

Hearing of my sanity was the biggest relief. I could only hope the doctor would come to the same conclusion. Though the doctor didn't come until the following day, I had water, was comfortable, and Robert chatted with me off and on to pass the time.

When the doctor saw me the next day, he asked why I put up such a fight.

"I didn't intend to. I feel bad about what happened—once I tried to make my escape at my mom's house, all hell broke loose, and I couldn't de-escalate," I explained.

"Well," the doctor said, "no one here will hurt you."

I started to cry. Mostly from shame. I was the only one hurting myself with the drinking and the drugs. I knew what a vicious cycle I was caught up in. I hated how I felt when I took the pills, but I felt worse when they wore off, and I explained all this to the doctor.

"You have to be willing to be clean and sober," the doctor said pointedly. He then added, "Willingness is all there is to it. You're in a hospital, not a hotel. There are many sick people in the community who need the beds far more than you do. I want you to think hard about whether or not you're prepared for a change."

Of course, he was right—I needed to choose my future before it chose me.

My mother came to visit me during dinner that evening. She sat directly in front of me, watching me try to eat my Thanksgiving-style TV dinner. I both resented her and appreciated that she came to visit me. (We were nowhere near addressing root causes of my issues at this point.) All I could think to do was satisfy the one addiction I was currently allowed—food—and I focused on food rather than my mother, who stared at my mashed potatoes and green peas in disgust.

There was a stiffening sensation in my body, in my back, creeping up to my neck, but I ignored it, focusing on getting every piece of food from my plate to my mouth. My back and neck cramped further, the pressure increasing, and my head got closer to my plate, my mother looking in horror. It wasn't until I could not move my back or neck and was starting to worry I might drown with my face submerged in gravy that I recognized the problem, and my mother yelled for a nurse.

"Oh, it's a reaction to the drug we used to calm him down," the nurse said, giving me another shot, of something called Cogentin, an "antidote" to the first drug.

"How could you let something like this happen?" my mother shouted. She was suddenly my advocate.

"Well, a very small percentage of patients will have side effects—" the nurse said, while my mother scoffed with her arms crossed. What a performance she put on.

"Mom, how could it not happen?" I asked when the nurse left. "People die every day in the system—that doesn't mean the system has it out for me."

"Nonsense. It's at least negligence," my mother declared.

Did she react this way out of guilt? Or was her reaction to absolve herself of any guilt she might, at any point, feel? Did she think if she occasionally said a few things that sounded like they were sort of possibly supporting, well then, she did her job as a mother and what more could be expected of her?

My noble advocate eventually left, and two days later I was discharged, and a couple of my friends picked me up from the hospital and let me stay with them while I decided what to do next. My life was mine to do with as I pleased. Unfortunately, these friends drank and used drugs, and though I didn't want to join them, my first night out of the hospital, I did in fact join them drinking and using drugs.

The difference was this time, I felt guilty, for the first time. The next morning, I awoke with anxiety in the pit of my stomach and the realization that this wasn't the way I wanted to live. All my life, I had taken abuse from my parents, and now, I was the one doling out abuse to myself. My doctor was right: I needed to make the commitment to live without drugs, and my old friends with their habits could not be a part of such a commitment.

14th & 2nd

I made the decision to go to a rehab center. I opened the phone book and called around to see which rehabs had openings and which would take me.

13. ARRIVAL

April 12, 2013 is the set date to pick up Star. The minivan is rented. Jenn has prepped the house. She bought Star a doggy bed and toys and treats. I've overstocked the minivan with an extra-large crate filled with blankets and pillows and enough water and food to stay on the road for a month. It might be an understatement to say I'm prepared. All I need to do now is drive 1,200 miles to pick up our miracle dog.

Eight months of my life have already been given over to Star, and now she is finally going to be tangibly in our lives, and not as a mere metaphor. My heart races with (far more) energy than the minivan's engine, and the next 1,200 miles to the National Dog Sanctuary are spent simply driving. I'm cognizant of little else. Upon my arrival, the staff greets me with a celebration already set up, including a giant cake inscribed:

Congratulations to Charlie & Jenn

Shiloh Has a New Home

April 2013

And there she is, my Star. My girl. I break down as I hug her. She smiles from ear to ear, that tongue lolling off the side of her mouth. I'll protect you, Star. I'll do whatever I can to give you the best life ever.

The celebration isn't long. It's nice to rest for an hour before heading back out to the road. A few of the staff members raise their eyebrows as I keep referring to Shiloh as Star, but Dan Woods explains it away as the new name I want to give to Star. Once the staff says their goodbyes, Star hops into the car through the sliding minivan door, sniffing at everything I've brought, and makes a beeline for the treats in the crate.

Now she's done with her life in the double-locked room, and it's only two hotel stays and a handful of big meals between here and her new life in Nebraska.

"Hey, Star, so what do you think, ready to go home?"

Huge smile.

"Alright, then. Let's go. It'll be a couple of days, but just wait to see what your new home is like."

After she explores the crate (and inhales the treats it has to offer), I hold up a treat and she takes it, so gently, from my hand. She's polite and mindful of her space and of mine. I want to be worried for her, but she looks at me as if to say, "Hey, it's okay. I'm good, are we going?"

That's right, Star. We're good. We're going home.

I drive like a true minivan driver, for safety, yes, but also because I don't want to attract any attention from the local authorities, cognizant I'm passing through areas with Breed Specific Legislation (BSL) against Pit Bulls. I can't get this far and then lose it all. If Star is a protected, secret dog, she is now my sole responsibility, which makes me her secret service. To that end, I also only lower the side window four inches, but Star makes full use of those four inches. She takes in all the scents on the wind as we chase the sun, the breeze going right across her nose and those olfactory sensors—this is freedom.

My stops are all pre-planned, so I have reservations at places that specifically welcome pets with a small deposit. Once we cross Ohio, I stop for dinner and learn a new thing about Star: She's a picky eater. She's been fine with the treats I've given her during the ride, but when I pour the high-quality dog food into her bowl, she turns up her nose. A shelter dog that doesn't inhale what's put in front of her? I go to the drive through at a Wendy's and order a couple of hamburgers, but no dice: Star isn't interested. Maybe she's too excited?

I eat my own dinner and then we take a walk around the block, and Star isn't sure where to look because everywhere there are people and food smells and activity. Not once does she bark. Out of desperation (will she trust me if I don't get her the food she wants to eat?) I collect a sack full of snacks, including peanut butter, which is usually a go-to food for dogs. It turns out peanut butter, on sliced apples, is her weakness. Jackpot. My next trick is to put a little peanut butter on her dry kibble, and she eats most of that as well. Alright, another success. I'll take it.

Back in our hotel, a room with two queen-size beds, I pat Star's bed to get her to jump up. She hesitates, lowers her head, then makes a circle, stepping back.

"No, come on, Star, this is where you're gonna sleep," I say kindly.

I move to pick her up, but she lets out a short sound that isn't a growl or a yelp—it's more like a closed-mouth *yip*. She doesn't want to be picked up, not yet.

"Okay, girl, don't worry," I say as I pat the top of the bed again, realizing Star probably never in her life had slept on a bed. I put a treat on the bedspread, and after two more minutes, Star's hesitation is overcome by the desire for the treat, and she jumps on the bed.

"That's it, that's my girl," I say encouragingly.

She eats the treat, then stands on the mattress, feeling the alien bounciness of a brand-new surface, sniffing around, feeling out the perimeter, then cocking her head at me and giving me a little tail wag.

"Who's a good girl? Who's a good Star?" I ask warmly.

She crouches down in play mode. I jump onto my mattress and squat, in play mode. Then, I jump to her mattress. She spins around. I jump back to mine, and then she follows me. We play at jumping back and forth between our beds for a few minutes. Despite all she's been through, she's still under two-years-old. She is not quite, but practically, still a puppy. Despite all she's been through, she hasn't forgotten. Despite all I've been through, right now, on this bed, I'm a boy again, only this time I don't worry I'll be hurt by the people in my home.

We spend the next few minutes in sheer glee until we're both tired out. Finally, she makes her several circles before settling down. I get up to brush my teeth, and every time I move or make a noise, Star's head shoots up, curious and uncertain. "It's okay," I assure her, making sure when I'm in the bathroom, she can still hear my voice talking to her. Eventually, she buries her face between the pillows, and I can hear a soft, muffled snoring.

I drift off in my own swirl of thought about Star, and somewhere there's a distant thought about Kane, and about my parents back in the 1970s, before dogs were allowed in motels. My parents would sneak in Ringo, the sizable German Shepherd, under coats and hidden behind a bag, all the way from the car into our room. Sometime in the night, I wake up, turn over, and realize Star is here with me. *This isn't a dream.* We are headed home.

On our drive the next day I see Star's nose out the crack in the window and I see her excited reaction to seeing people in their cars. Kids we pass wave at her. I think of what Jill said about not letting anyone know I have her. I think about not posting any photos of her and not revealing her whereabouts to anyone.

My new neighbors are all quite conservative. The one is a retired judge. There was so much upheaval over the fence. While I see her as the ultimate survivor, after having been a victim of so much awful circumstance, my neighbors may see her as a Pit Bull who charged a cop and got what she deserved.

It's too risky to take any chances. I won't say a word.

I won't lie, though, either. If someone asks me, I'll deflect as best I can, but I won't lie about who she is.

#

After our two-and-a-half-day drive, Star and I make it home to Jenn. She is waiting for us in the driveway.

"Is that our girl?" she asks, bending down as Star and I limp out of the minivan after our long confinement.

Star stretches, then ambles over to Jenn, giving her new mom her signature smile.

"Look at this gorgeous face," Jenn says, her eyes welling with tears.

All the tension, my maniacal searching, the strain on our relationship, is all gone in this moment. We are a *family*.

"Are you hungry, Star? I have some food ready for you," Jenn says invitingly.

Star rushes in but is at first distracted by all the new smells and sights. Though we try to get her to eat, she takes a few bites of her food before moving on to more exciting things. After her incomplete meal, we follow her through the house as she gives herself a tour, and then we show her to her new yard, with its featured masterpiece, the 8-foot fence. She sniffs and wanders and circles and circles back and stands, smiling, looking at us. What impresses me, once I really think about it, is her vision is actually pretty good, and she shows no real struggles with depth perception despite having only one eye.

She truly is quite the girl.

Her living arrangements have gone from the streets of New York City to the quiet, rural, upper-middle-class suburbs of Lincoln. Star is home.

And I can get back to my life. The difference is I'm not fully going back to the person I was.

14. THE REHAB CIRCUIT

My first attempt at rehab guaranteed if the patient relapsed within the first year, the second treatment stay with them was free. With that promise, I called the rehab center to pick me up and drive me into the Pennsylvania mountains. I read the motivational slogans posted on small signs on the road all the way up the mountain. The signs were, in fact, inspiring and motivating, and I entered the mountaintop log cabin rehab full of hope.

By my second night there, I was planning my escape.

Being an unrecovered addict turns you irrational and leads you to all manner of terrible decision making, even when you're not loaded up on drugs. I was whacked out of my mind. At dark, I took a butter knife I pocketed from dinner and sliced at the screen, sawing back and forth. I prepared myself for jumping down from the window, making sure I could get a good grip on the windowsill with my hands before making the big jump down. I hoped I wouldn't get hurt in the fall. I had only imagined my window was high off the ground. As soon as I climbed over the ledge and let myself hang down, I felt the ground under my feet. Oh.

The next step was to belly-crawl the fifty or sixty feet around to the side of the building to head out to the woods. The sweat beaded on the back of my neck, my elbows and knees turned muddy. I stopped when I heard voices, and I ventured to peek around to the front of the building. I saw several of my rehab buddies smoking out on the porch. I, too, could have walked out the front door, via the porch, without the belly-crawl. The problem was now I was in too deep; I couldn't let them see me like this and popping up out of nowhere when I had formerly been in my room would only have aroused suspicion. I made a ninety-degree turn to the right and into the woods, on my belly, until I hit the thick darkness, where I could stand up and head downhill. Though I couldn't see, the only logical direction was downward. I stepped into a pool of wet, muddy leaves, fell down, and slid down the muddy mountain, in the dark. The mud was slick, and I tumbled fast, though not without bumping into rocks and sharp branches. My descent was only brought to a swift end thanks to a large tree in my path.

The wind was knocked out of me, and I lay there on my back, too scared to move lest I wind up in the middle of another uncontrollable descent. I stayed there, against the tree, on my back, muddy and cold, until sunrise. The occasional drifts into sleep were brief. With daylight as my aid, I picked out a large, broken branch on the ground to serve as a walking stick, guiding me down through the mud. I managed to slip and catch myself multiple times on the way down. An eternity later, I found the main road. I was hungry and thirsty and completely ignorant of my appearance as it was, covered in mud, leaves, and scrapes, my t-shirt ripped. I looked like a madman or a refugee from a sasquatch den. I didn't even notice I had blood on my hand, not even after I wiped my face with the bloody hand.

This is the picture of me as I stood by the side of the road, waiting for a passing motorist to wave down.

This is a picture of addiction.

Me being in such a condition and this being rural America, most passing cars did not slow down. Finally, though, one green early 1970's Dodge Dart full of teenagers, maybe eighteen years old, stopped for me and rolled down the window part way. They looked scared.

"Hey, I need a ride into town," I said desperately.

One guy in the back reached down to the floorboard and picked up a rifle.

"What's that for?" I asked.

"We're hunting for rabbits along the road," he said, "and I'm going to hold it while we give you a ride. I don't know you, and you talk like you're from New York City."

It would be another few years before the advertisement for Pace Picante Sauce flooded the airwaves, in which a bunch of cowboys lament a competitor's salsa comes from "New York City!?" in a shocked, overly drawn-out voice, but that was the impression the boys in the car gave when they made their comment. I was from New York City!? and they needed the gun, just in case. (That and I looked like I had possibly/probably already murdered someone.)

The driver looked at me, then said, "We'll give you a ride, but you have to sit on the trunk." He nodded his head directing me to the back of the car.

"Huh?" I grunted.

"We'll go slow, but you got to be on the trunk," the driver clarified.

If he thought riding on the trunk would dissuade me, then he clearly hadn't spent time around anyone with an addiction before.

"Alright," I said, walking to the trunk and situating myself, cross-legged, with my fingers wedged between the window and the crack of the trunk lid to keep from falling off the back. Each time I looked down I saw the kid in the back seat with the barrel of his rabbit-hunting gun pointed at me.

The driver kept his word and drove at about 20-25 miles per hour. It took thirty minutes to get into town. I reminded myself it would have taken me all day to get there on foot. I probably would have passed out on the way from hunger and thirst. Once we got to town, they pulled to the curb to let me off. The kids all apologized for putting me on the trunk and pointing the gun at me, but they said they were nervous about who I was.

"But at the same time, we wanted to help you," the driver said.

"Well, thanks," I said and gave them a short wave. I went on my merry way through the very small rural Pennsylvanian town with two whole blocks of shops. I only had a few dollars on my person, which was all I was allowed at rehab for vending machine cookies and sodas. It didn't matter—I just needed to find someplace where I could get some cheap food.

I had enough to buy a Coke and two packs of Hostess cupcakes, my sugary go-to, at the grocery store. I shoved the first two cupcakes in my mouth, barely chewing—like a shelter dog might do—then chugged the Coke to wash them down. As I was wrestling open the plastic of the second two-pack of cupcakes, a car roared up behind me and then screeched its brakes.

Two rehab counselors got out.

The town I was in was the first town reached by anyone coming from or going to the rehab, so they figured I would swing through town if I'd left on foot.

"How in the world did you make it off the mountain, Charles?" one asked as they opened the back door for me.

I sighed and asked, "How'd you find me?"

"It's a small place. We called down to ask the shopkeepers to keep an eye out for you."

The counselors were clearly driving faster than those kids in the green Dart. I was tired and had no other options, so I wasn't going to fight with them. I got into the car.

Like *Cool Hand Luke*, my escapades made me popular with the residents and counselors for the rest of my stay. I finished the next twenty-seven days without incident. I got a ride back to Long Island, and my mother immediately called me and said I should move back in.

Moving in with my parents would not be a good idea.

"Charles, this way, you'd be away from your friends and the temptation to do drugs," my mother implored.

Though reluctant, I conceded to her that going back to my friends was not an option. Plus, I had nothing to my name, and limited job prospects. Back into the basement I went–the cold, bleak basement. It wasn't a week before my mother was honing her verbal abuse. Whether it was one day or two later, I don't exactly recall, but I was soon back to self-medicating with prescription drugs. Back then, it was no problem to find a doctor to write a prescription for just about any ailment, regardless of whether it was a figment of the patient's imagination.

A patient would say, "Doc, I have pain, and the pain causes me anxiety, and the anxiety makes me not sleep, which makes me sad," and the doctor would write one prescription for pain medication, one prescription for tranquilizers, one for sleeping pills, and one for anti-depressants.

In my head, I knew I'd get past all this one day, so I told myself it didn't matter what I did now to get through the immediate pain.

My parents were onto my glassy-eyed numbness right away, and the mountaintop Pennsylvania rehab kept their word. Within twenty-four hours, a driver was at my door to take me back for a free round after my relapse. Stepping into that station wagon was a relief, as it meant an escape from my mother's condescension and constant contempt.

The driver was a man in his 70s. He was a WWII vet, who had retired to rural Pennsylvania and needed something to do, so he drove around the tri-state area picking up whoever the rehab center told him to pick up.

"Sometimes I got my wagon full of young men, and sometimes it's just one, like today," he said.

"Where do you do most of your pickups?" I asked.

"Oh, let me tell you, it's a mix. I pick up kids from the most beautiful homes in Nantucket and from small apartments in the South Bronx. I've been to blocks even the NYPD won't go to except maybe for the tactical unit. If there's someone in need, I go to pick them up."

He felt so familiar. He was the same type as Mr. Carmichael and Mr. Berg, my early mentors. Men who had been through a lot and yet still cared about other people. The men who told great stories and who actually listened to what I had to say.

"Look at all you've been through," I said, ashamed. "You must have seen enough action for many lifetimes, and now you're doing this. You fought enemies overseas—here I am, fighting a battle in suburban Long Island, and the only enemy is myself."

"Hey now, look," the driver said, "it's different times now than it was then. And what you have is a disease."

A disease. I'd heard the line in some of the 12-step programs and even read about it in literature on addiction, but I never really took it to heart. Mainstream society always treated addiction as a failing. Here was this retiree, vet, and driver for a rehab, who lived a full life with so many experiences and saw just about everything, acknowledging as fact that addiction was a disease. Sure, the rehab must have schooled him, but it came out so naturally.

He continued, "You just haven't accepted your addiction is a disease yet, you have a disease that needs treating, and when you do, you will be done fighting it. It all rests on your acceptance, and unfortunately, this disease tells you that you don't have it."

He was speaking directly to my heart.

"When you're ready, you'll be ready," he said, "but I know you will get this one day."

"You do?" I asked.

"Yes," he said, then paused. "If the addiction doesn't kill you first, and that's the problem. No one knows when they have gone too far. There's no science to drinking and drugging too much."

Though his words were grim, he was giving me an education without shame. So much of society, from the hospitals to television, had a stigma against addiction and addicts. As far as they were concerned, we all got what we deserved. To be around someone who said we had a disease and our lives still had value, was the light of hope amid all the grimness. The four-hour ride was a delight. This whole trip felt more personal, more consequential.

Upon arrival, I was admitted by a very attractive nurse in her thirties who took my vitals. My reaction was to put on the old charm.

"Charlie, you can do this," she told me. "I want to tell you something, and I don't tell this to everyone. I'm in recovery. I'm alcohol- and drug-free for eight years. I can do it, so can you."

I nodded. I kinda could imagine it.

"Have you considered having a personal relationship with a Higher Power?" she asked.

"Right now, to be honest," I said, "all I do is call on the Lord to help me. He isn't always on time, but He hasn't let me down so far."

"It is great you recognize Him," she said, smiling softly.

Playing the golden schoolboy down on his luck, though I did believe this was true, I told her, "I sure do recognize Him, but I also realize my problems are of my own making. I'm just not where you are yet spiritually, and I may never get there."

I could be quite lucid and eloquent—it's what made people like me. Also, though, I needed to show everyone I wasn't "just" a junkie. I was someone who believed in all the right things and had all the right words. After my conversation with the driver, though, I was feeling so open—it was all such a different experience than being with my mother. I added, "I have so much pain in my gut and head. I don't know how to cross over to sober living now."

"Charlie," she said, "the program and twelve steps and twelve traditions. These are the steps you must take to stay sober and clean. They will teach you those steps here, and it's one day at a time. Even for me eight years later, one day at a time. Just keep saying that, and it will get easier."

She was pretty and friendly, but the way she delivered her promo for the twelve-step program was mechanical, and all I could see in her was a robot for the program. I did plenty of praying to Jesus, but I was far from convinced Jesus was the only alternative. I thanked her, and each time I saw her in passing during treatment, we always smiled at each other. Each time, I thought of her living one day at a time and wondered how she could date, live, do anything else, while her head was immersed in the program and living only for the present day.

My problem was in being an all-or-nothing guy. All diet or no diet. There was no question of whether to have one cupcake or six; I would always choose six. There was no "**one**" of anything; if it smelled good or tasted good or felt good, I wanted more and more and more.

During my stay, counselors were still talking about my great escape off the mountain, and we had a few laughs as I became a cautionary tale. Meanwhile, I gained much more knowledge the second time around, especially when it came to choices and treating my addiction as a disease.

When I left, though, all that knowledge was discarded like the crinkly plastic of a Hostess cupcake wrapper. Days after leaving, I relapsed in spectacular fashion and frenzy.

#

I tried another shot at a different rehab. I found a new rehab by the ocean, at the end of Long Island in a scenic town called Greenport. If it weren't for the actual rehab part, this would have been a wonderful getaway. A girl I knew from high school days gave me a ride. Most of the time, there was always a girl willing to give me a ride or a place to stay. I was *poor, sweet Charlie*.

On the ride, despite the beautiful day and scenery as we drove along the coast, the self-pity sank in. How could I have a problem with addiction? Why couldn't the foot doctor who was being investigated for Medicaid fraud have gotten a different job, anything other than driving taxis? Why couldn't he have stuck to his own field when there were so many sick people out there? I knew, though, if I wanted to blame someone, I should take a look in the mirror.

At the Greenport rehab, there were kids there from some of the wealthiest families on Long Island. I thought of my driver to the Pennsylvanian rehab telling me about patients coming from everywhere. The backgrounds were all so different from mine, but it turned out not to matter—we all ended up in the same place.

There was an undercurrent throughout many of our stories. The young men in my group shared instances of how their parents had treated them poorly, or were distant with them, or were abusive. What if, I thought—what if I'd had a normal childhood without the trauma of physical and mental abuse? Would I even be here in this predicament? My brother didn't have a drug addiction problem—and our father never raised a hand to him, and our mother didn't berate him. However, there was something we shared: He could never have enough girlfriends, he could never stop spending his money, and there was never enough of enough. There was a void that needed filling in him, too.

If, during all this time it seems as if my little brother wasn't there, it's because he wasn't. As soon as he turned 16, he emancipated himself and moved away from our parents. He hated everything about our father. Even though my father doted on Christian, he saw through to the man he really was. My brother also did well to stay away from me during my destructive period. He became his own man, moving to another state and starting a successful business of his own. His hatred of my father was so complete that he legally changed his last name to remove himself further from the family toxicity. He might not have suffered quite as much as I did, but he suffered, and maybe it was my example that helped him stay away from drugs, as we both seemed to share a proclivity for addiction.

In a previous detox center, my counselors asked me about my family situation. At first, I was evasive, but when my parents came for an assessment, the counselors seemed attuned to the family dynamic without me telling them everything that happened. As my parents complained about me to the counselors, that I had been such a problem to them my whole life, my counselor sat back and gave as much of a hint as he dared.

"You know," the counselor said, "you should all come in together as a family for counseling sessions."

My mother was incensed. "That will not be necessary," she insisted.

"Actually, it can be very beneficial for families to work together to examine the root causes of deep-seated issues such as addiction," the counselor explained.

Later on, I heard plenty about what a hack the counselor was. My mother was a saint, naturally, and her abusive alcoholic husband didn't need any help whatsoever. No, I was the problem, so I was the one who needed to be sent away to be fixed.

Was my addiction really my parents' fault, though? As far back as I could remember, now that I was doing plenty of reflection in rehab, I had been addicted to food. When I was an infant, I would suck down bottle after bottle of milk, and then yell out to my father, "Mo' milk, Daddy!" I thought about this at night, lying awake in Greenport. Was I genetically predisposed to addiction? In the years to come, some people suggested my mother might have already been monitoring my food intake and just wasn't giving me enough in the first place. It's a possibility—and a mystery I may never solve. Yet the counselors wanted me to delve deeper into my family.

I told them about the beatings and the psychological warfare. I described the withholding of food and the destruction of mealtimes and my long-term addiction to food. My one-track mind, even as a kid. For example, if I collected baseball cards, I would stay on it until every player on a card was in my collection. Then I would go on to the next collection, focused solely on accomplishing that goal, then moving onto the next one.

Feeding myself to get a sugar rush was almost always preceded by a bout of parental abuse. My resentments toward them could fill an oil tanker. I wanted to be heard by my parents, but they shut me out. My resentments turned into anger, but that anger missed its intended target—my parents—and boomeranged back onto me.

"The problem, Charlie," the counselors said, "is if you are ready to hold others accountable but dismiss your own actions and play the victim, then no amount of rehab or counseling will work. It just won't. That being said, addiction *is* a family disease."

Still, I was better off than people with other diseases, such as children born with diabetes or who develop cancer—my disease could be arrested at any time once I finally made the choice to surrender my will and follow the steps to recovery. I needed to stop wallowing and learn from this rehab experience.

There was something about the vibe of this rehab, though, that didn't sit well with me. The patients were snooty and odd, oblivious to the privileges they had, but so were the counselors (maybe the patients' weirdness rubbed off on the counselors). This would not be the place I'd get better, and I recognized it.

What I really wanted was to go back to work. I loved work, and it filled me with a sense of purpose. The truck I had gotten earlier, intending to use it one day, was always breaking down, but at least it was still mine. If I could borrow money and get it fixed and make it run, I could find work making deliveries or hauling something. That was my plan. I needed to figure out a way to get myself out of rehab early without sneaking out in the night, like I did at my last Pennsylvania mountain rehab.

The center had a policy that, when we were out on a walk around the facility for our fresh air and exercise, we couldn't smoke within a hundred feet of the building. Violation of said rule would incur immediate expulsion from the rehab. Alright. There were plenty of snitches in this place, guys who would be sure to rat me out pronto. All I had to do was ask someone for a cigarette. This would be easy because most of the guys there smoked.

I'd never smoked a cigarette in my life, but all I had to make it *look* like I was smoking. I bummed the smoke and had the guy light it for me, then walked around with the lit cigarette in my hand. Once we got closer to the building, I broke off from the rest of the fellow walkers and paced within a few feet of the main building. I expected to be bum-rushed by a pack of orderlies, but no one appeared. Naturally, when I need security to be all over me, there was no one.

Once the rest of the walking group swung back around, I stamped out the cigarette and followed them back into the building. As I entered, a counselor pulled me aside.

"Charlie, were you smoking by the building?" he asked.

"Yes, I was," I said clearly.

"I'm sorry, but you know the rules. We will have to dismiss you from the facility."

Oh, heavens, no! Not that!

"Alright," I said, "I understand."

My papers were put through within the hour, and someone from the facility drove me to the LIRR train station and bought me a ticket back home.

15. SECRETS IN NEBRASKA

It takes Star some time to adjust to less activity. She no longer has to tolerate the constant checkups and transfers and routines of a staffed animal hospital with dozens of other dogs all waiting for adoption or living out their sequestered lives. Our house is certainly less active than a hospital or the streets of New York City.

We take Star for walks in the park near our house and view the yard as not much more than a convenient necessity. When we head out, she seems happiest on the streets, when we walk to the park.

"She's a city dog," Jenn says, "she's used to streets."

We find her quiet streets with little to no traffic where we go for our daily walks. Star is in her prime and she enjoys the walking, the movement, the familiar texture of concrete and asphalt.

After our first week, Jenn suggests we take Star to Starbucks in downtown Lincoln, close to the university, where on a Friday night, Lincoln has *almost* the hustle and bustle of (a mini) New York City. I don't *worry* so much as I *watch* to see how Star does. I try to read every head tilt and ear twitch and tail position.

"If she's not ready, I can pop in and grab us a coffee and we can sit in the car with the windows down, getting her used to the people," I say.

We shouldn't worry. The second Star gets out of the car, she lights up. Everything is worth sniffing and exploring, but Star isn't nervous about it. In fact, she's the most at ease we've seen her so far.

Suddenly, two fire trucks with full sirens blaring and lights flashing pass us. Star doesn't bat a remaining eyelash. She is all smiles.

"Oh my gosh," a group of college students say, seeing Star, "look at her! Can we pet her?"

I'm not sure.

I stand next to Star and say, "See how she does, but come slowly. We just rescued her."

"Gosh, do you know what happened to her eye?" one of the students asks.

I shrug. "An accident."

The students bend down, but not too close, and Star shies a bit. "It's okay," one of the college students says, as she reaches out the back of her hand for Star to sniff. She smiles as she lifts up her paw for the girl to take, and everyone (me included) coos at the sight.

"I guess this is a success," I say.

A night out for Star in Downtown Lincoln to give her a bit of the city becomes our weekly routine. Each week she is ready to jump in the car as soon as we grab her leash—she knows it's time.

Each week, I marvel not only at how unassuming Star is and how natural and easy she is in a crowd of people. I am also amazed at how so many people are drawn to Star, probably because of her nature. Her brown and white coat is distinctive, and she has her stitched-together eye and the flat spot on her skull, but there is also that *huge* smile. She is like a happy little Buddha. She doesn't have poor boundaries, though she isn't a big cuddler and that's okay. She's relaxed with her boundaries but is happy to offer her paw to anyone who wants to say hi. She's saying hi back.

Another piece of evidence to how accustomed she is to city life is that she doesn't wander. She sticks close to Jenn and me and she acts like a human out for a stroll on a Friday evening. She even stops at crosswalks to look both ways before setting her paw down on the street, remarkably, Star never pulls on her leash. There is always slack.

I realize I can't wait for the outings with Star. My step is lighter. When I talk to Star, my voice goes up about two octaves. Every week, I volunteer to take my stepdaughter to and from school, because I know I'll get more time in the car with Star. More time with the two of us on the road.

"All my kids," Jenn says, shaking her head at me as I roll on the floor with Star and our other dog, Petey.

"What, we're just—"

"You don't have to say a word," Jenn says.

In time, Star settles into our home, and it isn't too long before she's quite accustomed to home living. She enjoys the nice perks of a couch for multiple daily naps, and of course, the luxury of her own bedroom with her own bed. Jenn and I unabashedly spoil her, but she deserves it. She's a dog who requires no training. She's incredibly smart. She tells us when she needs to go out, and rarely, if ever, barks. In many ways, she's as quiet as a cat.

I do take her to the vet to get looked over and show them the x-rays. They immediately recognize this is Star from the news, but they know to keep the secret after I explain my adoption agreement to them.

"Will she be okay with the bullet fragments?" I ask, concerned.

"Well, really, the shape of her head has more to do with muscle atrophy from the damage of the bullet. With the bullet fragments, what I recommend is doing another x-ray and comparing the results," the vet explains.

I tell them give Star the x-ray. I am willing to do whatever the doctor's suggest. This is what I can do for her. The doctor does the x-ray and tells me that while the fragments are moving, they all seem to be moving away from her brain.

"This is very good news" the doctor says, "We can keep watch, but there's not much more to do. What you might find, though, is that her body may eventually push out the bullet fragments. Keep an eye out."

The vet is correct—it becomes a regular occurrence to feel an object under Star's coat and within weeks, it starts to protrude from her skin. The first time this happens, I'm horrified. I take her back to the vet, and the doctor performing the procedure to work the bullet fragment out of Star's skin with tweezers, stresses her out. She's so worried about hurting Star and she doesn't have experience with an injury of this type. While I'm glad she hasn't experienced dogs with bullet wounds with any frequency, her stress from her inexperience is impeding her job, and Star grows agitated and uneasy because the vet hesitates. Star stands up and readjusts her position each time the vet prods or digs. It's agonizing to watch. While Star has been given a topical painkiller, the main issues are the sensation and the stress.

This goes on a few times before a bullet fragment protrudes. I take Star to the vet to get it removed, the vet is uneasy, Star gets agitated, I internally freak out, barely able to watch my girl suffer. After a while, I stop taking Star to the vet. Instead, I sterilize a pair of tweezers and treat Star as if I'm removing a splinter from my own hand. I pull it straight out, without the prodding and digging, and for Star, the relief is instant. Okay—that problem is solved. Our family learns to live with Star's injuries, to the point where, despite the appearance of trauma, "bulletectomies" wind up being not too big a deal to handle.

Most people ask about her eye and are satisfied when I say she had an accident. I worry less about discovery, though I don't quite reach the comfort and ease in which I take the secrecy of Star's history for granted. Thus, we move on with our life, and she's our Star, and that's that.

Then, in late fall of 2013, as the weather taking its subtle turn toward winter, we were on our regular walk route where we get to a corner gas station that sells gas and snacks (handy if Star and I need to refuel ourselves) before heading back home. As we approach, I see one of my customers, Rob. We exchange a few pleasantries about the changing weather and the trash business.

Then he asked about Star.

"What happened to your dog, Charlie?"

"Oh, she had an accident before I adopted her," I say spontaneously. (It's becoming second nature to answer this way.)

"Do you know what kind?" he asked.

I hesitate. *Don't lie. Don't lie. Conditions of Star's adoption.* "No, not really," I finally say.

"Where did you adopt her from?"

"An adoption agency back east," I say while looking at Star who is sitting like the polite girl she is. I'm past ready to move on.

"I see," Rob says, "you must miss New York, so you got a dog from there."

Though Rob is probably just making a little fun, as he's a light-hearted guy, he strikes a nerve. He's a smart guy who never forgets anything. I know he can build on any tidbit of information I give him, and his wheels are likely already spinning.

"No," I blurt, "I didn't adopt her from New York—there are more places on the East Coast than just New York."

"Easy, Charlie, I'm kidding with you," he says, hands up and stepping back.

Now, of course, I feel foolish.

"What's your dog's name?"

"Star."

"Beautiful name." He leans down to Star and says, "Aren't you beautiful? But you know that, don't you?"

Star shines her big, lolling smile.

Turning to me he says, "She appears to have Pit Bull in her, but she is mixed with some other breed. Do you know what?"

"Nah, I don't. I was just happy to adopt her and give her a new home." I say quickly.

"I bet—since you traveled so far to get her."

"I sure did."

He gives Star a once-over and says, "Okay, well, I'll let you two get back to your walk. It was good seeing you, Charlie. You too, Star, beautiful girl."

Star smiles up at Rob.

I've known Rob for as long as I've lived in Lincoln—back when I purchased my first pickup truck. He was full of questions then, too. "Are you buying a 4x4 model? Are you getting an automatic? How much power are you looking for?" were just a few of the questions he asked. I try not to take his current inquisitiveness as an intrusion. It's just how he is. A property developer, when he became one of my customers, he always had exactly the right questions for every project. We hit it off because like me, he was interested and involved in everything he pursued. He was, in general, a naturally curious person. Why wouldn't he ask a bunch of questions when he sees me with a one-eyed Pit Bull who's missing part of her skull and was adopted on the East Coast and had a clearly violent accident, I know nothing about? It would have been odd if he hadn't asked questions.

Though I hate this whole, "Star-in-witness protection" nonsense, my greatest worry is not knowing how Nebraskans would take to her with her history. Would any of them call animal control and make a big deal out of the once-famous dog? Am I being paranoid? With the New York and Philadelphia institutions involved and with, as Rhonda from the legal defense team said, "Eyes in Nebraska," I believed someone could be watching me at any time, so I wasn't going to do anything to blow Star's cover and risk losing her. But boy, working undercover was a pain in the ass. Still, I knew the heartbreaking loss of losing a dog, as Lech had, and what it would do to Star to be torn from her humans once again.

16. CITIZEN KANE

I had an old truck I wanted to put to use, so I put an ad in the paper, offering myself up as an independent delivery company, and within a week, I landed a contract for a soda company releasing a new product called, "Jamaica Natural Soda." There was nothing natural about the Day-Glo-dyed and sweetened drink. Their market was predominantly inner-city areas in the South Bronx, Harlem, Bedford-Stuyvesant just to name a few areas. It was the kind of route most drivers the company contracted with refused. None of their other drivers were crazy enough to go there.

What did I have to lose? I'd already spent plenty of time hunting for the next high around the Jamaica Station, so I had no qualms about entering these neighborhoods to make deliveries. Within a week, I went from rehab patient to businessman.

The soda was cheap and sweet and sold well in low economic areas. I, too, lived off the stuff, especially between pay schedules. During this time, I was skinny everywhere except for my gut. I had a soda gut.

Along with soda, I also delivered mylar balloons to grocery stores and other party favor stores along a similar route as my soda route. I was the white kid from Long Island making his forays into neighborhoods labeled as the most drug- and crime-ridden neighborhoods in the state. There were even gang turf wars going on, yet everyone left me alone. The customers on my routes were some of the kindest and most generous people I'd met—certainly putting my own family to shame.

These neighborhoods, I came to learn, were about far more than the news headlines white suburbanites use to write off whole communities. Yes, there was crime, but there were also families, people working to survive, people who still had dreams, people who had their shit together far more than I did. Families there went back for decades and were rooted in those communities. They didn't want to just pick up and leave (or couldn't afford to move their businesses) when crime moved in. They were, in fact, *communities*, and were far more willing to get to know each other and help each other than the people in most suburban neighborhoods.

One store manager I visited each week took five minutes of his time to chat with me and get to know me. He asked if I was a weightlifter, and he talked about his days on the track team back in high school. The other delivery men on their own routes became familiar, especially the whistling bread man, who was always whistling. Though we don't know what goes on in people's personal lives, he drove through his day with a lightness in his step and a positive energy as if he had figured out life and was content with what he had. He had a contentment I had never known.

That being said, I did see the crime firsthand, though it was never directed at me. After finishing my delivery at a Brooklyn bodega, I walked outside and witnessed the whole block being robbed by a group of men. People were on the ground being stripped of their money and drugs if they had them. They came over to me, seeing my dolly for unloading the flats of sodas, and said, "You, get lost."

I shrugged and said, "Okay, thanks."

The one who seemed like the leader laughed and walked up to me. Looking me up and down, he said, "Man, you got balls of steel." He then asked, "What's your name?"

"I go by Chase."

"Chase, alright, alright. 'Big T' here. We own this block."

"Alright," I said.

He waved me on, and I took my dolly and left. Owning a block. Was he serious? Of course, I like to know facts and do my research, so I took a mental picture of him and then asked around. Big T was Anthony T. Santiago. His family owned a string of bodegas, but Big T was considered the black sheep of the family, didn't take to legitimate work. He had gotten himself shot five times in the chest and stomach, and though he survived, he'd had part of his intestines removed, requiring him to wear a colostomy bag. Even still, people went along with the fact that he and his gang roved a neighborhood and did what they wanted. They were living life like the wild west in a major American city. He immediately made me think of Tuco in *The Good, The Bad, and The Ugly*, only he was a hell of a lot bigger.

If I had done my homework in researching Big T, he had done his. Next time I saw him, he was waiting out in front of a store with some of his crew.

"Hey, Chase," he said, nodding his head toward me.

I walked over to him.

"So, word on the street is you got a dad who's a union boss. Got a street name of Chink."

This was news to me. Sure, my father's office wasn't very far from this neighborhood. But he had a street name?

"We know some of the people your old man is involved with," Big T continued.

"Oh, well, makes sense," I said quickly.

The union part made sense, but my mind was still spinning around my father's street name. But come to think of it, I could never remember my father getting his hands dirty from work. There were a lot of short phone calls with him. Who was this man I had lived with all those years?

I saw Big T again, and he told me to come riding around the neighborhood with him. He said he would show me in the ins and outs. Finally, he said, "And it's Anthony to you, not Big T."

I'm not sure if he was showing me off to the neighborhood, as if to say, "This one, this is the union boss's kid, and he's not to be touched or there could be ramifications."

My father, violent as he was, and with something to prove, was viewed by the outside world as someone with great power, which reflected onto me. What did it say about men like him, about Big T, about these men with their niches of absolute power?

"You know," Anthony said, "when we first saw you, at first we thought you was a cop. You are a muscular motherfucker, too big to be looking for drugs."

The truth was, it didn't matter what I did or didn't eat, my neck and arms were permanently big, even if my muscle tone lapsed a bit.

"No, not a cop," I said.

"No shit. Word on the street though is that you was in the hospital for drugs."

"Yep. That part is accurate."

"Man, you got a big man for your pops and you making deliveries around here? He ever try to get you in his union?"

"I don't want to work anywhere near my father," I said flatly.

Anthony nodded and said, "Okay, I get it. But, my man, I'm going to get real with you for a minute. You need to get your life together. Look at that ratty-ass truck you drive. You used to drive cabs, you used to go gambling, you come from white-bread suburbia. Like, you need to get straight."

Here I was, being lectured by a man who would, without hesitation, shoot someone for looking twice at him.

Periodically, I'd run into Anthony when he wasn't with his gang, and he'd take me to his family's house. They were in a rough neighborhood, and though they could afford to move, they refused. Anthony took me around to show me the harshest conditions of city life. As we looked around, he said, "You see how bad some people really got it? They don't got anyone to help lift them up—it's by their own will to survive. But all this, too, his home. Like my folks—they could move if they wanted to, out of the ghetto, but they wouldn't have any other life. This is where we come from. This is our place."

Not even a hundred miles to the east of us were the Hamptons, where some of the wealthiest people in the world, were separated by a straight roadway.

"You know, Charlie, you and me, we're the same. We are two men trying to find our way in the world, with no directions."

Though Anthony wanted me to hang out with him more, and though I found him and his crew fascinating, I needed to get back to my deliveries and back to making money. I declined most of the rest of his offers to hang out. However, he did introduce me to much of the Spanish food the inner city offered. It was delicious, and it soon became my new food addiction. I couldn't get enough, and I spent a good amount of my earnings on food. Still, I was busy, day in and day out. I scraped by well enough.

People who saw me in my hometown thought I'd beaten my addiction and was on the straight and narrow. I thought I had, too. All those times in rehab and detox counseling, though, and I was still in denial about how one addiction replacing another was not getting at the root problem.

#

Though Anthony wouldn't be my companion, it was nice to have someone to talk to. I only half-realized I was starved for companionship. I was lonely. It was serendipitous, then, when, at one delivery stop on Atlantic Avenue in Brooklyn, I saw a beautiful young Pit Bull the color of a lion. I asked the bodega owner whose dog it was, and he pointed to a guy in the store.

"Is that your dog?" I asked.

"Yeah, why?" The owner answered cautiously.

"He is beautiful," I said, looking closer at the dog.

His eyes sparkled. He wasn't like Ringo, of course, but there was a special and quite unique energy to him.

"You wanna buy him?" the owner shrugged.

Was he serious?

"Yeah," I stammered, "how much? Wait, I got seventy dollars in cash in my pocket."

"He's yours," the guy said. "But I'm telling you now, despite how he looks, he's no watchdog. Doesn't have a mean bone in his body. I got no use for him."

What he meant was he wanted the dog for dogfighting, and a dog that wouldn't fight wouldn't have a future with this man. I definitely wasn't looking for a watchdog. Hell, I hadn't been looking for a dog at all. But a companion without meanness? That sounded refreshing and wonderful.

"What's his name?" I asked.

"Kane," the man responded unemotionally.

There was an empty water bowl near him, so I took the bowl and called the dog, and Kane climbed into my truck. He looked at me and smiled, panted, and looked forward, out the windshield.

Away we went.

Kane became my constant companion. He was so well behaved and mannerly that I could take him anywhere, including with me on all my routes. I didn't worry about having him on a leash (because I was young and stupid and took his good behavior for granted). He went with me on late night runs to the supermarket, or anytime I went anywhere with friends. Kane became my best friend, and I was so happy.

People around me noticed a change. Grocers on my route said, "Man, look at you!" My friends noticed a difference when I'd come around to see them. And yes, I even took Kane to my parents' house when I'd stop by from time to time.

My mom might have been horrible in many ways, but she was a devout lover of dogs. "Charles, you seem so happy! And who wouldn't be with such a good boy?" she said, petting Kane. She then asked, "Are you getting him the right dog food? Dogs can get sick if they have cheap food with a lot of fillers."

Forget nourishing humans—my mother was at a loss when it came to properly feeding her own children but, taking care of the dog's dietary needs was paramount.

What a gift the random stranger gave me. I couldn't imagine anyone willing to give up such an incredible dog, unless he really only viewed a dog's worth in its ability to fight. I tried to be generous in my reflection of Kane's previous owner: Maybe he was like me, barely able to afford to keep himself, and the dog was an excess expense for him. I, however, needed Kane in my life, and any expenses were worth it.

Sadly, Kane coming into my life did not mark the happy, permanent change I needed to make. There was still that flicker inside me despite my job and Kane, the old fire of all my self-destructive tendencies. My life was still on its descent, and nobody, including me, was about to stop it. It's hard to describe the pull of addiction and self-destruction to someone who has never experienced it. My parents, hell, most of the society around me believed I just needed to pull myself up by my bootstraps and get on with life. *Just stop doing drugs, Charles.* Sure. Except my will for saving my life was nonexistent. Imagine being strapped in the passenger seat of a car with the cruise control on, no one else in the car, and you want to reach for the steering wheel or the brake, but you can't move your arms or legs. You see the crash that's about to occur and recognize the inevitability and inescapability of impending doom.

I was inside that car.

The resurfacing problems were timed with the repeated breaking down of my truck. I had no way to make deliveries when my truck was down, and I couldn't afford the repairs to my truck when I wasn't using it to make money. I was at risk of losing my route when other drivers took my place, now that I was living proof that a guy from suburbia could survive the neighborhoods. I was replaceable.

The other blame, though, needs to go back to me because my money management was shit. I had nothing to fall back on. All my cash had gone into food, as well as rent on a shitty apartment. It was shitty because I hadn't needed something nice when I was spending so much time in my truck. So as the money dwindled, runs to the supermarket turned into dashes to 7-Eleven. I no longer had money for the kind of dog food Kane needed.

I stretched out meals for us, which included us heading by foot and paw to Burger King. I'd go to a manger and ask for food for my dog, and more often than not, one of the managers on duty would help us out. I was still clean and sober—I hadn't had any drugs since getting thrown out of the last rehab—but I was going down the drain and didn't know what to do.

My phone was shut off. Kane and I ate every last morsel of food in my apartment. We both were growing thinner by the day. Shortly after I stopped paying rent, I received an eviction notice. I was hopeless. I couldn't put the pieces together, couldn't think clearly how to claw my way out of this mess. At the same time, depression made its tsunami-like crash over me, flooding everything. After a few days, I was too weak and too tired to even go for a walk to get food for Kane and me, or to find any help. All I did now was let Kane out the backdoor so he could pee. He rarely had a bowel movement. Neither of us was doing much but passing water at that point. Kane and I were in a living hell.

I cried when I looked in my kitchen, opening and shutting the refrigerator door in case I'd somehow missed a crumb somewhere. Then, as if by magic, I found in the back of the cupboard a squeeze bottle of salad dressing I had previously missed. I opened the bottle and gave a good squeeze in my mouth. At least it would be calories. I looked down, and there was my best friend looking up at me, asking, "Where's mine?" I knelt down, held up the bottle, and Kane opened his mouth. I gave him a squeeze of the dressing. He licked his lips with his dry tongue. I gave myself another squeeze, and then another to Kane, back and forth until the bottle was empty.

No one had seen us in a while since we weren't getting out. I was surprised to learn even my parents were concerned about us. They couldn't call because our phone was shut off. Still, I was shocked when my father banged on my door one day, before my looming eviction. I peeked out the window to see who it was and recognized his big new Cadillac out front. Kane and I were starving, and my father had another shiny new Cadillac.

I had no time to clean up. No time to come up with a story of what I'd been doing. I was an adult, and it should have been my roof, my rules. I wasn't in a good head space to stand up to my father. I opened a door to the communal foyer, and my father stepped in to get out of the doorway.

"Jesus, Charles, what the hell is going on?" He looked at me, at Kane, at the shambles of the apartment. "Your mother was concerned. She sent me over to check on Kane."

Of course, her concern was about Kane.

"Look at you, how can you live like this? What a mess."

He started laying into me, badgering me about my truck, about work, about my entire history being half-assed and inadequate. Sure, what he was saying was right in principle, but he was absolutely the wrong messenger. My father, of all people. Finally, I got up the courage to stick up for myself.

"Look, I had work, but I didn't have enough money to get the repairs on my truck," I said, explaining the cycle.

He argued back with semi-valid reasons, but at least now, there was a back-and-forth disagreement about which of us was right and wrong, and not just a one-way lecture coming from my father.

"Okay, if you're so right, let me come in and show me how you're living. Go on," he said, challenging me.

This would not go well, and we were only getting more heated the longer we stood together in my pigsty of a home. That's as far as my thought processes functioned. I was malnourished and had a recent history of bad decision making, plus I was self-destructive. My reaction was to bolt out the front door to escape my father. I ran down the steps and across the street, which was four busy lanes of traffic. I was halfway across when I heard the screeching of brakes and a thud. I turned, and there was Kane, lying motionless in the middle of the street, hit not by one vehicle but two. He'd followed me out of the apartment.

My buddy, my only friend, my true companion. He was gone and it was all my fault! I lay at his side, sobbing, half-aware of the people crowding around me. Somewhere, my father's voice was saying he was still alive.

Both cars that hit Kane stopped. The car that hit him first had damage to the front grill. The damaged grill was, in that moment, burned forever into my mind, like a brand that will never leave me.

My father's voice was gentle. The fight was gone.

"Charles let's pick him up together and get him into my car. We'll take him to the hospital."

And, just like that, we were fighting on the same side to save Kane's life. At the veterinary hospital, my mother showed up, but I didn't want to see her. Every time she sent someone to talk to me, my father or the police, the results were dire. When it was just me, it was bad enough, but my guilt at hurting Kane overflowed. The depression tsunami felt impossibly endless.

"It's going to take money to give him the surgery he needs," my mother said. "And money to take care of him afterwards, from the follow-up medication to the actual care along with giving him the food he needs."

I was over a barrel. There was no money.

"We can pay for all this, Charles, but I think we should keep Kane."

I loved Kane. I loved him so much I knew he needed the best care, and he wouldn't get the best care if he stayed with me.

After his surgery, I went to see Kane. He was going to be okay. My abusers were going to get my beloved dog, but they would take care of him. I didn't think my mother would let what happened to Ringo happen to Kane. At least I told myself they'd take better care of him. They certainly wouldn't let Kane get hit by two cars in the middle of a busy street. They certainly wouldn't feed him salad dressing. Or Burger King. Or buttered rolls from 7-Eleven. Kane would have stability, and with me and Christian out of the house and my father away at work most of the time, there would likely be minimal fighting to fill the house with stress.

I would visit Kane until he was okay, but after that, I was ready to walk away from my family. What little I had left in my apartment, I threw away. There was nothing worth saving or donating to charity, and I certainly wouldn't be able to take it with me on the streets.

My father gave me some money to fix my truck, which didn't take much, but the next time I filled the tank and drove somewhere, it died again, in the middle of the road. I was sure it was the timing chain. I left the key in the ignition and walked away, leaving the truck where it broke down. I had no vehicle, no place to live and no Kane. As lost as I had been paled to how lost I felt without Kane. What was left was emptiness. I didn't have enough in me to be emotional. Any dreams for my life I'd had as a kid were now gone. Everyone was gone. I had no belief in anything. There wasn't even self-pity—if I could just stop myself from sleepwalking through life, I might be redeemed. *If.* Yet I was not willing to stop breathing. No way. The problem was I couldn't feel deeply about anything anymore.

To fill the time, I took to riding the train system aimlessly throughout New York City. I was homeless but didn't want to be alone on the streets.

17. STAR, THE HIDDEN HERO

Though I haven't posted Star's whereabouts on her Facebook page, that doesn't mean the activity stopped. Her page has become a beacon for dogs in need with people sharing dogs in kill shelters and encouraging visitors to Star's page to share their stories and find them a home. It's nice to see how motivated people are to help these animals. Some even post photos of the animals they rescue, so it's also a relief to see not every post is doom and gloom.

One dog who catches my attention on the Star page is Sadie. The posted photo is of her in her cement cell in the North Haven Animal Shelter. She's an all-black Pit Bull mix with a white cross on her chest who was picked up as a stray. Star had been tagged to tweets of Sadie on Twitter. Every few weeks, her photo pops up somewhere on social media or a rescue site, and I hope against hope someone will rescue her.

For some reason, black animals are the least likely to get adopted. It's what's called "black dog syndrome," also referred to as BBD (big black dog), when these dogs (and also cats) are passed over for adoption. Shelter workers regularly say black dogs and cats stay in shelters longer than their lighter-colored counterparts, and they often wind up getting euthanized. This is where breed does come into play, because for years, the media has featured Doberman Pinschers or Rottweilers as mean and aggressive. Also, if the animals are photographed in poor lighting and posted on their adoption websites, their expressions don't show up as well as other dogs, making them look less sympathetic. None of this has anything to do with the dogs themselves.

Sadie's other problem is that in her bio, she's listed as being aggressive with other dogs, which right away will rule her out for most adoptive parents who are unable to take on that kind of responsibility, especially if they have other dogs or don't have the time to put in extensive training—or if they have small children.

Then, the last week of October, someone posts that Hamden Animal Control officers have given the go-ahead for the shelter to euthanize Sadie by the end of the week, and this is a last-ditch effort to save her. I look at her photo again, and she has this wide smile, with her tongue hanging straight out the front. A dog smiling like that is a happy dog and needs a good home.

I call the number on the shelter but can't get anyone who can approve the adoption, and no one seems to know who I should contact. Plus, Sadie is not available for general adoption. This is because, for whatever reason, she didn't score well on her assessment. What I've learned from Star's page, from volunteers as well as doctors, is if an owner surrenders the pet and the assessment doesn't go well, these dogs get labeled as problems, and the label is nearly impossible to shake.

Dogs are often dumped off at a shelter, and then, disoriented and surrounded by noisy dogs in a foreign environment, they undergo the assessment and frequently act out during these moments. Who can blame them? Also, if an owner wants to dump a dog and not look like a jerk for doing it, they can just say the dog bites. Now, once a dog is a biter, the likelihood goes up for him or her to be euthanized.

Rescue organizations have to pull a dog like that from the shelter. I leave multiple messages and send out emails to Hamden Animal Control as shots in the dark. One person tells me, "Well, we just can't let you take her."

"Why? You're going to kill her."

"There's a process—" he starts to say.

"Look, I've already rescued a Pit Bull that sustained injuries, I have a fence and a big yard, I've been vetted by New York and Philadelphia…"

"I'm not sure where we have Sadie, or if she's even still here."

I had been calling for days and leaving voicemails! Nobody returned my calls not to talk about offering me any help. This went on day after day until finally, someone got back to me. (They probably took so long to get back to me because they were vetting me.)

"Alright," the person at the shelter says, "after listening to your voicemails and references and based on your experience with dogs, you can adopt Sadie, but you have to be here within one day, or she will be euthanized."

"Tomorrow? I'm in Nebraska." I calculate the drive time. "I'm on my way. Don't kill Sadie, please."

We hang up and I fly around the house, calling for Jenn, who is still asleep. "I'm leaving for Connecticut—I have to pick up a dog!" I scramble for a water bowl and a couple of waters and snacks since I won't have much time for stops.

"You're getting another dog?" Jenn says.

I don't stop moving as I shout out, "They're going to kill her. I got to get her."

As I run out the door, Jenn calls out, "Let me know when you get there safely!"

I had no minivan this time, and no real plan. The anticipation is different with Sadie than it was with Star—this time, it is more like agitation and frenzy. I have to make it in time. Once I get her, I'll stop for more snacks and foods, and we'll take a couple of days to get home. At least the smells of Star and our other dog, Petey, are all over my car, and they'll be the smells of her new home.

"Charlie," I ask myself as I drive into the night, "is this another instance of one is never enough?"

"Maybe," I answer myself, "but here's the difference—this is a living creature in dire need, and I have the means to save her and make her life better."

After leaving at 5 a.m. Friday morning, I arrive in Connecticut on Saturday. In the meantime, I ask a local rescue to pull Sadie from the shelter and take her to the vet, who can give her a checkup and a bath. When I finally see Sadie, she's clean and smiling. She's missing a tooth. There are bite mark scars on her. Part of her ear is missing. There are all the appearances of her having been in a fight, used for fighting, or used as a bait dog for training.

She's had trauma.

She's out of her gray concrete kennel (more like a prison cell), and as soon as she's in my car, it's clear she's ready for the open road and will go anywhere with me. I'm curious to see how Star will take to her, but Star is such a happy girl, and had no problem taking to our little Napoleon, Petey. Sadie's bio indicated she is aggressive with other dogs. They're all going to be a bunch of misfits, that's for sure.

I fit right in with them.

Our drive back is easy, though Sadie is always a little nervous when I leave her in the car to pump gas or buy snacks. In the hotel, she follows me into the bathroom. She clearly has abandonment issues. This will be a project. We arrive home in the very early hours, catching Jenn in bed again, but she's already gotten another bowl and a set of dog toys and treats in preparation for the new arrival. She gets up and runs to Sadie, and Sadie runs to her—their bond is immediate.

Jenn gasps at Sadie's wounds, running her hands over them. "Huh," Jenn says, feeling the raised nipples on Sadie's abdomen. "I wonder if she's had a litter of puppies."

I allow Sadie time and space to decompress and slowly introduce her to the other dogs, Petey and Star.

Jenn becomes more convinced of this watching Sadie with her toys. "See her pile up the stuffed animals? Even if she plays with them during the day, she always piles them up at night. She was a mama at some point." Her behavior is remarkable and so polite.

Sadie is a mama in every aspect. She is more mama than alpha. She takes charge, herding Star and Petey toward food and getting them to come outside to play. At first, Petey, the stubborn Jack Russell, tries to assert himself, but he's no match for Sadie's calm control and insistence. He falls in line with the pack. Every day I watch them together, I marvel at their communication between each other and the way they manage their relationships.

A journalist from a local Hamden news outlet contacts me almost immediately about doing a short write-up about Sadie's adoption. "It's such a heartwarming story," she tells me, "And it's big news for our hamlet."

If she only knew how heartwarming.

I can't post any photos with Star, but I want to honor her role in rescuing Sadie, so I post that Star was able to help a dog find a home with me because of the community on her Facebook page. I insinuate it's an adoption honoring Star's legacy, which is part of the truth. The Facebook community is thrilled that after so long, Sadie has found a home.

I think to myself, looking at Star and Sadie together, with Petey, of course. Sadie was within hours of being killed. She was within minutes of not being here, of not being part of our pack and not having this great life. How many people saw her bio and thought she would be too difficult to manage? All our dogs are a little needy. But with Star and Sadie, Petey's socialization has improved by leaps and bounds.

What can't any of us become when given a real second chance?

18. MICHAEL AND THE MONASTERY

Aimless on the trains. Aimless at the stations. Grabbing my belly, hoping someone might throw me some change I could use to buy something with sugar in it for a few cents. That was my life in 1992 when Michael found me.

He approached me while I was waiting for a train at the Jamaica platform in Queens. There were few other people there at 1am. We made brief eye contact, and I thought, "Wow, there is a peaceful looking fella."

He walked over to me. It was as if he knew I was a hurting unit—but how?

"I'm Michael," he said, introducing himself.

"I'm Charlie. Do you ride the trains?" I asked.

"Only when I'm going to or coming from work in the city," he answered.

We talked for a few minutes before his train approached.

"You know, I'm a born-again Christian and am in recovery from addiction. It was hard for a while. It got bad. I was living in a cardboard refrigerator box in an empty lot in the Bronx before I was saved. I just couldn't find my way."

I told him how great I thought that was, then asked what prompted him to tell me this. "I'm just a complete stranger," I said.

"Charlie, from twenty feet away, I could spot the tombstones in your eyes. I knew you needed help. I must freely give away what was given to me in order to keep what I have."

Within two minutes, I gave him the summary of my life story, about my addictions. "Rehab doesn't help me. I can't find what they keep telling me will save my life, this force called a 'Higher Power' they keep referring to."

Michael nodded and said, "That's why so few of us make it."

"What—am I going to die?"

"You don't look too good right now, and it only gets worse. I will make only a suggestion, Charlie. You could seek help as I did, at a monastery in upstate New York. They help all who come there. It's a place called Graymoor, and it's in Garrison. Will you remember the name and where it is?"

"I have a memory like an elephant. But—do they take guys like me?"

"They take everyone from former jailbirds to people just looking for a spiritual reprieve and everyone in between. If you want help, it will be there. If you're looking for a partner in crime, it will be there, too. It's all up to you. Which road will you take?"

"Do I need to make an appointment?"

Michael laughed. "No. They are always open. They will be there when you're ready."

He was quiet and I was silent. Something was moving between us, something unseen. Maybe that "something" is what we think of as one soul reaching out to another. My soul had been reaching out, and like a messenger sent just for me, Michael's soul reached back.

Then, his train rolled into the station, and as he boarded, he stopped to look back at me and nodded. The doors shut, and his train disappeared into the middle of the night.

Instead of waiting for an LIRR train, I walked around the Jamaica Station, replaying the conversation with Michael and asking myself a series of important questions: "Can meeting him here, now, all have been only a coincidence? Why is it I haven't been able to get what these damn rehabs have been trying to teach me? Why haven't I been teachable? I've witnessed plenty of people getting clean and sober, the program working for them. So why not me? What's it going to take to wake me up?"

No, I wasn't going to take the LIRR train. Why bother going to Long Island? All of my friends would be sleeping in their nice homes. I was the one on the streets. And my hardships were self-imposed. Instead, I wandered for a while and ended up boarding the J train, for somewhere to sit, for the movement and for the feeling of having somewhere to go.

A couple of hours passed, but it was still too early for the morning commuters to board. Typically, nothing good ever happened on that service line at that time of night.

Then, inexplicably, my brain started shouting *Get off the train! Get off! Now!* The stop was for Cleveland Street, East New York. Brooklyn in the early 1990s.

I started walking. I couldn't say what my purpose was—I still can't, all these years later. I was compelled by something internal. For blocks, I followed Cleveland Street, along a stretch of run-down buildings until I recognized I was headed for an abandoned building. It was the kind of building where drug dealers routinely set up shop.

I had seen many buildings like this, but I had never been to this building before.

I was in Brownsville, Brooklyn at the time, being there could mean an easy death sentence for anyone not from the hood or anyone who wasn't packing. One of the taxi regulars back when I drove a taxi used to have me wait in front of buildings like this with the motor running. This customer had me drive him frequently to the most dangerous places in the Five Boroughs. He paid and tipped well, so what was it to me where he wanted to go? It wasn't any of my business what he did, and I was told to take him wherever he wanted to go by the dispatcher. Desperate addicts came to places like this in groups.

The car was kept running outside, with everyone still inside except one brave soul (or the craziest soul) who would go on a near-suicide mission into the building.

Once inside, the person would find the first burning candle somewhere on the floor, then find the next candle, following the path to a closed door either on the second or third floor. At the last candle, the person would slide money under the door or through a hole in the wall, then wait for a package to return from either under the door or through the hole. Once the person received the package, he or she would run like hell through a gauntlet of thieves, other addicts, or gang members who wanted to steal the goods. In order to get back in the car, the person would have to have the package in hand. This was an attempt to keep even addicts honest and that was where I was headed.

Then, there was that chanting inside my head, the same that told me to get off the train. *Go around to the back, to the back of the building, go to the back! Go! Go!* It was as if I was pushed from behind and then directed to walk around to the back of the abandoned building. This strong direction was like a force of dark, negative energy. It was palpable and malevolent. It was like my addiction and all the monstrosity in my life had taken physical form and was exerting its force on me.

In that moment, I did not have control over my body—I was a passenger deep inside my hijacked body, and I was terrified. My body was made to go faster to the back of the building. I got to the corner and peeked around. Four men stood in the darkness of pre-dawn, illuminated by a small fire in a trashcan. They were injecting some drug or other or a mashup of drugs into their veins. As I got closer to them, they didn't see me.

"Ask them if you can join them," the voice in my head said. "Ask them! Ask them!"

If they see me, I thought, they may kill me. They may let me join them but sharing needles with them may also kill me.

I was afraid when a nurse had to take blood, but the voice in my brain wanted me to try a syringe used by other people. How had I gotten here? I had just been on the train. From deep inside myself, I hit some internal panic button.

"God, please help me," I prayed, "Lord, save me. God, please help me. Please. Save me."

The chanting stopped. Without the voice of the impulse, I was able to think, a little, though the thoughts were still in a fog.

"Lord, help me," I said aloud.

At once, my forward motion stopped. The praying was working. As if I was fully reentering my body, or filling it back out, or coming up for air after too long underwater, I shouted at the top of my lungs, "God help me! God help me!"

The men around the fire were shocked and looked right at me. I didn't care. Instead, I reversed course and took off running, back down Cleveland Street. I ran and ran and ran. How long it took me to run out of steam, I don't know. I was drenched in sweat and my lungs burned. Slowing to a walk, I came up to a firehouse, and the doors were open. One firefighter was cleaning one of the trucks, and my entrance startled him.

"Please," I said, "I don't know what happened, but I got the scare of my life a mile or two away. Could I possibly have some water, maybe wash my face?"

"Sure," he said, leading me to the bathroom and getting me a cup of water. "I know the neighborhood," he said, "you're lucky you're standing here now."

He watched while I guzzled the water, then rubbed the sink water into my face, making sure my soul was still connected somewhere in the skin and muscle. Maybe it was a baptism.

He looked closely at me while I reiterated I didn't know what happened or how I got to that neighborhood.

"You know," he said, "NYFD is always looking for strong young candidates to take the test—there's one coming up soon."

He was an angel who arrived too soon.

"Sir," I said, "thank you for helping me. I have to get saved before I can rescue anyone. I wouldn't be much use to the department right now."

He nodded and then listened with great empathy while I gave him the quick synopsis of my dire straits. What I knew was I needed to get to Graymoor, the monastery Michael had recommended. I believed with my whole heart it was my only hope.

#

After I left the fire station, my one option was to call my father and ask him to take me to Graymoor. I had to wait until he got up for work, which would be around sunrise. His schedule across the years made him a regimented early riser, giving him enough time to get ready for work, so I knew he would answer the phone.

I hopped back on a train to get to the Jamaica Station, safe territory for me. I arrived just before 5 a.m. My father would be up at 6 a.m. My pockets were empty, so I asked the early commuters if they could spare any change so I could make the call. Someone generously gave me two dollars, which I used to by a coffee with sugar while I waited. Then it came: 6 a.m., on the dot.

He answered the phone with a loud "*Hello.*"

"Geez," I thought, "this guy starts his day ready to fight."

Clearing my throat a little, I said, "Dad, it's Charles."

"Yes, Charles, what do you want?"

Nothing to do but say it. "I need a ride to this place that can help me in upstate New York. Can you take me?"

"When?"

"The sooner the better."

A pause. "I have to go to work today—it's Friday, and I need to be there. How about after work?"

"That will work."

"Should I pick you up at your apartment?"

"No!"

"Okay, then, where?"

"The front of the Jamaica Train Station."

"What—what the hell are you doing in *that* neighborhood?"

"Long story, but the short one is I walked away from my life. I have no more vehicle, no place to live, no possessions, and not much more change to feed into this pay phone. What time will you be here?"

"I could get there around 6 p.m. You know, that's not around the corner, and there will be a ton of traffic. Just wait, I will be there. Even if I'm late, I'm coming." He paused for a few seconds and asked, "So—what is the name of the place you want me to take you to?"

"Graymoor."

"Are you sure you want to go there, son?" he asked warily.

"Why?"

"I've heard of the place. It's been around forever. It's really for guys at the end of their rope."

"Thanks for telling me. I really want to go now because that is exactly where I am. It also sounds like the perfect place for me. Will you know how to get there?"

"I will look on the map before I pick you up."

"Okay, I will be waiting for you," I said, and I hung up.

For the first time in my entire life, I felt ecstatic after a conversation with my father. Something changed in me—making this decision was about to give me a new lease on life, that much I knew in my gut. I was going for help with no reservations. Getting help from Graymoor would be doing things *their way*, not *my way*. I was fully ready to make this commitment.

All I needed to do was keep myself busy in Jamaica for the next twelve hours until my father arrived. At first, I walked down to the front of the station to watch people board their trains. An endless army of people headed to work. I should have been doing the same things in the prime of my life. I envied those people carrying on with their lives, but I believed in every one of my cells I would be one of those people at some point.

After a few hours passed, I realized I was starving. There was a fried chicken place on the other side of the station that never shut down, and though I'd never been in there before, I'd had luck asking for food from Burger King, so maybe, I thought, I'd have the same luck at this chicken place. When I walked in, I had my immediate doubts—the entire mood of the place was serious and direct.

"What do you want?" the guy behind the counter said. I must have forgotten where I was—they didn't tiptoe around you in Jamaica, Queens.

"Two-piece meal," I said as quickly as I could.

There was no time for a sob story. When it came time to pay, I would just put the fifty-five cents remaining in my pocket on the counter and ask if I could pay him the rest when my father came to pick me up. The worst he could say would be no.

A few minutes later, the cook handed the guy at the counter my meal, and the guy started to ring me up.

"Look, I'm so sorry," I said, and briefly explained my dilemma.

"Guy, you gotta be fucking kidding me," he said, yelling out a few more curses. Then he reached over the counter and grabbed me by my neck.

Oh, I thought, it's on.

I grabbed him, dragging him around the counter and into the dining room like he was a wet mop. He didn't see that coming. Then, the cook ran out from the back, grabbing me, and both finally got the better of me and dragged me into the kitchen. The counter guy, who initially choked me, was the main attacker, and I focused on him, managing to get him close to the deep fryer—he was very close to getting a dunk when the cook grabbed a thick mop handle and started wailing on me. It was an all-out brawl, and it wasn't long before concerned customers alerted the nearby police, who appeared within minutes to break us up.

"Okay, what happened?" the sergeant asked.

The cook answered, almost shouting, saying he saw me drag the guy.

The sergeant leaned into the cook and sniffed. "I smell alcohol on you. Have you had anything to drink?" he asked suspiciously.

"Well, yeah," the cook replied.

"Your word is worthless under the influence," the sergeant said. He then said, "Shut up and go back to work."

The counter guy admitted to putting his hands on me.

"I could lock you up," the sergeant said. "If you had a problem with theft of services, which I do not believe even occurred, you should have called us, and we would have handled it."

The counter guy leaned back, crossing his arms, and said nothing.

The sergeant looked at me. "What's your story?" he asked.

I leveled with them. I told a similar story to what I told the firefighter but added the latest development that I was waiting on my father to take me to Graymoor. The sergeant walked me outside. "Wait right here," he said. He then asked, "What was your order?"

I told him my order and he disappeared inside the small restaurant. After a few minutes he came out with a new order for the two-piece meal. Handing it to me, he said, "I took care of it for you."

To say I was grateful would be an understatement. I appreciated how lucky I was to have a sympathetic officer, and I'm sure my still somewhat clean-cut suburban appearance made me a sympathetic figure. I got a break not everyone gets. Once I received my food, I thanked the officer and sat on a bench to have my lunch. I had to laugh about the whole situation. This was the toughest free lunch I'd ever had. I replayed the fight in my mind, imagining how it must have looked if there was CCTV in the place. It must have been a scene straight out of *The Three Stooges*.

The chicken meal was *absolutely delicious*, even if the quality was terrible. On that day, it was a feast.

The rest of the day passed in relative peace, considering I was homeless, at the end of my rope, and about to make a last-ditch effort at trying to save my own life. I collected the newspapers the commuters threw away and read through each of those front-to-back. I was exhausted, and less so from the fight. Living on nothing, scraping by, scrounging and begging and fighting for scraps was physically and emotionally draining and exhausting in every way.

I could no longer live like this—I needed to get well.

I had never even been camping before—I was an indoor guy. It was much too painful for me to be homeless. I no longer had it in me to be without a home.

There were very few cell phones back then, so I had no way to contact my father. 6 p.m. came and went. I got anxious when 6:30 hit. I was worried maybe my father would be a no-show, but I stayed put in the front of the station. Maybe ten minutes before 7 p.m., my father finally drove up. All that mattered was that he showed up. I climbed in the car and said hello, then listened to my father's long explanation.

"Sorry I'm late, but traffic was terrible, and then your mother asked me a hundred questions, which delayed me longer. Are you sure you really want to go to this place? You're going to be around older men with all kinds of criminal backgrounds who have hit bottom and that's their only option—it might be as bad as a city shelter."

"Dad, city shelters do not encourage their guests to find the Lord," I explained, "I'm going for the right reasons."

My father drove on. The sun was setting. Fortunately, my father had music on, which was a welcome distraction. At first, we listened to a Dan Fogelberg cassette, and when the cassette finished, we listened to Hootie and the Blowfish. My father listened to popular contemporary rock and pop? He didn't listen to Frank Sinatra and Pavarotti cassettes? This day was full of surprises.

The sky darkened and it started to rain. Though I'd had the earlier certainty I was making the right decision, I was still full of anxiety. I was heading toward a monastery in the dark, in the rain and while at the end of my rope. But of course, with my life, I wouldn't have a drive with sunshine and blue skies to ease my mind.

The music did help me relax, and I finally asked how Kane was doing. It was as if I'd flipped a switch in my father. He lit up and said, "He's doing great! I don't know what that dog is made of, but what I saw him go through, it's a miracle he made it."

My father had a front-row view of the near-tragedy. While I only saw the aftermath of Kane getting hit twice, my father saw each moment play out. The grill of the first car hitting Kane was severely damaged and I couldn't help but think of the *Terminator* movies, the robots impervious to any force.

For the last part of the ride, my father put in an Aaron Neville cassette, which I couldn't believe was a coincidence. This had never been my father's taste in music. Could the delay have been because he had stopped at a music store to get these cassettes? I didn't ask him, but there we were, two men who could never get along now riding peacefully for hours in the car while Aaron Neville sang from the heart.

I will never forget that ride.

I would never spend that much time with my father ever again.

#

The rain continued to fall as we turned up the mountain. I was terrified.

There was a very long driveway leading to the monastery. We were in total darkness and suddenly the monastery appeared, lit up among the trees. We were greeted at the reception door by an older man who seemed more like an old-time innkeeper, with deep red hair. I got out of the car and walked up to him. He nodded at me and welcomed me—there was no asking why I had come.

"Is it okay to let my father go?" I asked.

"Yes, he can go. I'm here to check you in."

I turned and leaned into the passenger window to tell my father I was going to get checked in.

"Thanks for helping me," I said, "He said you don't need to stay."

My father's eyes filled with tears, and he choked back one small sob. "Okay, then. You take care of yourself. Do what you need to, so you get well."

It was so alien to see him emotional in this way. Rage, sure. But this? He turned the car around and drove back down the mountain. I went to check myself in.

"I'm Jimmy," the man said. "I too have been where you are. Now I'm in charge of intake."

He was full of reassuring empathy. My relief was tentative, but it was there, maybe like a low burning fire waiting to see if it would get revived or if it would burn out.

"As a precaution, we're going to first take you to a shower and get you deloused," Jimmy said.

I was shocked, but I understood. Here it was, a Friday night. A twenty-something guy like me should be holding hands with a date at a movie, yet my will had brought me to an institutional-type monastery, getting the delousing chemical squirted all over me.

"No, no self-pity," I told myself. "I will only have to do this once. I will be redeemed. I have a life waiting for me."

After the delousing, I was led to the open dormitory with no privacy and rows of beds like a military barracks or a dorm in a medium security prison. I would stay here for several days to make sure I didn't have lice or the flu or anything else that would be communicable to the other guests. Several other men were in the room, quietly keeping to themselves. All was neat and orderly.

Jimmy showed me to my bed, where there was a new set of pajamas for me, and then he pointed to the *Alcoholics Anonymous Big Book* on the table.

"That's there for you to read," he said, while pulling another small book out of his pocket. "This is a pocket Bible. I always got it on me. Would you like one?"

"Yes, please," I said.

The next morning, I had the first of my three-square meals a day. After wolfing it down, I felt almost human again. I reflected on my lunch the previous day with a mixture of amusement and shame. We were then all called into the chapel for a church service led by Father Owen, a man who worked directly with the men in Graymoor. He wore old fashioned thick-rimmed glasses, which contrasted with his shock of white hair. Also present was Father Bernie, a Franciscan Monk built like an athlete. Later on, I asked one of my dormmates about him.

"I heard he's a black belt in karate," my dormmate said, "You don't want to get on the wrong side of him."

I could see that.

I walked the grounds on my own between church and lunch, another square meal, and then attended chapel again in the evening before dinner. The first three meals I had at Graymoor were three of the best meals I'd had in some time. Regular meals didn't stop me from eating like a recently rescued shipwrecked sailor. Or like a shelter dog.

Printed on the literature and posted on small signs was the mission statement for Graymoor: *We have been called to heal wounds, to unite what has fallen apart, and to bring home those who have lost their way.*

I certainly hoped I would find my way in that place. In between meals and church and quiet reflection, I read every word of the Big Book, hanging on every passage. At the beginning of the book is a section called "The Doctor's Opinion," listing a medical opinion on AA's recovery plan. The physician writing the opinion discusses treatment using medical terminology.

Addiction is a medical condition, though the physician believes patients also require a "moral psychology" more than a "frothy emotional appeal" to apply powers of good to accompany the scientific approach. It all made sense. Reading through the rest of the *Big Book* was reading my life, and the understanding and recognition were acute. Instantly, I knew this book would be a big part of my recovery and, really, my entire path moving forward. The *Big Book* provided a new vision for my life unfolding in front of me. Once I finished the *Big Book*, I started on my pocket Bible, which was less clear but still provided me with comfort.

After my quarantine, I moved into my college-style dorm with bunkbeds, which would be my living space for the next couple of months. I had the top bunk, and though my roommates were pleasant enough, we were all shell-shocked and quite reserved. For me, and likely my roommates, this was the last hope for saving one's life, and it was a tremendously personal experience requiring deep focus and concentration on myself.

Most of the time in the room, we were on our beds, reading, and most interactions were confined to mealtimes. Even outside the room, I mostly kept to myself, as I walked the grounds, reading, and going to chapel twice a day.

Jimmy was a stable force and mentored me each day, reminding me the simple task to take life and sobriety one day at a time. He said, "If one day at a time is too much to get through, take it five minutes at a time, and then belly breathe, Charlie, belly breathe."

The meals, the surroundings, getting eight hours of sleep every night, and the lowkey lifestyle…after two weeks of this tranquility and consistent feeding, I gained some of the weight I'd lost over the past six months. I was feeling like my old self again. Once I felt a little nourished, I was homesick.

Maybe I could go home. Maybe is was just a string of bad luck, and I'd lived most of my life at the house on Long Island, and I needed to get back. I dole out a few apologies and, hopefully, they would be accepted. I could find employment and my life would straighten out. I didn't need to be at the monastery anymore.

Yes, home. That's where I needed to be.

I found Jimmy in his office and said, "Jimmy, I want to leave."

The redheaded staff member was shocked, but he said, "Well, if that's what you want."

"It is."

"Okay," he said. "Of course, that's not up to me, but I'll arrange for you to meet with Father Owen and Father Bernie."

Later that day, Jimmy led me to Father Owen's office. "Wait on the bench outside the door and they will come get you," he said as he turned to leave.

"Alright," I thought, "perfect." Sitting and waiting would give me enough time to rehearse what I want to say. I role-played my whole speech of why I wanted to leave, listing my reasons, imagining all the possible responses Father Owen and Father Bernie would give, then providing my counter-arguments. Imagining the prospect of leaving was exciting. I would be going home. I felt so rested and good with my health renewed. Sure, there might be some hoops to go through to get out of Graymoor, otherwise Jimmy could have just signed me out, but my arguments were all sound. I could toss back anything the two fathers threw at me.

"Besides," I told myself, "This place will be here for me if I ever needed it in the future." I actually was still in a state of denial, a common place for addicts to be once they start to feel somewhat better.

I waited in front of the office for nearly an hour. Then, Father Bernie in his brown Franciscan robe opened the door and called me into the office. It was inexplicably bright in that room, and I would have liked to have had sunglasses. Father Owen was sitting behind his desk, and with the light in the room and his white hair, he appeared like a white-hot star radiating white light.

We had never officially met.

"Charles, my name is Father Owen, and this is Father Bernie. Jimmy has informed us you have something you would like to tell us."

I went to launch into my fancy speech I'd rehearsed, but nothing came out of my mouth. "I—" I started to mumble something like, "*Well, what I had hoped, I mean, you see…*" This darn devil had been chanting in my ear for the last 24-hours, and now that I was in this office being asked a question, the devil was gone.

In hindsight, Father Owen had seen me before, or my devil, or a thousand other guys like me, so many who wanted to bail out before the miracle of sobriety happened.

"Charles," Father Owen said, "I want you to know this: Brother Bernie and I care deeply about you. We want you to succeed, but we understand you want to leave us. Is that true, Charles?"

"Yes, Father Owen."

"Why?"

"I'm homesick."

Father Owen didn't change position and continued to look at me directly. "Charles," he said, "you don't have a home. I've spoken to your father, and he said you are homeless. That is why we are providing a home for you."

As he spoke, I couldn't stop it—I started to cry.

"Charles," Father Owen continued, "no matter where you go in this life, you will always remember the love you received here." *To bring home those who have lost their way.* Emotion overcame me. That room, so full of light, Father Owen's words, the tone of his voice, kind but unequivocal, "Charles, all things are possible through Christ."

As he said it, I stopped crying—at least a little. He believed, so I would believe. It was as simple as completely trusting Father Owen. In those few moments in his presence, in the surety of his words and the energy through faith he conveyed, I was ready to completely give myself over.

"Alright, Father Bernie is going to get you working," he said. "It will help you pass the time with us. You will be assigned a very special job. Father Bernie, why don't you take over and explain it to Charles."

The powerful Father Bernie, who had stood like a boulder against the wall, then stepped toward me. There would be no cajoling or coddling. The Franciscan monk would be direct in every interaction. "We have a cemetery here at Graymoor, and it is very important to all of us it is cared for. You will be caring for the landscaping of the cemetery. It will be a very rewarding job. See Jimmy when you leave us. He will put you with the landscaping crew, and you will start tomorrow morning."

I thanked both men profusely and headed right for Jimmy's office, feeling as if a tremendous weight was lifted off my back.

"How did it go, Charles?" Jimmy asked, the hint of a smile on his face.

"Really well. I'm going to stay," I said happily.

Jimmy nodded, and the full smile emerged. He said, "I already knew you were staying. Here, I have all the info for you to start with the landscaping crew tomorrow morning."

That night, dinner tasted even better than it had before, and then I was off to a church service, absorbing everything in the sermon given by one of the Franciscan friars. I then went off to bed to prepare for my first productive day in a very long time. As I lay in bed, I gave thanks to the Lord for putting so many good people in my life, from Father Owen and Father Bernie to Michael at the train station in the middle of the night, who had sent me here, to the firefighter who let me wash my face, to the cop who had bought me lunch instead of arresting me. And I thanked the Lord for the good people who tried to help me before. I would be dead without them.

In the morning, I reported to the landscaping crew at their shop to get my assignment and the tools I would need. For at least the next couple of days, I would be the only one on duty working in the cemetery, raking the leaves around the headstones, then trimming the grass around them with sheers. There was a tractor used for the grounds, but it couldn't get between the headstones, so it was a job needing to be done by hand. This job was all physical labor with no complexity.

It was easy to get lost in the job, full of solitude, but it was the kind of solitude I liked. My supervisor checked on me a few times to make sure my progress was okay and to see whether I had any questions. Aside from the lunch break, I worked through my whole day with hardly any awareness of the time. I was surprised when my supervisor said it was time to wrap up for the day. I was tired, and the exertion left me with a total awareness of my body. The physical awareness was akin to the feeling of weightlifting, although with weightlifting, I always felt like I was chasing something and trying to put a wall of muscle and strength between my soul and all the pain in my life. Working in the cemetery was different—I felt my myself opening up to the world, even in my solitude. I needed to pay attention to every stray leaf and wayward blade of grass. I was connecting to the grounds and to nature.

After two days, I widened my scope from the blades and leaves to the headstones. As I stood back to check the row of headstones I had just finished, making sure I hadn't missed any errant blades of grass, the numbers on the headstones suddenly stood out to me. The names didn't mean much—it was the dates, born and died, emerging like those photos that look like a blur, and you have to stare at for a while before the images pop up in three dimensions.

In an instant, I start to calculate the ages. 78. The next one, 83. Another, 84. One was 92. Along the row, 70s, 80s, and into their 90s. I had a few years to go before I hit 30, and I might not even make it that long. I would be remembered only as the guy who couldn't get past himself, past a selfish life. Whatever good I might have brought to this world wouldn't happen. If a future child depends on me living in order to be born and have a life, that won't happen. My view of my own mortality was vivid and palpable, as if there was not just a metaphorical path laid out in front of me but a literal one. There were divergent roads with signposts for all my potential life events on one side, and a very literal dead end a few feet away.

That was *my death* unless I changed my life.

This was the moment. For the first time, I was not thinking of recovery as merely something theoretical, something in my mind I assumed was an eventuality. No, now I was feeling it in my heart: Embrace the right road. It was right there. Sobriety would be work, but it would begin here, and it would be true sobriety.

This was my awakening. At last. All the AA books and statements and steps, they were no longer simply words on a page— they were my life. They were how I wanted to live, in order to live. I knew what others were talking about now, finally. I could see past myself, from the outside, and see the wrongs I had committed. Yes, I'd had some bad breaks as a kid, but I also received many blessings. I was healthy, as told by an array of doctors when I used the emergency room as my primary care physician. I survived homelessness and the collapsed lung and many near-death experiences and…the list went on. I had been healthy enough to survive all that. My health, my strength, was my blessing.

Yes, my parents didn't show me parental love, but how many other people had stepped in to spend their time with me, to show me the way? Even local police took care of me, or attempted to help me out, to have a court session on the hood of a police cruiser to give me a tongue lashing to avoid seeing the county judge. There was so much worse that might have happened to me. My resentments were darkness. I had no right to have any resentments because they were stopping me from seeing and feeling the sunlight in the world.

I stood up taller. Did Father Owen give me the cemetery job to wake me up? Did the Lord say, "I now have him alone, it's time to wake him up spiritually?" I don't know, and it doesn't matter to me, all these years later. After those days in the cemetery, I was a changed person, I underwent that psychic change described in the *Big Book*. I had a real direction, an actual path, to the physical road of a long life. Fear and uncertainty were replaced with hope and direction.

Also, I'd been racking up sober time, and with the gift nobody can ever buy—sobriety with peace of mind. I'd been afflicted with the disease of addiction, in all its insidious degradation and dread, and left untreated, there are no survivors. Nor are there shortcuts or get out of jail cards. You might die quickly or slowly. I'd gotten the slow painful version, but it bought me time. I had one last attempt to change course.

I started looking forward. Whatever happened in my past, my future was spotless.

Each day at Graymoor, I continued to build a better me. Was I doing the building? No, I surrendered my will in Father Owen's office. Now the change was happening. I met with Father Owen a few more times, and one day, he reminded me, "Approach everything in life from a position of love."

Graymoor was indeed about love, and all these years later, I can still feel the love I received there.

I don't believe I could have had this awakening in a traditional rehab—first of all, I'd been to plenty, and recovery had never been close to happening. I was a time-consuming use of resources, which were limited, as there were masses entering their facilities day in and day out. They could have been able to get fifty or more addicts clean and sober in the time it would have taken with me, on a merry-go-round, until something stuck. I'd lived the deadly triangle of addiction, with the initial euphoria produced from the food, gambling, alcohol, and drugs, and then the next high was chased to keep me from filling the void of the internal absence of the original addiction to which the addict inevitably returns.

Food would be my hardest addiction to kick. It's not like I could go cold turkey on food. It's not as if my weakness had *only* been for sugary snacks. There are no traffic checkpoints to ensure you haven't consumed too much food. No one regulates food intake. There isn't a bartender cutting you off. There are no safeguards.

The monastery had counselors to whom I brought up my food addiction and was told, "Remember, Charles, what got you to hit bottom—drugs and alcohol. Let's worry about those first."

Perhaps they worried it would be too daunting for me to give up all of my addictions, or perhaps nowadays, treatment would focus on the food as well. I'd worry about the substance abuse first and foremost, then work hard to keep my mind healthy, away from the traps leading me to feed my emotions rather than my belly.

I needed to take one precious day at a time.

#

As weeks at Graymoor turned into months, I was ready for my next phase of recovery. Graymoor placed me in a drug treatment center in the middle of Long Island. I was given a urinalysis to ensure that I was drug free, and then Graymoor arranged for my transportation from one safe environment to the next one, a place called Charles K. Post Addiction Treatment Center, a hundred miles away.

Technically, Charles K. Post Addiction Treatment Center was a converted wing in the infamous Pilgrim State Psychiatric Center in Brentwood, New York. The complex was huge, imposing, and though a new facility had been rebuilt, the older, abandoned buildings moldered on the property, looking reminiscent of a Gothic horror story.

Pilgrim had been built in the early part of the 20th century to accommodate the rising number of mental health patients who were placed in horrific asylums. On the large swath of undeveloped Long Island land, doctors and advocates believed if these patients were able to engage in outdoor activities, such as farming, they would show improvement in their overall health. The farming ended, and in the mid-1950s, overcrowding became a problem. Pilgrim housed nearly 14,000 psychiatric patients, who were receiving lobotomies and electroconvulsive therapy. Once the pharmaceutical industry broadened to provide alternatives to institutionalization, the number of institutionalized psychiatric patients dropped exponentially, leading to the shutdown of several facilities. One by one, the hospitals were abandoned. Even Pilgrim shut down wings, and by the time I arrived, the complex was in various stages of decay. The abandoned buildings were missing windows, had leaky roofs (or roofs with giant holes), and had assorted overgrown brush throughout the old farmland. And honestly, it could be scary as all get-out, especially during the nightly walks on the grounds. One of the buildings not abandoned but re-appropriated would be my home for the next forty-two days.

 I was ready to start this next chapter of my life and it felt new, and exciting, though I was aware of how much work I still had ahead of me—but I was ready to do the work to get better. I had many months of sobriety logged under my belt, yet I was reminded I was still in a controlled environment. The real work starts in real-time once I'd get back on the streets.

 This center wasn't the kind of rehab that shuffled patients in and out, and I really enjoyed the way it operated. There were group sessions with counselors who really got us to open up in front of the other men, helping us purge the things we addicts clutch to in order to rationalize and justify our behavior. Nothing was off topic. We would have all our issues addressed and discussed thoughtfully by our counselors running the groups and by our peers.

 After several of these group sessions, I could feel an improvement in my overall outlook. I was also communicating better. I was learning how to talk about my needs and feelings. One of the reasons I always favored closer friendships with women was because women avoided the toxic masculinity behaviors found in so many men. There was no posturing, no need to challenge each other and fight each other, no need to prove who was top dog.

 Looking at another man and asking, "Could I take that guy?" is rooted, of course, in insecurity. I'd hidden my insecurities better at times than other men, but there were plenty of dirty looks and internal hostility. I'd covered my pain with pride and hadn't been willing to talk about it with anybody. At the same time, I'd rejected men like my father as role models and preferred the intellectual thinkers of American history. My father was anti-intellectualism; for him, thinking smart meant being "snooty," and there was zero talk about God or what might happen when you die.

Though I'd had friendships with guys, I was never close with them the way I was with girls and women, who made me feel safe. Women saw behind the mask I wore in public and tried to know the real me. Plenty were girlfriends, but many were buddies, best friends, and counselors who could see what was going to destroy me far more precisely than I could. I'd say it wasn't so bad, or I knew things were bad, but I'd land on my feet eventually. A few stuck by me when I couldn't be there for myself. I could meet a new girl, and we'd spend countless hours doing nothing but talking and getting to know each other before the romance kicked in. Then, suddenly, the addiction would wake back up, and I'd be gone, leaving the woman wondering where I had gone and what she'd done. I could be away from drugs and alcohol for weeks, even months at a time, but then that old alarm clock would buzz, and I'd be back deep into my addiction. I'd lift weights, wear nice clothes, and find a girl who would understand me and accept my crazy lifestyle. Then when things got too complicated, or drugs messed me up too much, either they would move on, or I would preemptively leave to avoid getting hurt—as I'd done as far back as my couple of weeks with Teresa.

At Graymoor, I got the awakening I needed. Now, Pilgrim would give me the tools to live my life back in society, teach me to cope and process daily events and avoid letting those events trigger a need to use drugs. Pilgrim helped me exercise and build up my emotional muscle for the first time in my life. I could stop internalizing all the bad that happened to me as somehow my fault. In theory, this might have been the coping skill I needed to survive long enough to reach my awakening. I'd never succumbed to defeat, but I had no tools to break my negative emotional cycle. In our sessions, our group was connected by our shared griefs and traumas, and I realized I wasn't alone—and I wasn't the only one who'd had a messed-up childhood. I'd have to accept my past in order to move on from my past.

The whole process of the treatment center was geared toward transitioning us back into the real world. I was there over the holidays, and Pilgrim held a party for us with music, food, and dancing, giving us the opportunity to have fun without the use of alcohol or drugs. I, meanwhile, also made sure I stayed away from the food. Buffets were not my strong suit, and if I overate, my enjoyment of the party would be over, and the guilt would last for days.

1993 turned into 1994, and at the end of my forty-two days, I found myself at a level of happiness I'd never before known. Recovery felt real, now, not like a temporary placeholder for some later date. My heart was full of gratitude for everyone who had helped me.

The treatment center insisted I go into a halfway house program. I was surprised, at first, when they used the word *insisted*, which isn't generally used after someone demonstrates the ability to complete treatment and show clean urinalyses.

"Your case is severe, Charlie," one of the head counselors told me. "We want to help you ensure against relapse," he added "and this is the best way to do it."

I accepted whatever they told me as gospel truth. I moved to their halfway house—which was still on the hospital grounds, though not fully supervised the way we were at the treatment center. Transitioning back into the world would be incremental, but I was ready to do all I was instructed to do. My counselors gave me the tools to cope with a sober life amid the many temptations and triggers; now, I would be responsible for using them if I wanted a life in recovery.

One of the next tasks was to get work. I was excited to learn there were many jobs available with construction companies doing work on the grounds of Pilgrim, so I went to my counselors to report my decision, excited for the next opportunity.

"Charlie, that's not a good fit for you, at least not right now," my counselor said. "You're still early in recovery, and the work will be more demanding than what we think you're ready to take on."

It was my first of many disappointments. I was doubly insulted when my counselor said I needed to get a minimum wage job.

"There are several reasons for this. First, you have to relearn how to use money. You need to manage what you bring in and spend it wisely. Additionally, it isn't good to suddenly have all this extra responsibility thrown on you after so long out of the workforce."

I trusted their judgment once again and let them find me work through their collaborating temp agency. I ended up working at J.C. Penney's in their children's department. All the regular eating in addition to the weights I had been lifting in recovery brought me back up to 235 pounds. I was the giant guy putting baby clothes on tiny hangers and answering to managers four to five years younger than I was. Though it was a humbling experience, I learned to be okay in whatever I was doing, and I took my children's department job very seriously.

The temp agency told the halfway house that they were pleased to hear from J.C. Penney that I was doing a great job and I was very self-motivated. Back when I was making good money driving a taxi, I was reckless with my spending. Now that I was making $4.25 an hour, I learned how to make ten dollars do backflips. My money needed to last me, and I couldn't just spend my cash on whims—or junk food.

I shuddered thinking of not having five dollars for my lunch at the chicken restaurant by the Jamaica Train Station and at the ruckus I caused. My entire life, I'd relied on working hard, whether it was my paper route as a kid or at the gas station. With those jobs I immediately bought food—or added to my precious record collection. Buying records was the only time I'd ever done any saving or planning ahead. Now, with a regular, very small paycheck coming in, I understood the principles of money management. I took care of needs and worked to save even the tiniest bit to carry me through to the next paycheck.

For ninety days, I did my work through the temp agency. At the end of the ninety days, my counselors revealed their plan.

"Charlie," they said, "taking this job showed us how serious you are about your recovery."

That felt good to hear.

"We wanted to see how you took directions, accepted the lower paying job, and how you responded, if you were harboring any resentment."

Resentment, I'd learned, was the number one offender to sabotaging recovery. Anger and recovery do not go together and have taken a sledgehammer to the recovery of many good people. The counselors had perhaps underestimated the impact the monastery had on me. Plus, I never wanted to be deloused ever again in this lifetime.

"As you know, there is a demolition company working on the premises. One of the owners was in recovery himself and now goes out of his way to hire men who have had addiction problems or have been in prison and need a fresh start. We'd like you to meet with him. We think you're ready."

I would get my shot at a construction job after all. I met with the owner, and he asked me what my story was.

"Where are you living?" he asked.

"Oh, about three hundred yards from the building you're doing the interior demolition on," I answered.

"You're hired," he said.

"Great. Thank you. Just like that?"

"The real interview will be your job performance. If you don't work hard, you'll no longer have a job."

For my new boss, actions were currency; words were not.

"Day starts at 7 a.m., ends at 3:30 p.m."

I loved the day-to-day operations of the job site and was fascinated with exploring more of the history of Building #25 as we turned it into a brand-new hospital. It was the old psychiatric ward, built in 1929, unchanged as a time capsule but left to rot, all its artifacts still inside. Building #25 was tall, and from the outer stairwells, you could see for miles, especially as the other old buildings had been demolished and cleared away, leaving a wide-open view. On the ninth floor was the "motivational center," which bore a giant mural, a mosaic of sailboats on the Long Island Sound. It was a work of art.

"Yeah," Phil, one of my co-workers said, "this is where the lobotomies were performed."

All of us workers got a little shudder passing through the ninth floor, helped in large part by the lobotomy story (how apocryphal it was, I never learned). This was before the days of internet search engines, so my information mostly came word of mouth, but I took every opportunity to ask about as much of the place's history as I could. Most of it was there, laid out right in front of me, in my hands as I cleared it away.

My job was using the air hammer, which is basically a jackhammer for walls. We were knocking down the enormous walls of the old architecture, which favored a hive of smaller rooms, to build a contemporary style hospital with a more open and inviting floorplan.

When it wasn't the walls, I was down in the basement, jackhammering the bedrock to make way for the new elevator shafts being installed. The work was energizing, and I had so much energy in those days that, as soon as I saved up enough of my money, I bought a car and joined a gym, where I worked out after working hard all day. It was a gift and a blessing to be so physically tired—a healthy, good tired after solid productivity. I was building something. I was making a hospital. My work mattered. My life was on track, and I was diligently following all the suggestions my counselors set out for me.

All but one.

19. SUGGESTION NOT TAKEN

The one that says not to get into any relationships during the first year of recovery.

Well. I had been so good at following everything else, and besides, the monastery...The old rationalizations.

It wasn't hard to rationalize Denise's thousand-watt smile, her dark curly hair that flowed down her shoulders or her tan skin. She looked like a sixties flower child in flowing, flowered dresses and funky sunglasses.

We met at a recovery event, which I attended regularly as part of my ongoing commitment to living my life in recovery. Denise was also in recovery. She was four years sober. Her last drinking binge hadn't been pretty. She kicked alcohol without rehab, and she made it through with twelve-step meetings that were enough for her because she had a foundation of normalcy to return to. She had a foundation I never had. I went to some of her meetings with her and was receptive to the recovery speakers. It was good to have a companion who understood some of what I'd been through.

We were the same age, and she was a schoolteacher. I was drawn to her intelligence—she had one master's degree, and she approached every problem using intellect and pragmatism, and she didn't hesitate to seek out experts to help guide her. Another mark in her favor was that her parents lived in Nebraska—there it was, the mysterious wilds inhabiting my youthful imagination. I could learn insider's information on what life was really like there. Besides, what could possibly go wrong?

Maybe I should have asked, "What could go right?"

No, I wasn't ready, but I couldn't tell myself that in those days. I was committed to making our relationship work. Even when stuff started going wrong.

We'd talked a few times before meetings, and after meetings, and found we kept talking long after meetings were over. I asked her out, and we hung out several nights right away. Then, I met her at her apartment one evening, arriving there just as she was getting home from work. At her front door was a bouquet of a dozen roses.

"Wow, you make an impression early," she said.

"I just got here," I said, my insides stiffening, then starting to heat up. It became clear to her that the roses weren't from me. Her face fell, as she read the card.

"Yeah," she said, sighing, "my ex."

"Is he sure he's your ex?"

She unlocked the door and threw the roses straight into the trash. I don't know if she wanted to throw them away or if the act was for my benefit—she must have seen the steam coming off my head. An ex?

"I'm sorry," she said.

"Hey, you know, no big deal," I said, trying to blow it off, like I was Mr. Nonchalant.

"Things were pretty bad. He was abusive, and manipulative, and after I broke things off, he came back, trying to win me over, and we got back together for a little bit, but I just couldn't be with him. I guess this is him trying again. But it's over. Really, it's over."

Who the hell did this guy think he was? I was already feeling serious about Denise—we'd been dating for a whole week.

But…no big deal. We moved on with our night and had a great time. She talked about maybe one day leaving New York and going back to Nebraska. "I don't know, what about you? Could you ever leave New York?" she asked.

I saw she was fishing for a potential future.

It was one I could maybe, vaguely, imagine. But leave New York, really? There were guys I knew who had spent a lifetime in New York who had "sworn it off for good," moving to New Jersey or Florida, even Arizona. All of them had come back, and they had come back with a story. It appeared to me no one ever permanently left New York. Still, I didn't know a single one who had been to Nebraska.

Our relationship progressed, and then the little things, tiny questions, doubts, and oddities (I hesitate to call them issues) surfaced, causing plenty of self-reflection. The cute schoolteacher and I turned out to have very little in common.

I realized, for instance, how having a full refrigerator was calming to me. It meant security. I kept it stocked with healthy food, but it was there, and I could tell myself I wouldn't go hungry, and I didn't have to go scavenge. Denise kept some bottles of water and one or two yogurts in her refrigerator. That made me nervous. I wasn't concerned she was like my mother and would withhold food from me, but the sight of the barren fridge triggered a deep anxiety within me.

Also, time with her made me realize how far I'd been from the actual world. In prison, inmates are generally "with it" and can get information on news from the world, including pop culture. I, on the other hand, had been going through life sleepwalking, sedated on drugs, homeless, my finger off the pulse of society. She listened to the Violent Femmes—what happened to good ol' rock n' roll?

The world changed quite a bit while I was out to lunch.

Being in a relationship with another human being brought out many challenges, as I could look back and see I'd been living like a caveman for years. I wasn't relating to other human beings. I wasn't building solid relationships. I wasn't even interacting like a human. It now mattered how I greeted people, that I was aware of their needs and how they existed in the world.

The bigger problem would be my trust issues, though I couldn't have articulated it as such back then. There was this looming sense of dread—I had a small level of fear even when taking a shower at Denise's apartment, as if, while I was lathering up with soap, some guy from Denise's past would show up. I developed the habit of continually peeking out the shower curtains to make sure no one else had come in like I was preparing to fight anyone, naked and covered in soap. This was not a stable foundation. Sure, I could recognize this, and I didn't even need to be literally working on solid foundations at the time to catch on to the metaphor. It didn't help that on some date nights, we'd run into a guy she used to be engaged to, or another ex, or the rose man would contact her again. Denise never once acted like there was anything between her and these other men, but I was in a constant state of discomfort.

Denise was a social butterfly, always wanting to take me out to meet her friends and enjoy the nightlife. I was a natural at being social, but I now was keenly aware these tendencies of mine landed me homeless and penniless. I started to think maybe we were both hurting our potentials for happiness. I couldn't speed up my recovery while spending nights out on the town. I was like Rocky Balboa, who needed a simple life, and if I were to have my own Adrian, I would have to wait until the time was right.

That was what I thought, or at least, that was my main thought. But then, my other thought: Here is this great girl who seems to like me a lot. I had nowhere near enough strength to walk away from her.

During this time, though things were moving ahead with Denise faster than I would have liked. I felt I still needed a place of my own. There was no pressure for me yet to move out of the halfway house, though it wasn't an anomaly for me to move out when I did. I wanted to transition to a small place, a furnished room, and see how that worked out. I put the word out, and my co-worker Phil told me his mother could rent me a room.

Phil had been a good friend to me on the job. He was also in recovery, and he was a prince of a man. If I'd had any impressions that living a life clean and sober meant a life of boredom, Phil quickly shattered the misconception. If he was this nice, this interesting, it must have come from somewhere, so I happily accepted the room in his mother, Janet's house. When I moved into the room in Janet's house, I did not struggle with the new minimal supervision. My commitment to recovery was strong, and Janet was very good to me.

The struggles I had were adapting to having to use a laundromat. I had to fit it into my schedule, wait there while my clothes spun in the washers and dryers, and even learn how to use the machines. Denise helped me laugh through all my antics and was a supportive teacher. She was sympathetic to my complaints of sleeping on a mattress about as thick as a Band-Aid. Of course, the uncomfortable mattress and the offer to do laundry at her apartment only made it more appealing to spend time with Denise. Recovery felt less intense if we could laugh about nuisances.

Despite the nuisances, and even with Denise and the new living situation, I kept up my routine of working hard, going to twelve-step meetings, and then would squeeze in gym time whenever I could.

It's a general rule, and I found this true for me: You have absolutely nothing to give when you are in early recovery, which means you have no business taking on a relationship. I learned this once Denise and I found ourselves in relation*shit* territory.

Some of the tensions came because she wanted to move back to Nebraska and wanted me to move with her.

"We could give it a go there," she told me. "I think the change of lifestyle would be so good for you. It would definitely help you unwind."

"Leave New York? No one leaves here. It's the greatest city in the world," I exclaimed.

"What's here for you?" she asked seriously.

The one thing about my sixties flower child was that the flower child appearance was just that—appearance. She was as fierce and intense as I could be, sometimes even more so. At first, the talk of moving was just talk. Then it became serious. Denise was ready to be finished with New York, and when I wasn't as receptive to that, she grew angry, and as I learned, she had no boundaries when she was angry. Things could get volatile unless someone yielded, and that someone was me.

One night while she was sleeping, I had gone into the bedroom to get a pair of underwear out of my dresser after having a late-night shower after work. She awoke, sat up, and yelled at me for making too much noise. I apologized and went back into the bathroom to get dressed. When I got back, she shot out of bed, yelling, "Now I can't go back to sleep because you had to take a shower and you had to make so much noise with this damn dresser."

"I'm sorry—I didn't mean to."

"I have a big day at school tomorrow—did you ever think of that?" She proceeded to rip every drawer out of the dresser and throw all my clothes across the bedroom floor.

My chest tightened—suddenly, I was back at my parents' house, watching my father rip up the house on a tirade. I knew better than to try to talk to someone that angry—better to get out of the way and let them blow off steam. I went into the other room and slept on the couch. The next day, there was no mention of her tirade. Again, I had the flood of recognition of life with my parents. Is this really what I wanted?

"Maybe," I wondered, "things really would be better in Nebraska?"

It's true, I had what might be a codependent relationship with New York. I loved the people, the food, the smells of a pulsing city. Whenever I'd be in a conversation with other New Yorkers, and we'd talk about the city or changes, I'd always end by saying we lived in such a great state and how lucky we were, despite any complaints.

I even talked it over with Phil and a few other guys at work. I told them of the possibility of me leaving for Nebraska. Almost in unison, they shouted, "Nebraska!?!"

"They have tornadoes out there!" one friend said.

"It's way too dangerous. Put your foot down—don't move," another declared.

Well, I was one to check my facts, and the truth was there was a far greater chance of getting caught in a hurricane in Manhattan than a tornado in Lincoln, Nebraska. I'm not sure if I was trying to talk myself into or out of the relationship, or if I was simply keeping my options open. Possibly all three. What I did know was I didn't want to disappoint Denise. Disappointing people had become my M.O., and I wanted those days behind me.

Six weeks into our relationship, when tensions started to flare, Denise left to visit her family in Nebraska and would be gone for two weeks over the summer.

"It will give us just a little time apart," she said, "and then we can see how much we really care for each other."

Again, I thought long and hard about the possibility of moving to Nebraska. If she still wanted to see me when she got back, I'd know we were okay. We weren't really able to talk much while she was gone. I didn't send her any letters, though she called me a couple of times long distance from her parents' phone, which made us keep the call relatively short. She was having a good time, it was so perfect there, and so on.

What I found in her absence was she added a spark to my life, and I looked forward to doing things with her and wasn't ready for that to be over. On the day of her return, she called me to say her friend who was supposed to pick her up from the airport had "overcommitted" and couldn't come, so could I? I thought this was a good indication she wanted to see me. Even if there was no overcommitted girlfriend, I took this as a good sign.

Two days after her return, however, we had ourselves another flareup. She was driving us in her Chevy Blazer down Merrick Road on a weekday afternoon when I saw her face change and she seemed startled.

"What is it?" I asked, concerned.

All I'd noticed were a man and woman going into a travel agency.

"Oh," Denise said, "nothing."

"Nothing? What did you see?"

She took a breath and said, "That was my old boyfriend. The one who sent the roses."

"Stop the car!" I demanded.

While Denise hit the brakes going 35 miles per hour, I was already in the process of opening the door. Despite the fact the Blazer hadn't stopped all the way, I jumped out. We were going faster than I realized. I managed to do the tuck and roll, and it was a miracle that all the oncoming traffic managed to swerve out of the way and avoid hitting me. When I came to a stop on the road, I struggled to catch my breath, as the wind had been completely knocked out of me. People from the sidewalk and from the cars that stopped surrounded me. Someone yelled to call for an ambulance, but I waved them off. It took a couple of minutes to collect myself, and then I was right back up and marching into the travel agency. Denise's ex was in there making travel arrangements with a new girl. Just two months earlier, he was dropping roses off at Denise's doorstep.

I got into his face and yelled, "Don't you ever send another bouquet of roses to Denise, you got that, pal?"

The new girl looked confused, and the ex was clearly flustered. He was caught off guard but also sheepish because he shouldn't have sent the roses. "We can take this outside, if you want," I said, seeing he was no fighter. I was a survivor and I'd only fought when it was absolutely necessary against my bully for survival or when I was on drugs, and even then, it was only to protect myself. Still, the ex-didn't know that—he just saw this pumped-up guy with a weightlifter's neck and angry eyes. And he saw my toxic need to prove I was the top dog. He understood me loud and clear, and I backed off. Denise, meanwhile, had parked the Blazer and was yelling at me to get the hell back in the car.

Denise was up to DEFCON volatile, and this time, she was 100% correct.

"You could have easily died jumping out of a car! And even if you did survive the jump, those other cars came so close to hitting you! Those motorists didn't need that kind of scare. Also, did it ever occur to you that I'm a teacher in this community? Do you know how fast news like this travels?"

I sat there in silence, taking my tongue lashing. She was right about everything.

"I'm so disappointed in you," she added. "But also, I had no idea those roses upset you so much. You need to work on how you feel and communicate those feelings with words."

Though the communicating part was easier said than done, the incident injected a serious dose of humility into my soul. As bad as my grudge against this guy was, jumping out of the car like that just so I could face him was utterly insane. I so easily could have been killed or seriously injured.

Part of the problem was my sense of accountability, or lack thereof—I was comfortable being impulsive in a place where I knew half the police department. Half of them were now mostly men and women I'd grown up with, and the older ones were like big brothers to me. The other part of the problem was I didn't think I had been bothered so much by the roses as I was by Denise's cavalier attitude when talking about all her past relationships. She made no big deal about guys—and I was starting to feel just like a number in a long line of inconsequential men.

Nebraska was now looking more like my future home. Over the next week, Denise continued to chew me out, justifiably, but then the criticisms changed into requests to at least take a trip with her to Nebraska to meet her parents. I agreed, and we flew out to her parents' home in Lincoln.

Her parents were originally from Nebraska but moved to Long Island when Denise's dad took a job with a big advertising agency, riding the LIRR to Manhattan each day. Both Denise and her sister were born in New York, but still felt the pull to Nebraska. They were great people, and I instantly felt at home on their back porch, breathing the Nebraska air, enjoying the quiet and chatting with Denise's dad about books.

Her dad had read more books than I saw in most bookstores. He had a ton of energy and was wound tightly, which I recognized as a kindred spirit. The area looked like what Long Island had been years ago when it was acres of potato fields.

The family introduced me to their friends, who were quick-witted and polite and totally accepting of me. There was nothing extreme about them—in fact, there was a neutrality from being

14th & 2nd

neither east nor west nor north nor south but from smack in the middle of the country.

I checked the phone book for Italian surnames and found none. Alright, well—I'd be unique to the area. It was a fact I liked.

I didn't dislike the place and could see myself there, but I still wasn't in a rush to make any decisions, and when we returned to Long Island, my thoughts were devoted to work and recovery. I needed to be focused where my feet were. Denise's desire to move, however, grew to a near obsession. However, she also realized talking about moving to Nebraska all the time would be more than I could handle, so she limited her references.

In the meantime, Denise put pressure on me to get rid of my "bachelor pad," as she called it. "You're here most of the time anyway," she reasoned.

When I talked to Janet about it, she tried to discourage me from moving out. "You need to stay focused on your new life, Charlie." She understood addiction and knew all about the problems in my past. She didn't say it outright, but in so many words, she told me she was concerned if the relationship ended, I'd be at risk of losing my sobriety.

Janet clearly saw the writing on the wall for how the relationship would turn out. I felt every word she told me, and also, she'd met Denise on a few occasions, when she'd stop in and I wasn't home.

"She sure is...intense," Janet offered.

Any suggestion you don't take in recovery, I've been told, comes with a price. I didn't take Janet's suggestion, or that of my counselors on relationships in the first year, and politely cleaned out my dresser, packed up my few possessions, and closed the chapter on my bachelor pad.

Of course, I had no business being in the relationship, and you cannot fix two people who are not compatible, but when Denise got pregnant about a month later, it completely changed my world. I would never look back.

Getting married seemed like the right thing to do, so Denise brought me to her Catholic priest to discuss marriage. He, however, was adamantly opposed to her getting married so soon after her planned marriage was called off.

"It hasn't been that soon," I said, thinking we'd been together for three months. Plus, there was the ex-boyfriend with the roses that I'd met who'd come in between us.

Denise and the priest looked at me. "Denise ended her engagement five months ago," the priest said.

When we left, I asked her about the guy with the roses and how he fit in with everything. "We were on and off for a long time, and we'd just gotten back together after I ended my engagement with Jack."

This information explained why the rose guy thought he still had a chance, and why other guys would come and go. I shrugged. None of those guys were willing to give Denise the commitment I was willing to give her, so I thought.

The omens were there, and a marriage license was not going to fix our problems, but we both refused to heed the warning signs.

Life was suddenly very serious, and I was preparing to get married. I called up my father and asked if he could get me into a construction union. We'd barely spoken at all, except for my occasional calls to let them know I was alive, in recovery and had a job. I'd ask about Kane, and my mom would say, "He's great! He doesn't miss you—he has a great life." That was the most they said, as they didn't want to talk to me.

"You're getting married?" my father asked.

"Denise is pregnant," I said.

Immediately, my mother got on the line and said, "Having a baby with someone is no reason to decide to get married."

(When our baby girl, Rachel, was born, healthy and beautiful, I would never regret the relationship with Denise, no matter how bad things got.)

I sent my parents an invitation to the wedding, which was going to be small, but I never heard from them, and they did not attend the wedding. My parents were no happier with me sober than they were when I was whacked out on drugs. But, at the very least, my father did in fact make the call – one call – and there I was, in the union, with considerably high wages, working multi-million-dollar construction jobs.

With what I earned, Denise and I could have bought the house of our dreams, and that wasn't even considering Denise's teaching salary. We would have been financially secure with a perfect-on-paper life, but Denise was adamant about returning to Nebraska. Now that I was providing for a daughter, I had no inclinations to jump out of cars, so I put leaving Long Island completely out of my mind.

"No," Denise said, "we're moving."

I was in the middle of working on a 14-million-dollar interior demolition project, and I hadn't even mentioned to my new job that I was moving.

"My parents bought a duplex," Denise declared, "one side will be ours to have until we decide whether to get our own house. Or not." With that announcement, she called a moving company, who came to pack up the whole apartment we'd been renting.

It was such a generous offer from her parents (though I didn't entirely know what version of reality Denise told them), and I appreciated how thoughtful they were in wanting to make life easy for us as a family.

"Okay, but not just yet," I implored, "I have to finish this project."

For three weeks, I pushed back on the move. We lived with everything packed in boxes, and if we needed a pot to boil water, we'd have to rummage through boxes and unpack it to use, then pack it back up when finished. At the three-week mark, Denise was done waiting and called the movers to load the truck and drive it to Nebraska. She and Rachel would fly to Lincoln, two days ahead of the moving truck, and I would wrap things up on Long Island and then join them in a week or so, while Denise got everything unpacked at the new house. I quickly pulled my alarm clock out of the boxes, as well as a couple of moving blankets, and with a small bag of clothes, that was the extent of my possessions.

When I dropped her off at the airport with our daughter, Denise said, "I'll see you in a week."

Now that I was alone, I wondered what the hell I was doing. Sure, Nebraska was beautiful, but was I really about to give up my high-paying career? Eighteen months earlier, I was making minimum wage working retail.

There were no job prospects lined up for me in Nebraska, though Denise said it wouldn't be too hard to find work, plus, we wouldn't be under financial stress because of the money we managed to save up and the fact her parents were letting us stay in their duplex. Okay, great, but there was the arguing, and Denise's willfulness (which went beyond strong independence and speaking her mind). Though many of the fights were about the move, Denise demanded her way at every front—and on Long Island, we were on mutual territory. In Nebraska, that would be Denise's territory alone, and her parents would be right next door. How would she be then and there?

The first week came and went. I told Denise the project was taking longer than expected, which wasn't a lie. A second week came and went. The phone calls were more frequent, more pressing: Why wasn't I coming? Where was I? What was taking so long? She was pissed.

"We're all unpacked here, no thanks to you," Denise said sternly, and then said, "My parents think you aren't coming, and it's really embarrassing."

If it hadn't been for Rachel, I might have broken it off right then and there. Still, I couldn't commit to the move. I knew I was paying for not following the "no relationships in early recovery" suggestion. I understood exactly what they meant, and I knew why this was a disaster, even though it was a little late. What kind of person was I, though, if I didn't follow, at least for my daughter's sake? So, after a few more days, I conceded, quit my job, arranged for my last paycheck to be mailed to Nebraska and called Denise.

"Okay, I'll get a flight today, and we'll drive back together, so you don't need to do it alone. Mom and Dad will watch Rachel."

Two hours later, she had her plane ticket, and I wrapped up what little I had and swept the apartment so Denise would get her full security deposit back.

I packed the car with the blankets, alarm clock, and a small bag of clothes and gave the key back to the landlord. Soon I was at JFK Airport, waiting for Denise. She bounded out in a cute hat and sunglasses, her carry-on slung over her arm, smiling ear-to-ear when she saw me. Okay, maybe she isn't mad about the delay, I thought. Maybe this really will be a new beginning and I've been the jerk for delaying our new life.

We'd be in Lincoln in three days after twenty-three hours of driving. I decided to go slowly to enjoy the ride, to say goodbye to my old life, and to transition to the new one. We chatted about how things were going at the duplex as we left New York behind and cut across New Jersey on Interstate 80. We stopped for the night in Pennsylvania, and everything was quite good between us.

The next morning, we had a pleasant breakfast, then drove for three hours before hitting the Ohio Turnpike around noon.

"You motherfucking sonofabitch," she started yelling, "would you have ever left if I hadn't forced you? You don't think about how this makes me look? You selfish bastard. My parents had to do all the unpacking and cleaning, and what the hell were you doing?"

I knew with *100% accuracy* that my life was about to be a living hell.

"And since you're no longer employed, my mom has a list of chores for you to do around the duplex. You need to pull your fucking weight for a change."

I kept quiet and drove well under the speed limit. This would be my last couple of days or so of freedom before reporting for duty at the duplex. I made as many stops as possible without incurring any more of Denise's wrath. We got as far as Iowa by nightfall. The only thing keeping me heading west and not turning the car back around was the prospect of seeing my daughter. It had been a month since I'd said goodbye to her.

When we arrived at the duplex, I was shocked to see how, in that month, Rachel had grown so much. My noticing this led to more passive aggressive comments from Denise, but I didn't engage. Her mom was cordial, but she also conveyed her displeasure at my delayed arrival.

#

I fully accepted my share of making the bed that I now had to lie in, but it was no small wonder that within eighteen months, Denise and I would become another divorce statistic.

Things did not improve between us once Denise had gotten her wish to move. I'd ignored the evidence before, but now, there was no way of denying her raging temper. Head down, I focused on getting my life together, staying straight, and trying not to escalate conflict. That summer of 1995, I put in for a job with the Nebraska Department of Corrections to get a job at the prison.

While waiting to hear back from the Department of Corrections, we had time to spend together, so Denise and I went to the park at Oak Lake to meet some friends—well, Denise was going, and I agreed to go with her. After half an hour, one of Denise's friends pulled out a joint and started smoking.

"We have to go now," I said.

"Why?" Denise asked.

"Why? I can't be around any drugs. Besides, I'm trying to get hired with the state. If the cops come, I'm guilty by association."

Denise agreed to leave, and we got in the car. As soon as I pulled away, Denise grew enraged.

"How does it look that we're leaving?!?" she yelled.

"I don't care," I said, accelerating the car.

Denise grabbed the gearshift and threw it in park. The transmission made a horrible sound as the car lurched to a stop and shuddered in the middle of the road, shutting off. I tried to restart the ignition, but then Denise ripped the keys out, ran out of the car, and then threw the keys into Oak Lake.

The car was now stranded in the middle of the street, and my only option, as I saw it, was to go into the lake to retrieve the keys. I started toward the water, but then Denise ran to me and started punching and kicking me nonstop. All I could do was hold my hands up to protect my head and chest from her blows and get to the water, since at least in the lake, she couldn't both hit and kick me. The keys had splashed into the lake a good way from the shoreline, so I was swimming around with my head underwater, trying to feel for the keys on the silty bottom.

There were plenty of people in Oak Park who witnessed this, and one person had a cell phone and called the police. I was under the surface of the water when the squad car pulled up and the officers shouted for me to get out of the lake.

"But I have to find my keys!"

"Get out of the lake now, or we will send the dogs in to get you."

Reluctantly, I trudged out, dripping from head-to-toe, still in my clothes.

A passing motorist witnessed the entirety of the exchange and also called them. "We got a lot of calls about this, and we are going to place your wife under arrest for assault as domestic violence," the officer whose name tag said Blanders told me.

"Arrest her?" I asked, and then said, "But—she's a girl."

Not that women can't be abusers, but I looked at her tiny frame, and even with her kicks and hits, I never felt endangered.

"Besides," I added, "she's a schoolteacher and the arrest will ruin her career."

Sure, she was volatile and had been violent, but to go as far as to arrest her?

"Well, we are obligated to arrest her, after seeing the cuts and scratches you have on your face and neck. We are following Nebraska's domestic violence laws," Blanders said.

They handcuffed Denise and put her in the back of a second squad car. Was this really happening?

"Look, Officer Blanders," I said, "there isn't a payphone around here. May I use your cell phone to call my father-in-law and let him know what's happened to his daughter?"

He handed me his phone, and I called my father-in-law, who, in a low-key tone of voice, said, "You two need to deal with this."

That was it. That was all he had to say.

"Do you have a place to stay? Can you go to a friend's house or maybe stay with another family member?" Blanders asked.

I had no one. I explained about the duplex and about being new to the area.

"Alright, listen," Blanders said, "We can't let you go home tonight, because if Denise gets out of booking, she might be even angrier when she gets home. We'll have to take you to the City Mission for the Homeless. It will just be for tonight."

As he drove me to the homeless shelter, Officer Blanders said, "My name's Jerrad, by the way. You know, when you came out of the water with your dark green shirt on, you looked just like the Hulk. Any other circumstance, and it would have been a funny sight."

It certainly would have. If Denise and I hadn't been so doomed from the start. If she hadn't been so volatile. If she wasn't in jail.

"I'm sure sorry for all this," I said.

"You don't need to apologize for anything," Blanders said. He was kind to me, but I couldn't help feeling responsible for something. After he dropped me off at the shelter, I walked outside, away from the other men, so I could cry. There I was in Lincoln, Nebraska, away from everyone I knew, jobless after having a great union job, homeless, and feeling the after-effects of the beatdown from my wife to top it all off.

The next day, my father-in-law picked up Denise at jail, and they both drove over to the homeless shelter to pick me up and then brought me back to the duplex. They acted nice to me, as if we were a perfect family.

"Let's have a nice dinner at home together," Denise suggested, "we need to fix the situation because, well, there's a lot at stake."

Yeah, there was a lot at stake. Denise couldn't lose her teaching career over this mishap. For a week or so, she was all sweetness, bending over backward to make me feel appreciated, showing affection, acting as if the three of us plus her parents next door were the happiest of families.

Of course, there were strings attached.

"Do you really have to press charges?" she asked.

"I'm not going to," I said, knowing what she did was wrong but feeling bad for the woman I married all the same. She was the mother of my daughter. It turned out, though, that the decision wasn't up to me. Officer Blanders called to say the state was pressing charges and I was a witness, and the prosecutor would be calling me.

"What she did was abusive," Officer Blanders said, "Just because you're a big guy and can take it doesn't make it right."

Denise was worried for weeks about her future in teaching.

"I don't know how you could do this to me," she said after a while.

"I'm not doing anything. Besides, what you did was wrong. It was physical abuse."

She blew up and started yelling. She said, "Oh, so this is you getting back at me? Fine, if I get fired, then where will the money come from? I won't be working, and you'll be the sole breadwinner because I won't be able to find another job again. Did you ever think of that?"

"I'm saying, maybe you should have thought of that before you threw my keys in the lake and attacked me in public."

I knew I was poking the bear but come on. I reminded her again that I wasn't the one pressing charges and had no control over what the prosecutors did.

"Well," she said, huffing, "you don't *have* to *cooperate* with them! Not if you care about your family!"

This was a problem for Denise, but being Denise, she was going to approach it the way she did all problems, by seeking help and advice from the best people possible. She decided we both should go to a psychiatrist, though she said it was to discuss my issues. She used her connections to get us an appointment with the chief of psychiatry at Lincoln General, who was noted for his acute skills of perception and for not mincing his words.

We arrived at his office, and Denise said, "You need to help my husband."

The tall sixty-five-year-old doctor had more plaques on his wall than one might see at a sports hall of fame. I felt honored that he was willing to make an appointment with us and listen to our story. I'd learned plenty from my counseling and especially my time at Graymoor to humble myself and be straightforward with my counselors. Maybe Dr. Baldwin would have some brand-new insights into my life. At the very least, it would be someone in Nebraska who would listen to me who wasn't on anyone's side.

After greeting us, Dr. Baldwin sat back in his chair, his feet propped up, and his hands under his chin. "Charlie," he said calmly, "why don't you go ahead and tell me about your story."

I wasn't sure where to start. "The short or the long version?" I asked.

"No, you just talk. Don't rush. Tell me in your own words."

He listened to me for forty-five minutes without saying much. Then, he turned to Denise and asked her to tell him about her story, to talk about how we met, and to share what happened from there. She told roughly the same series of events, including me jumping out of her moving car, which I had mentioned as well. She included how I made her leave the picnic because someone was smoking pot, and now because of that incident, she might lose everything, and I was holding it over her head. When Dr. Baldwin asked how I was holding it over her, she said because the prosecutors were still calling me.

"And they're calling him because they say they're required to press charges, though Charlie isn't," Dr. Baldwin said, verifying Denise's account.

"Yes."

His expression didn't change, but he looked at Denise for a minute and said, "Denise, everything you've told me, you have a personality disorder. I recommend you have your doctor—or I can, if you like—write a prescription for Depakote, which is an effective mood-stabilizing drug."

Denise was incensed. (Little did she know that Dr. Baldwin was the author of a somewhat controversial book titled, *Marriage Without B.S.*) "Me?" she asked, once she picked her jaw off the floor. "What about him?" she pointed at me. "He's the one who's nuts!"

While I was shocked at the sudden turn-around, I had to bite my lip to keep from smiling.

Dr. Baldwin sat up then and said, "There's not a thing wrong with this guy. He's been through every battle emotionally a person can go through, and he's very stable. Now, is he stressed? Is he wired tightly? Absolutely. He needs to relax, take in the Nebraska air. As a matter of fact," he said, "I'd like to take him out duck hunting."

"Duck hunting?" Denise almost screamed, "You'd put a gun in this man's hand?"

"Absolutely," he said. "I don't know why you think he's unstable—he's anything but. Now, with your attitude and as intense as you are, you're very unhealthy for him. Some people just aren't good matches for each other."

I wanted to feel bad for Denise, but in that moment, I understood much of my patience and goodwill had been spent. All I felt was relief and what I later learned was called *Schadenfreude*. She sought out the most prestigious psychiatrist in the state, so he'd tell her, "Yes, you're right, Charlie is nuts and you have every right to treat him the way you do," and instead, not only did she receive the opposite, but this doctor also invited me duck hunting.

Denise stormed out of the office, and though I had to follow her, I first thanked Dr. Baldwin for his time and his support.

"I don't know if you really meant you'd take me duck hunting," I said, "and though I'm not into hunting, I do love getting out in nature. Of course, I'd be happy to have lunch or a cup of coffee with you."

"Charlie, I meant what I said," the doctor said seriously, "You have so much to offer, and I know without a doubt you'll get your life together one day."

It was as if God reached inside my chest and touched my heart. I still needed to go out and face Denise in her current state, but now I knew there wasn't anything wrong with me. Dr. Baldwin believed unblinkingly I'd be okay. I could have that same faith in myself as well.

My goal now was to avoid any fights with Denise. I don't know if I was biding my time for…something, for her to throw in the towel, but my priority was our daughter and making things good for her. When the prosecutor called, I told him I had nothing really to say, that I didn't remember what happened, and said, repeatedly, "I can't answer that."

"Look," the prosecutor said, "if she gets away with assaulting you this time, it will happen again."

He was right. She was arrested again for domestic violence (this time for hitting our daughter) over a decade later when she returned to Lincoln for her mother's funeral, after marrying another man in Nebraska and moving to California where she divorced her second husband. She was at her sister's house, and her sister called the police. Similarly, Denise got off for that one, though I never forgave her for hurting Rachel.

#

Within a couple of weeks, once the case was closed with no prosecution, Denise kicked me out of the house, saying it was over. I had a total of six dollars in my pocket, a quarter tank of gas in my old pickup truck, and nowhere to go. There were only a few acquaintances I knew fairly well, so it was humbling to call them up to tell them my wife had given me the boot and I needed a place to sleep. I was reliving the all-too-familiar sadness and helplessness I had encountered so many times before.

However, I did get hired by the Department of Corrections, and they sent me to the academy for training. When I met with the admissions committee, they had a revelation for me. They had done a full background check and had a few things to ask.

"What do you know about your father's time in New York corrections?" a member of the admissions committee asked.

"My father was a correctional officer? No, that can't be right."

"No," the committee member said, "your father served time, in the 1950s. He did time for robbery and attempted murder of a New York City police officer."

I couldn't have been more shocked if someone had told me my father was John Gotti himself. He had done real prison time, not just jail time. This was the secret world my parents kept, locked away in separate rooms of their lives.

After learning this information, I was on the hunt, collecting information over the months and years whenever I could. When the internet became functional for the masses, I searched through old newspapers. My search yielded a result showing the front page of the February 6, 1956, *New York Daily News*, which reported my father's holdup of a cabaret in Queens with Joseph Imbruglia. Imbruglia attempted to shoot an officer, but the gun jammed while it was pressed against the officer's stomach. This was the same Joseph Imbruglia who trafficked in cocaine and heroin. He was also involved in the infamous "French Connection" case, and my father's partner-in-crime was on the FBI's most wanted list in the 1980s.

My father. This was my father. I'd shared a house with him for almost two decades. I was lucky Nebraska Department of Corrections had considered me at all.

It would have been easy to feel completely alone in my confusion during those days, but fortunately, there was another guy from the East Coast, and he and I hit it off immediately. He offered to rent me a room in his parents' investment property until I got on my feet. He let me have the room for sixty dollars a week. I had child support payments and daycare expenses, so the low rent was absolutely a gift. With an arrangement like that, I knew I could wear out my welcome quickly, so I worked as much overtime as possible to save as much money as I could.

Working for the prison was great money (when one factored in the overtime) especially since I didn't have any other opportunities, but that kind of work takes its toll. My days were spent strip-searching men before and after visits, looking in their mouths, under their balls, having them spread their cheeks—not exactly how I'd envisioned my future self when I was a kid imagining a career in law enforcement.

20. INTRODUCING STAR

Once-homeless Charlie and once-homeless Star made it through their first year together, and after all this time, the looming shadow of authority ready to swoop in and take her away dissipated. As the Summer of 2014 slides toward Labor Day, Star's Facebook page has continued to grow, with questions and rumors circulating. Plenty of people ask why the very vocal Charlie Cifarelli has suddenly gone quiet. Why is he not posting questions about Star's whereabouts? Has he given up? Was he bought out? Was he threatened? Is he another loser guy who dropped the ball?

Several people pose the most important question of all: "Does Charlie have Star?"

If I were on the outside looking in, I too would wonder all these things. You can't fool all of the people all of the time. And my end-of-summer run-in with Rob, my savvy customer who questioned me about Star, gives me the next test.

Rob marks me at a local hardware store, comes straight for me, and says, "Hi, Charlie, how are you?"

"Good, and you Rob?" I say cautiously.

"I'm okay," and if he pauses, it's only for a second, because he's already made up his mind to ask. Clearing his throat a bit, he says, "I've been wanting to talk to you and was hoping to run into you at some point."

"You should have just called me," I say, knowing what is coming.

"I really wanted to talk to you in person," he insists.

I'm edgy. It's a small, internal gnawing. "Well, I'm here now."

"How's your dog?"

Here we go.

"She's fine," I say flatly.

Then, it happens. He asks the question I have been avoiding for such a long time. He says, "I must ask you this, and I must tell you I have been thinking about it a lot. I just felt when I met you with Star that there was more to her story than you were telling me. I wrestled back and forth with the idea of saying something or not—that's why I left it there. I decided though, if I saw you, I would say something; otherwise, I would try to let it go. I wondered if you really didn't know her story or if there was more you weren't saying. My gut tells me you do know. Charlie, as you've gotten to know me over the years, you know I'm always on the computer and watch way more YouTube videos than guys half my age. I couldn't get your dog out of my mind after I met her, and somewhere in the back of my mind, I knew I saw a brown and white Pit Bull somewhere, but I had forgotten where. Then it came to me: I saw a video with more than a million views of one brown and white Pit Bull being shot in the head by the police in New York City. I have seen a lot of messed up stuff on YouTube, but this video stayed with me. But then, I recently found out online that the dog survived!"

"How did you find out?" I asked.

"There are many videos on YouTube about that shooting, and I was reading comments. The brown and white dog did survive," taking a step closer to me, he said, "Charlie, you have Star, I know it. She is missing an eye, and your dog is missing an eye. She has the same markings. And…the same name."

Most Nebraskans never get too worked up about anything—they say remaining calm is an excellent quality for longevity. Rob, though, is fired up. He's sure he's connected the dots and knows he's right—he just wants to hear it from me.

I take a deep breath and say, "Yes, Rob. My Star and the Star in the video are in fact the same dog. I have adopted her."

Rob hugs me, right there in the aisle of the hardware store. What is happening?

"Charlie, that's a wonderful thing you did!" he exclaims and then says, "Poor dog was confused—she was protecting her owner!"

One uneasy questioned burned in my mind. "Rob, outside of you, does anyone else know of your revelation?" I asked, quietly.

"My son knows. He knew about the story when it happened."

"Alright," I say, "Look, for Star's sake, please don't say anything to anyone else. I have a bunch of stipulations in the adoption agreement I was asked to adhere to, and quite frankly, I don't know how the local media might react to her story. The locals—they will either love her, or they will say, *"Not in my backyard."*

"No, Charlie—I think what you did is quite admirable, and it's a big deal. This dog has been in many news articles. I think it would be a big deal in the local media." He put his hand on my shoulder and gave a reassuring nod. Star has another ally and so do I.

"Thank you, Rob. I'm very sorry for not telling you the whole story back at the gas station."

I go home and hug Star. Another bullet fragment is working its way up to her coat. They mostly come out in her face area, but a few come out on her neck. Her current doctors tell me these fragments pose a risk and that each day she doesn't succumb to them is a good day. If something happens to her because of her injuries, and I've stayed quiet, she'll never get the celebration she deserves from her fans.

That's it. Star's whole witness protection and secrecy and hiding has to come to an end. Now I have to figure out how.

I go back to the computer for more research. So many publications have written about Star, but I'm looking for the one that's written about her the most, the one that would be the biggest cheerleader for Star in her new life. I realized it needed to be *Gothamist*, who'd done the initial reporting. They were a great online magazine in New York that really covered the story, and each article showed they were rooting for Star to survive and thrive.

"Alright," I told myself, "I'll email them. I'm over this secrecy. The facts are Star was almost killed and beat the odds."

It's a simple message I write. I tell them who I am and that I've adopted Star, the New York Pit Bull, and now she lives with my family in Nebraska. My message is short and to the point. I include my phone number—I'm always more comfortable talking than writing. Though Star has even helped me with that. All the writing I used to fear, in school and through work, I fear less, after all those Facebook posts and emails when advocating for Star. I hit send and then go to bed. It's late Thursday night—technically, Friday morning. I probably won't hear from anyone until after the weekend, if at all.

The next day, Ben Yankas, a journalist from *Gothamist*, calls me. He's well versed on Star's story.

"You have her?" he asks excitedly, "You really have Star? In Nebraska?"

He asks a bunch of questions, doing his due diligence in vetting me to make sure I'm not some quack looking for a weird fifteen minutes of fame over a dog that isn't mine. While we're on the phone, I email him a few current photos, and as the saying goes, a picture is worth a thousand words.

"That's her," he says, his voice nearly breathless. "It's really her."

We talk for nearly forty-five minutes. I don't ask any questions about the future. My goal has been to report she is alive and well, and I've revealed my secret to the magazine that had so diligently covered my girl through her story. When we hang up, I feel a new lightness, something rare and perfect. No matter what happens, I won't regret telling someone Star's okay. I don't tell Jenn about my interview, or my email to *Gothamist*. I don't know why. I tell myself it's because nothing may even come of it, so why get her worked up for no reason?

When I wake up Saturday, it's such a beautiful day that I ask Jenn if she wants to take the hour-long drive up to Omaha.

"Do you have anything in mind you'd like to do up there?" Jenn asks.

Food is always foremost.

"Let's start with lunch at the Cheesecake Factory," I suggest.

Cheesecake Factory has a big menu and even bigger portions. The place is tailor-made for an eater like me.

The thing is, I've forgotten about my interview with Ben Yankas. That's how much relief I've found. I had a deep, amazing sleep, and woke up feeling like a new man. We have a great drive to Omaha, enjoying the weather and appreciating each other's company. We then get seated at a table in front of the windows under the all gleaming-sky brightness shining down on us.

The bread arrives at our table, and my willpower simultaneously makes its departure, as I play my internal game, *I will only have one piece…of each kind of bread*, but of course, it turns into, *maybe two of each kind*, because I can never have just one of anything.

As I'm negotiating with myself, my Facebook alert on my iPhone dings. Now, I'm not a tech savvy guy, but once I switched from a flip phone and Blackberry to an iPhone, I was hooked, and Star's Facebook page was the gateway drug. I ignore the ding because Jenn and I are at lunch. My volume is set to the lowest volume, but still on, in case I get a call. Then, like a floodgate opening, the dings are nonstop.

"What is going on?" Jenn asks.

A flood of likes and messages. That's what's going on. I've never received this type of activity on Star's page, ever. I open the app and see people are sharing a *Gothamist* article to Star's page. The article being shared is, "Nebraska Man Adopts Dog Shot by NYPD." The article is shared on both Facebook and Twitter. The comments are incredible—as if Jimmy Hoffa suddenly appeared and laughed, saying, "You all were busy looking for my body in New Jersey, but here I am in Nebraska, alive and well and living the good life!"

I show Jenn my phone, and as she reads the article aloud, her eyes widen. I'm a noisy fella—a little shy—but Jenn is a true introvert.

The article is excellent except for one minor contention: I'm quoted as using the word "convict" in reference to my corrections employment, but I would never refer to an inmate as a "convict" because doing so gives them strength in a negative identity.

She gets to the end and blurts, "How did this happen?"

I say nothing.

"Tell me, Charlie, how? You apparently gave an interview. Charlie, what about our privacy? Our neighbors will all know now."

"Maybe," I say, cautiously.

"Maybe? This story will spread like wildfire."

Jenn of course is right. I have no clue how social media and media work and had never gone truly viral before. *Gothamist* covered my story, and then other news outlets reposted the story, so the same story was rehashed by a multitude of different media outlets, each hitting their own audience. The news is all over New York. It's too late to shy away now.

WPIX NYC runs *The Incredible Story of Star* on both the six and ten o'clock news broadcasts. They also post an update across their social media. While *Gothamist* went into all the ugliness of what happened to Star, WPIX has a softer touch they include few details but sell Star's story as the ultimate feel-good piece. Friends from New York who I haven't spoken to in twenty-five years are reaching out to reconnect. Once the story is big in New York, everyone else hears about it. The feedback is overwhelmingly positive. The trolls either don't come out or other followers get them deleted before I see any negative comments. The off-duty cops are remarkably silent. So is the official NYPD spokesperson: No comment.

Who knows, though, what's churning behind the scenes?

Star becomes Star, The Underdog, and though my privacy is now gone, at least Star has gotten the last word on her story. I fully expect the story's focus to be on Star, and Jenn rolls her eyes at me, because I am Star's spokesperson, and I'm the man who's tracked her down. It's true that New Yorkers always feel at least somewhat famous just by virtue of being from New York. So many years now in Nebraska have separated me from that. I'm still Charlie, yes,

Charlie from New York, but I'm less of a novelty after so much time. I'm the Charlie from work, Charlie from down the street. My concern remains my Nebraska neighbors and what they will say about a dog with this much history living in their backyards.

Days go by since going viral. Not a single one of my neighbors says a word. Honestly, I'm shocked, because I've seen a few of them named as fans of Star's Facebook page. In November, I go to vote and run into the retired judge from down the street. He walks up to me and asks, "How is that special dog of yours doing?"

The conservative judge is supportive? "She's great!" I say, as I smile at him as big as Star smiles. I once again find tension and fear leaving me. If the judge accepts Star, the whole neighborhood will, as they respect his lead.

Really, my fear stems from the stigmas against Pit Bulls. There was a time in America when a dog was a dog. Then, in the 1970s, Doberman Pinschers were demonized, and in the 1980s, Rottweilers. For the last thirty years, the Pit Bull has held that place of infamy. I've looked into this a lot—me being the research guy.

The problem is that media only report on Pit Bull bites. So…have Doberman Pinschers suddenly stopped biting? Rottweilers? What about German Shepherds? Sure, breeds might play a role, but research also shows most dog bites are instigated by teasing, and often those bitten are unsupervised children who don't know better. Dogs often snap as a warning and don't go for actual mauling. Incidentally, Chihuahuas have the highest rate of biting people (though a Chihuahua bite doesn't make as dramatic a news story).

In many of the dog bite statistics I find, there are inconsistencies and even mistakes. Sometimes, any dog with a block-shape head is deemed a Pit Bull, even if the breed is unknown or mixed. All of this serves to put communities on high alert, banning the dogs in some cities with Breed Specific Legislation (BSL). As a tragic result of these BSLs, many Pit Bulls are instantly euthanized in shelters because they're harder to adopt. Furthermore, Pit Bull is often an umbrella term for a grouping of dogs that includes the American Staffordshire Terrier, Staffordshire Bull Terrier, and sometimes even the American Bulldog. The real perpetrators are usually the owners who get their hands on Pit Bulls for dogfighting or other abusive practices.

When families do adopt Pit Bulls from shelter, they have no idea of any history of abuse—and many of these abused dogs need special and extensive training by an experienced dog person. If that's done, though, these dogs can very successfully reacclimate to living in a home with a family. (Most of Michael Vick's Pit Bulls, for example, were successfully rehabilitated and adopted.)

Though Lincoln has no Breed Specific Legislation, that doesn't automatically mean there will be no stigma against Star because of her breed and history. But the large majority of Nebraskans are also fair-minded individuals, and I can see that in the judge. There is one upside to Star's story being public: Some neighbors come to understand the necessity for the big fence around the yard as part of the adoption agreement. I'm not such an odd outsider after all.

As fall turns to winter, I think Jenn and I will be able to resume our quiet little life.

#

The resurgence of the news story about Star's shooting and Lech's loss gets me thinking about Kane again. Before Star, when I thought of the NYPD, I always thought of one specific day back when Kane and I were inseparable. I was in that barely functional truck, and the police pulled me over for a traffic violation. Kane was in the front seat with me. I didn't have my license on me, so the police wanted to speak with me at the station and make sure I was who I said I was and be sure I had no warrants.

"Why don't you drive your truck down to the station, so you don't have to leave your dog behind," they said, and then added, "Of course, if you try to run, we'll shoot out your tires."

They were at least half-joking. When we arrived at the police station and I got out of my truck, one of the officers said, "Leave your truck running with the AC on so your dog won't get hot. We'll watch your truck and your buddy here."

While I was in the station, sorting out my definitely-not-squeaky-clean record, an officer came in with Kane prancing at his side. "It was really hot out there," the officer said, "so it's best just to bring him in here." He set my keys on the desk in front of me. Never once did they threaten to take Kane from me or take him to the pound. They went out of their way to accommodate him. They knew he didn't have a mean bone in his body. Just like Star doesn't.

My Star. She now cuddles up next to me on the couch when we sit together. I rub her back, feeling another hard bullet fragment just under the surface of her skin. It will work its way out in time.

21. CONDEMNED AND REDEEMED

John Joubert's execution by electric chair was set for mid-July of 1996. As the visiting room officer, I monitored him in the visiting room on July 9 as he waited for a meeting with a journalist from New York. The officers brought him from death row to our section of the prison, where I took charge of him in the visiting room, handing him off to the other officers when he was finished.

This was his last day in the visiting room, as he would be taken to the penitentiary hospital for the last week of his life for around-the-clock supervision, to prevent him from harming himself or taking his own life.

Seemed odd. **Don't** kill yourself so the State **can**.

Joubert didn't talk much to the prison staff, but as his time on earth was coming to an end, the normally quiet man with the look of an older kid had become more verbal toward me. He either took note of my New York accent and asked whether I missed New York, or he asked how I was doing.

After the journalist left, I had to take his Styrofoam coffee cup from him before heading back to his cell. As he handed the cup to me, I could see his hand trembling. John was a serial child-killer. He had been a sadistic bully before that, stating he'd received sexual pleasure as an adolescent from stabbing a young girl with a pencil and slashing another with a razor blade. He was not a good person. He was exactly the kind of person I would have loved to have taken my aggressions out on, *in another life*. What I learned in my time so far at prison was that I could not become like the worst of these people. I could not lose my own humanity, even if some of these inmates had none of theirs left.

This was the last time I would be walking him out of the visiting room, and Joubert looked at me and said goodbye. He looked at me as if he was waiting for me to say something special or magical back to him. I hadn't planned anything. Why would I? The moment was awkward, and what came out of my mouth was, "It was nice knowing you."

I wasn't happy with the reply. It wasn't *nice* knowing him, under this or any circumstances, but he was a human being at the end of his life. This scenario isn't in any academy training, nor is it written down in any post orders. While the other officers waited to take him back to death row, I moved closer to him and said, "John, if you have a belief in God, ask him for forgiveness and ask Him to be with you, as He is the only way." It was all I knew to say that might possibly be of any consequence.

I wasn't in any position to dole out retribution or forgiveness. The former had been done by the courts, and the latter was up to the families of the victims. Beyond that, there was just God, as far as I could see, and if there was any goodness in Joubert's soul, maybe he would seek forgiveness.

"Thank you!" Joubert said.

He was executed days later. His execution would mark one of the last uses of the electric chair as punishment in Nebraska. He received a four-inch blister on the top of his head, along with burn marks near his temples. After his body was removed, the chair was decommissioned—a chair that had ironically been built eighty-plus years earlier by inmates. It took the lives of thirteen men.

I'd hoped my conduct was professional to Joubert and I hadn't crossed any lines. It wasn't long before the prison received two letters about my conduct overseeing the last few prison visits of Joubert. When I learned the first was from his attorney, I was sure my mouth had gotten me into trouble. Instead, it was a straightforward letter thanking me for my professionalism and for being courteous to her during her lengthy visits with her client.

"My client, John Joubert, appreciated your professionalism and wanted his thoughts known," she wrote.

I sat with her letter for a long time. There I was, a full-grown man who'd been beaten as a kid by my father, dealing with this murderer of multiple children, and yet, through the grace and mercy of Christ, I could remain neutral to do my job and not let my ill will surface. Grace is, after all, being given something you don't deserve. And mercy, the other side of the coin, is not getting what you do deserve.

Being in this prison was changing me. It was making me more compassionate, or at the very least, for those I couldn't give compassion, I could at least trust justice had done its job and any mercy or damnation was likewise in the hands of a Higher Authority.

The second letter came from the New York City journalist who interviewed Joubert and witnessed the execution. Leah was in her mid-twenties and wrote at length about her feelings and about what she'd gone through being part of the execution process. She also wanted to let me know she appreciated my professionalism in treating Joubert. It was a beautiful letter. As a journalist, she was to perfectly articulate the complexities of capital punishment and the realities of the criminal justice system. Maybe it's the case that feeling sympathy while seeing someone facing the last moments of life is what keeps us from being like them.

Leah then wrote that if I ever got back to New York, we should meet up, and she left me her contact information.

She'd had incredible hazel eyes, and this was a unique situation. If she lived in Nebraska, or if the man she'd interviewed was still alive, I'd pass, figuring I needed to keep a professional distance. Our connection had been made over something morbid, but maybe it was important that good could come out of it. I hadn't really dated any women since Denise, though there had been a couple of attempts, but Leah's words—and I won't lie, her hazel eyes—drew me in. Also, as it turned out, I had put in a vacation request a year ahead of time (required by the department to ensure there were no staff shortages) and I was going to be in New York starting that weekend and staying with my old friend Doug.

14th & 2nd

I called Leah and we arranged to meet the coming Saturday at noon in front of Penn Station. We'd have the whole city to decide what to do. Chance encounters like this were the softer side of prison work, I thought.

Doug picked me up at the airport Friday afternoon. He and his wife had a nice home on Long Island, within walking distance to the train station. It was a straight shot from there to Penn Station for my Saturday date. Doug had years of sobriety under his belt, in large part thanks to his wife. It was good to see my old friend, yet he wasn't the kind of friend who wanted to hear the bad news of the day. He was not interested in prison stories or tales of death and redemption. Instead, we discussed the choices for dinner and how I liked Nebraska.

Really, it hadn't even been three full years since my near-death experience and my stay in the monastery. There was limited structure to my life, as opposed to Doug's seven years of structure and calm. There was only so much sporting news I could discuss as my life revolved around paying to support my daughter, keeping a roof over my head, thinking of my next meal and trying not to think of the death and sorrow and regret I confronted in my job every day. None of that was Doug's fault. And, in a way, it was nice to have a light conversation focused on good news as opposed to matters of life and death.

While dinner was great, and the conversation enjoyable, I couldn't help but think of the day ahead, and what my time with Leah might bring. My plan was to get to Penn Station an hour early so I could eat a snack before meeting up with Leah—that way, if we wanted to go to lunch, I could avoid looking like a Neanderthal going to town on half the menu.

There weren't many people at the train station on a Saturday morning, not until the Long Island train picked up more passengers heading into the city. On the way, I was able to read an entire newspaper to avoid being *quite* so nervous. Did I even still know how to be around a woman? Really, regardless of where things turned out, I wanted to have a beautiful day in the city with an interesting person who'd written me a moving letter after us sharing a tough experience.

14th & 2nd

I downed a few cups of coffee at Penn Station and had a toasted onion bagel—my God, it was like a mouthful of New York. I knew how much I'd missed the city and the food, but there it was, that old taste. New York bagels are all about the water, coming down from upstate. The water provides the right amount of minerals, and those minerals go into the bagels, the pizza, the coffee, you name it. The water is why no food outside of New York can capture what it's like to be in New York.

At close to noon, I headed to the front of the station, outside, basking in the warmth of the sun in the clear sky. The sights and smells and sounds of New York were all around me. The rhythms of the traffic surrounded me. I didn't forget the traffic—the night before, it had taken us well over an hour to get the thirty miles from the airport to Doug's house, and the both of us know all the quickest routes from place to place with all our driving experience. Leah was a few minutes late, but that was traffic for you, and I wasn't sure if she was coming by train or by car.

After about fifteen minutes, a homeless man who looked like Nick Nolte in his mug shot approached me. He was slightly younger but had the wild hair.

"Hey, buddy, you have any spare change?" he asked.

"Sure," I said, "here's a dollar."

"Thank you, sir!"

As he walked away, I mumbled, "I hope so." It was a whole dollar, after all, not a few coins I wanted to offload from my pocket.

Time passed. I was definitely in the right, pre-planned spot, but I wondered if I should move around, in case we were just out of sight of each other. My watch said it was almost 1 p.m. Traffic in New York, I told myself. Saturday, though, I reminded myself. My attitude took a nosedive. Leah wasn't coming. And now, the homeless man was back on his rounds of the station.

"Hey, buddy, can you spare some change?" Mini-Nick-Nolte asked again. He didn't even notice I was the guy who gave him the dollar forty-five minutes ago.

"Buddy, I gave you a buck, now leave me alone," I said.

"Okay," he said, "but why are you in such a bad mood? You seemed to be happy a short while ago."

"It's a long story," I said, trying to dismiss this guy so I could have my disappointed pity party in peace.

"I have the time," he said.

"What?" I asked, just a bit annoyed.

"You said it's a long story," he said, looking at me closer, "Well, I have the time. What's your story?"

"Look, I was supposed to meet a girl here at noon. We met very far from here, and she took the time to write and set up this date, and now she didn't show up," I explained.

"Welcome to life," he said, "there are many joys, but even more disappointments."

Like I didn't know that.

"Hey, I've been to hell and back," I said.

"Yeah, but put a woman in there who you like, and when things don't go well, it's painful."

Who was this guy?

"So, what, are you a psychologist disguised as a homeless guy?"

If so, he was a very smelly psychologist. There was dirt caked into the creases of his neck. His hair was grimy. I got bad but was never *that bad* in my worst days.

"No, not at all," he said, "I'm just a guy who has a lot of life experience."

Incredible. I ask his name.

"Kevin. And yours?"

"Charlie," I say as I look at the sky and the beautiful day. I feel the slight, perfect breeze. "Hey, Kevin, do you want to hang out? I'm too upset to go back to Long Island now."

"I don't blame you. I'm from Long Island, too. Or should I say, I was."

"What's your story? Why are you homeless?"

"I had a job as a union crane operator, but I like to smoke pot to relax. I got caught and had to go to treatment, and then I was put on probation. I didn't learn my lesson."

This guy still thinks addiction is a choice, I said to myself. He's not done yet—that's why he's panhandling for drugs and alcohol. Alright, I'm in this. "Look, I don't want to come off as harsh, but if we're going to hang out, you need to clean up."

"No problem. There's a place I can shower nearby. I'll need ten bucks, though. I'm not feeling that good, as I have a drug problem and need some pain meds. I can shower and meet you back here in less than an hour."

I handed over the ten dollars. Okay, if he never came back, that would be okay too, as I had no idea who this guy was, and knowing my life, I could wind up next to him on Skid Row before I knew it. But there was something about his manner I took a liking to right away. I watched him walk away with my ten dollars, then a new thought hit me.

"Kevin, wait!" I yelled, "You don't want to shower and have to put your dirty clothes back on." A guy nearby was selling Hawaiian-style shorts with matching tops, along with cheap sandals. "What's your size?" I asked as he made his way back to me.

"Extra-large," he said.

I gave the vendor twenty bucks and handed Kevin his new outfit.

"Thanks, Charlie! You mind getting me the sunglasses?" he asked, fingering the display case. "This way I can match you."

Why not? He was already into me for thirty-one dollars, another five wouldn't break the bank. Plus, Kevin was making me forget about my Leah disappointment.

Even after that, I still wasn't certain if he was going to come back or not. Doug wasn't expecting me that day, giving me the key to his house so I could let myself in if it was late, telling me to "go get 'em" and we had plenty of time to reminisce the rest of the week. I walked back to the agreed upon meeting place one last time, just in case, and the only person there was the guy selling newspapers. Seeing this, I went back to the waiting place for Kevin. When I got there, he was waiting for me. I was entirely shocked by how good he looked. He looked like a California beach guy with his long blonde hair now clean and combed. He was a big man and quite fit from all the walking he'd done in the city.

"Kevin, are you hungry?" I asked.

"Sure am," he said, quickly.

"Let's go get a meal."

We headed for a diner, and after ordering, Kevin asked me what I meant when I said I'd been to hell and back. I started pouring my heart out to this Long Island native, and in turn, he poured his heart out to me. He'd failed several drug tests when he was forced out of his job, and shortly after he lost his position, his wife left him, then he lost his home to the bank.

"It all happened in less than two years," Kevin said. "I was too ashamed to stay on Long Island, so I came to the city to get lost in the crowds."

Two years earlier, he'd had everything. Three years earlier, I'd lost everything.

Three years isn't a long time but it's also an eternity. "I don't know what it is," I told Kevin, "But for some reason, as a kid, I could be thrown out of my house for up to two weeks at a time and I could cope with it, but the last time, in my twenties, homeless for a total of thirty-six hours, I couldn't cope at all."

"That's because as a kid you hoped things would get better, that you'd grow up and then have a life. As an adult, though, you saw those hopes fail to happen. Charlie, you became hopeless for a time."

I nodded. It made sense.

"But I did not embrace it, and I didn't quit trying to survive," I said.

"Apparently. That's why you're here with me now."

Our food came, and we ate and talked and talked, and ate until we were stuffed. We'd both grown up on Long Island, a great place to live, in proximity to Manhattan, and we'd shared the same disease of addiction. His addiction was still killing him while mine had been arrested. Well, most of mine.

"Boy," Kevin said, "I've never seen anybody eat as much as you do."

I got the check and said we should walk the city to enjoy the summer day. It was a great walk, and the two of us made quite the pair, him looking straight out of California and me looking like a mob enforcer. Our difference in appearance drew a lot of attention, and different women would come up to us and strike up conversations, asking how we knew each other.

I could not remember having a better time walking around New York City. We walked restaurant row, then went on to Chelsea, stopping in many bars for more talk and back slaps. My drink of choice was soda water, while Kevin drank anything the bartenders would make him with vodka in it.

Not far from my mind was the knowledge I wouldn't have been here if it wasn't for Graymoor. I didn't want to push Kevin or proselytize. He was an adult, and he gave me not even a hint of surrender. The more we talked, the more he gave the impression that he accepted he would die most likely from an overdose, or his body would simply give out. He couldn't make the change until he was ready, though, and my heart ached for him. He stopped off again for more pain pills, and again, it was by the grace of God and my belief in my healing that I didn't join him.

I was ready to dismiss him as a homeless drunk earlier. Most astounding was that in all this, Kevin was neither high nor drunk—he was completely straight and relied on the pills and booze and other chemicals to keep his body from going into withdrawal. What he needed was a hospital stay to detox him under medical supervision, though I kept this to myself. This whole day was a wakeup call for me on connecting to the people who needed help or at least compassion.

As evening swept over the city, I felt the familiar hunger pangs renew, and I wanted to have one last meal in Manhattan's Little Italy before heading back to Nebraska. I figured I would put it out there: "Kevin, I'd like to head to Little Italy for a meal, do you want to come?"

"I sure would," he said, "I don't want our time to end." Emotion ballooned in Kevin's voice, and I could see in his eyes he didn't want me to leave.

We'd had one heck of a walking day and wound up at a nice Italian restaurant, sitting outside to enjoy the beautiful weather for as long as possible. It was hard in this setting not to wish I had been here with the pretty journalist with her moving letter that had so spoken to my heart. Leah brought me to New York, but she wasn't the reason I was there. She was not the real reason I needed to be in the city that day.

The journalist was young with many options for a bright future. Meanwhile, the human being sitting across from me now had few options. My gut told me despite my disappointment, I was with the right person.

What came next was a fantastic example for a psychological study of the human ego at work. In Kevin's prior life, before homelessness, he'd made good money and lived well. All of that was on display this evening. He navigated the wine menu with the server, then ordered the Italian dishes in a perfect Italian accent. He even spoke with the server in a little Italian. This day was costing me plenty of money, but I didn't care. I'd have all the time I needed to pay off any of this trip's excessive expenditures. This show was worth every forked-over dollar.

Kevin's big deal was the wine selection, and he spoke with the server at length about what kind of wine he wanted with his food. They decided on the bottle, and when the server poured the taste, Kevin swirled the wine in the glass around while the server watched expectant as a kid watching cotton candy spin around on a stick. Kevin smelled the wine, tasted it, then waved his hand to the server, visibly disappointed.

"No," he said, "this has a musty odor. There's cork taint."

The dejected server removed the bottle and brought another. Kevin took a bigger taste of this wine, and then he exclaimed the wine had turned.

"Why do you think that?" the server asked.

"It tastes like improper storing allowed it to get too hot," Kevin replied.

"Ah. Yes. Well, when it gets delivered, sometimes it does stay in the kitchen if someone doesn't take it to the cellar right away. That might have done it."

The concerned server was now convinced Kevin was a wine connoisseur, and all I could picture was Kevin asking me twice in an hour for pocket change while wearing his grubby clothes.

"Can I speak with the Maître D?" Kevin asked.

The server replied, "Yes, sir," with all the reverence he might give a Fortune 500 CEO.

Whether Kevin was right or wrong, I had no idea.

The Maître D introduced himself and said, "I'm terribly sorry you have had the unpleasant experience so far with our wines. We try hard to meet our customer's expectations, but apparently, we didn't meet yours. Can I offer you a complimentary cocktail?"

Kevin jumped on the free drink as quickly as I jump on the chance to eat.

"Yes, bring me a double of your best vodka on the rocks."

"Yes, sir," the Maître D said, "also, the restaurant will be picking up your meal this evening, as we want you to have a positive experience."

Now the meal would cost me nothing. This was truly incredible. Granted, I was convinced they paid the tab because they wanted us out of the restaurant as fast as we could reasonably eat and drink. I don't think our Maître D thought for one instant Kevin was a wine aficionado. I made sure to leave a sizeable tip, and our server couldn't thank me enough.

When we left, Kevin and I were two content men, and for all the rest of the world knew, we were two old friends who were successful and worldly. We walked off with our full stomachs, and before long, we were in SoHo, the trendiest spot for nightlife.

14th & 2nd

Though my date had been a bust, and despite having an otherwise great day, I was determined to dance before heading back to Nebraska and to my post at the prison. I found a club and told Kevin I wanted to step in.

"I'm going to call it a night," he said. "Would you mind, Charlie, a last couple of bucks? I'm feeling the pain creeping back in, and I need a few more pills for the night."

I sighed, and said, "Look. Here is forty dollars. I'm not giving this to you for anything but food; if you do something different with it, that's on you. I want to say I had a really great time with you today."

We said goodbye. Kevin was on his way, and I was in the club. Within minutes, I was dancing on the floor, glass of soda water in hand, surrounded by a large group of girls from Long Island out for a birthday party. They made up most of the patronage, meaning there was a greater ratio of girls to guys, so I was never without a dance partner. It was as clean a fun as they taught me in rehab. Well, maybe not quite as clean, but still, I was in my comfort zone, happy with my soda water. This really did turn out to be a perfect day and night, I thought, happy to be alive and be me.

I even started talking to one of the birthday celebrants, wondering where things might turn out for the night, when suddenly there was a persistent tapping on my shoulder. The old aggression fired on like it had an ignition switch—it had to be a jealous boyfriend, so I wasn't going to turn around. The tap was persistent, and I started imagining all the potential scenarios, especially if he'd followed her out. I wasn't going to give him my chin on a silver platter—the guy would have to work for it. So, I took three or four quick steps forward, then spun around, ready to fight.

It wasn't a boyfriend. It was Kevin.

"You came back!" I exclaimed.

"Charlie, I need to talk to you," Kevin said seriously.

"Hey, can you see I'm a little busy at this moment?" I gave a knowing nod in the direction of the girl next to me.

"Look, this is life or death, brother, your fan club can wait. I need to talk to you right now." His eyes were wide, but his gaze was direct and pleading.

"Okay, go ahead," I said.

"No, not here, outside."

As I followed Kevin, the girl I'd been talking to, and her friends asked where I was going.

"I need to talk to Kevin."

"Are you coming back?" she asked.

With that, Kevin slams the forty bucks I'd given him back in my hand and answers them for me. "No, he's not!" he exclaimed.

When we got outside, I asked him what was going on.

"I can't live like this anymore, and I don't feel like living anymore. I'm telling you; I will end my life."

That wasn't any bullshit.

"Alright, you said enough that I won't be going back inside that bar. You have my full attention," I said, looking at him intently.

"Charlie, you hung out all day and night with me, yet you didn't need a pill, a snort, or anything. Okay. I want that. I want my life back. I'm going to have you take me to the hospital."

"Why a hospital?" I asked.

"I want to die."

"Pal, you've been jovial all day and not too serious with me. What happened?"

"I realized this was no chance encounter. You were sent to help me."

Though I'd been feeling like I was in a better place, the right place, hearing him saying that—*that I had been sent there for him*—seemed so improbable. Three years earlier, Michael had been sent to the Jamaica Station for me, I 100% believed that. Was I sent here for Kevin? For this? Was now his moment of surrender?

"Charlie," Kevin said, "You are just quirky and self-absorbed enough that you don't feel your presence and how it rubs off on those around you."

I couldn't help but feel Kevin knew more about me than most of my long-term friends. I was not sure he'd listened to everything I said, especially with the pills and the booze.

"So why do you want to end your life?" I asked.

"You made me think about the life I had. Now I want it back," he said.

That wasn't it.

"No," I said, "you started to *feel* because you were safe, and we walked a lot, and you sweat a bunch of those drugs out that were numbing you."

"You're right, and you messed with my head by not indulging and having a good time. If I spent the money you'd given me on drugs, I would have been numb again, and the whole cycle would have started again."

"Kevin, will you take some suggestions from your fellow Long Islander?"

He nodded.

"Let's get out of the city and take the next taxi back to Penn Station. You need to go to a Long Island hospital because they are a whole lot nicer than anyplace here."

He agreed with me. He said, "What about my pill dependency? Charlie, I don't want to feel the withdrawals."

"Once you are admitted to the hospital, bring it up. They will not want you convulsing, so they will treat that problem too."

"How will I know I'm admitted for sure?"

"When you're in there and you can't leave on your own, you're admitted," I said reassuringly.

Within two hours, Kevin walked into a Long Island emergency room, telling them exactly what he told me, that he no longer wanted to live, and he wanted to take his own life. Kevin was admitted that very night, before midnight. I'd given him my number, and I had the hospital's number, which I used to speak to Kevin more than a handful of times. He called me, and the calls were encouraging. His estranged wife was there, visiting him. He detoxed from alcohol and drugs and was put on antidepressants, which allowed him to stabilize and begin the process of rebuilding his life.

I would never meet or hear from Leah again, but she was my conduit to Kevin. I do believe Kevin might have ended his life that night if he had not known where to find me. As Michael told me at the Jamaica Station, "Only in service do I get to keep what was given to me."

I now fully understood those words. I must give away what was freely given to me in order to keep what I have. No hoarding of the miracle. That night was only the beginning of my career in helping the many other Charlies out in the world. Still, I wasn't quite done with my own healing.

22. UNDERDOGS

I have living room furniture I never use and rooms in my house I never set foot in. I have nice clothes in my closet with the tags still on them, being saved for what? I have no idea. It's been so easy to accrue all the trappings of success good money can buy.

A friend of mine from grade school lives in extended stay hotels with his service dog. There is no clutter in his life; he's a true minimalist. He's up at 5 a.m. for walks along the beach and spends his time and money on experiences, not material assets. He lets nothing own him and has lived like this for the last fifteen years, give or take.

I'm sure I could quickly jump on the minimalist bandwagon—I certainly see the appeal. It's the pull between my two sides, the child who was deprived and so craves having things and the child who got used to not having, especially when the one thing he cared about (his records) were destroyed by his mother. It's a reminder our loved ones are what's important. Things are not. Things are a distraction. Yet that hasn't stopped me from filling my life with things.

Maybe this behavior is like my overeating, and it's a trait I share with shelter dogs. It's almost a truism that you can show love and provide consistent food to dogs who have been abused and starved, but some will still wolf down their food in seconds like they won't get another meal. I understand – I still feel like that sometimes.

It's the shelter dog in me that wants to protect other shelter dogs, canine and human. I still work on helping out guys down on their luck who need a lift up, offering the love and the grace I was given.

My greatest gift of love has so far been in rescuing Star. But in the year of having her, I've learned I still have more to give. That's when I come across Browny.

He's part Jack Russell Terrier and part Chihuahua. His owner dropped him off at a high-kill shelter in Brooklyn on Valentine's Day. Her boyfriend didn't like the dog, and as the owner's story went, Browny had bitten him. *Supposedly*. Except I don't buy that for a split second. No way in hell Browny "just" up and bit the guy. Sure, he may have bitten the boyfriend as a last resort, after the boyfriend kept kicking him, and Browny would be totally justified in doing so. The problem is now the shelter is getting ready to euthanize him, and the animal rescue in Brooklyn is making a last-ditch effort to get someone to adopt him. Shelter workers believed there was more to the story, but their hands were tied.

Jenn has been mulling her own ideas over the last couple of years of finding ways to help other shelter dogs like Star have a second chance. Her heart is so big, with so much capacity for caring for others. I show her the photo of Browny. We have Petey, Star, and Sadie. Can we really take on another?

"What do you think?" I ask.

Browny, like Sadie, isn't available for general adoption, so I have to work to get him.

#

The last significant thing to happen to me in Brooklyn was almost losing my life. Now, I'm saving a life. Star, my co-pilot, sits next to me as I drive, wearing my metaphorical Superman cape. We're in rescue mode.

It's a long haul from Lincoln to Brooklyn, but we have our car stocked with provisions. Having Star by my side, going to save Browny, is a world away from the nervous anticipation I felt when leaving to pick up Star. This time, there are no stipulations. There is no secrecy. And I have my best friend with me.

We get there, and Browny is not the smiling Buddha that Star always is. He's scared and confused and ready to bite anything coming within a five-foot radius of him. After I read the shelter notes and form my own conclusions, I believe the boyfriend definitely abused this little fella. Part of me would love to crush the boyfriend, but I try to stay beyond such thoughts and instead, I focus on sending love where it is needed.

But how do I handle a dog like this?

"Okay, Browny," I say in my most soothing voice. I don't get close. I stay with Star and talk with the shelter staff, sending Browny love from afar and giving him affirming words and letting him know everything is okay.

A staff member asks if I've brought a leash to get him to the car. That's that. They are ready for me to take him, with no ceremony, no cake and no bath before adoption like Star. Browny cooperates with the leash and follows Star and me to the car, and again, I'm so relieved to have Star with me on this rescue. I'm also relieved another dog isn't part of his trauma. I hope Star can help Browny. There's so much work ahead.

The moving car on the highway soothes Browny a little bit. That, and I was telling Star stories up in the front seat, occasionally calling back to Browny to ask how he's doing. Almost magically, as we drive, he starts to unwind. I can feel the tension in the car lessen, and it is clear Star does as well. She turns around to check on Browny as well giving curious, even caring glances. My smiling Buddha: She is a calming influence.

When we stop for gas, I pour him a big bowl of food and do the old trick of keeping my focus off him by talking to Star. Every now and then, I say his name to give him a vote of confidence.

"Alright, Browny?" I say, "All good?"

Browny launches into the food, stuffing himself, and then I see the calm wash over him. I leave him and Star in the car to pay for gas and get some more snacks for the ride. When I come back, he's taken ownership of the vehicle, standing up on my seat with his paws on the steering wheel. He's waiting for me to come back. It's a sea-change, within a matter of hours.

I have *never* seen a dog want a home this badly.

\#

"Honestly, why did they name him Browny?" Jenn asks when we get home and we're watching Browny scarf down another huge meal. I have to agree. He's mostly white, with two brown patches. One of his ears flaps while one stays straight. His feet point outward, and he runs at an angle. His torso is extra-long, but his legs are short, almost like a Dachshund's. But my God, he's got the cutest little face.

For a split second, he's uncertain around the other dogs. Both Star and Sadie are much bigger than he is. Petey is about the same size, though I'm not sure if that makes it better or worse. After watching the other dogs play for a bit, Browny tries to join them, but he doesn't quite know how to go about it. He's up in their faces, and they all turn their heads up as if he's the annoying kid brother. Browny is trying, though, and Jenn jokingly refers to him as "the intern."

"It's like he's still figuring out how to be a dog," she says, "and is learning from the higher-ups in the pack."

Once Browny is more settled with the pack, it's time for me to train him to eat as if he will be fed again in his life.

"Alright now, Browny, one kibble at a time," I say in my softest voice. "You have to eat slower, or you'll hurt your tummy."

By now, I'm a pro at this. I have all the special dog bowls with obstacles the dogs have to work around, which keeps them from turning completely into a Hoover vacuum. Browny does great, and eventually, I can get him to chew and swallow his food a mouthful at a time. Soon he eats a few bites and takes little breaks in between. It is only by trusting us, and the confidence boost from the other dogs, that helps him get here.

On the day he mellows, and the other dogs fully integrate him into the pack, Browny's transformation from a scared and angry dog to happy little pup is complete. Browny turns out to be the happiest dog I've ever known. He does have a serious side, and it comes out when he feels he has a job to do.

He patrols the house to make sure nothing is out of sorts and will bark at a stray box or pile of laundry until we come take care of it. He is especially watchful and does not slack off when it's time to alert the crew that the FedEx truck has arrived.

"See what I mean?" Jenn laughs, "The Intern."

After a while, though, Jenn says he's gotten so good, he needs a promotion.

"He is definitely a sales manager," she says, "since he's always looking for a way to outshine his siblings."

His fear is no longer part of his story. Fear has been replaced with confidence, and that's due as much to his pack sisters and brother as anything else. Dogs have a language all their own. I so wish humans could heal as quickly as dogs and be as resilient. Dogs are so good at being in the present. We humans overthink and project.

These dogs are work and Jenn and I don't even think about taking vacations anymore, but it's worth it.

I can't dwell on my own past and the complete lack of trust and confidence I had as a kid. In my own way though I can't completely give up on them or write them off. I have mourned the loss of the idea of my parents as my family. My family is Jenn, her daughter Lauryn and the dogs. But also, the people who helped me the most weren't blood.

It really was the pack who helped restore me.

23. THE FINAL DRINK

Sometime in the summer of 1997, I was at a street dance and wound up with a drink in my hand. Someone passed it to me, and there it was. I couldn't handle the temptation, and I drank it. I'd had one, so, I thought, I might as well have another. If there was one rule consistently true for my life: If I had *one*, I *needed* to have *more*.

After this, the regular drinking started. At ten at night, I'd get home from work and drink until I passed out. I did this every day. I ended up living in a house ten minutes away from the prison. The prison was a straight three-mile shot down a road. And smack in the middle of my commute was a liquor store. The only thing I looked forward to in those days was stopping at that liquor store, buying a bottle of booze, and drowning my hurt and sadness.

The only thing keeping me sane were my weekly visits with Rachel. However, soon, even those moments would come to an end because her mother got a teaching job in California, found a new husband in Nebraska and headed for the coast. After insisting she needed to live in Nebraska, she moved to California, taking my daughter and her new husband with her and leaving me away from my home state, my friends and any relatives.

With Rachel gone, nothing was stopping me from drinking to my heart's content. I rationalized that I wouldn't get so bad because I would not do drugs or pills. I absolutely would not. Soon after, I joined the Corrections Emergency Response Team, CERT, where I could lose myself in bursts of adrenaline and get my aggressions out in training drills. Just because I was part of CERT doesn't mean I was looking for a fight. My goal was to deescalate fights. One time, achieving my goal almost broke my arm.

My focus at work was acute, but my goal was not to see the inmates as an enemy—far from it. I knew that but for the grace of God I would be in the same place. That, and luck or desperation or fear is what kept me from serving time.

One of the ongoing dilemmas was many of the inmates showed the signs of crack cocaine use. We knew the drug was coming in but could never figure out how. The crack wasn't coming through any deliveries or any inside routes. We knew this because we cleared those avenues. The only place left was through the visiting room, via outside family and friends. Though the visitors were all searched well by the front entrance staff, clearly, some packages were being shoved inside orifices. What I realized was there was a vending machine in the waiting area, outside the visiting room, which was accessible to the visitors but not the inmates. However, those snacks could be brought into the visiting room, an otherwise secure area.

Master Control watched via CCTV as one grandmother came in to visit B, who was sentenced to multiple decades. She made a beeline for the snack machine, bought a bag of potato chips, and then went directly to the bathroom. Strange. That was the opposite of the usual order. I watched her emerge, and she was holding the bag of chips by the top, pinching it together as if holding it closed. I called my area lieutenant on the internal phone and told him what I saw and what I suspected.

The Master Control at the prison's hub focused the video cameras on the specific visit. I asked for additional staff. The lieutenant sent a woman who'd been all through the academy with me and whom I knew well. She always had the right approach to situations and could remain calm and non-confrontational. Unfortunately, even my resting face can seem intense, which is not my intention.

My colleague approached B's grandmother and asked to inspect her bag of chips, which the grandmother claimed had not been opened yet. The query was well within the rights of the department's contraband policy. B's grandmother didn't hesitate in handing over the bag, and suddenly, I thought I'd gotten it all wrong. Nice shot, but no cigar. Once the bag was handed over, it was obvious even on CCTV that it had been opened, and my fellow officer didn't have to pull it apart. She reached inside and pulled out a package that looked like a duct-taped cucumber.

I run to back up my fellow officer as she makes her way toward me, package in hand. She holds onto the package and shows it to me. I direct her to the lieutenant's office so the package can be examined, and as she starts to go there, B leaps up and grabs the officer from behind, choking her around the neck while she tries to break free of his hold. She continues to clutch the suspicious package.

She and I were still fresh out of the academy, and she was using her training to try to buck B off her back, but B was strong, 230 pounds, and had nothing to lose at that point. All I could think of was our training exercises. As soon as I got to them, I gave B a brachial stun on the side of his neck with my backhand, dazing him enough to rip his body off hers and flip him onto the concrete floor.

B's grandmother was detained, and we determined the cucumber of doom was in fact crack cocaine. The state police came to secure it to be used to charge the grandmother and B with felony drug charges.

I was the one to take B to the Control Unit. We were quiet for a while, and he was cooperative, though he seemed a little discombobulated after his throw down.

"I needed to take you down," I said, "because you went after an officer. That's the way it'll go down every single time."

He gave half a nod then said, "Hey, you were just doing your job, and I was just trying to get my product into the prison."

Word spread that the new correctional officer, me, was alright but was also not going to fuck around. My whole M.O. was I didn't like bullies of any sort, whether in a jumpsuit or a uniform. It was easy to see how tempting it was to take your aggressions out on someone you felt deserved it. Part of this mentality was toxic masculinity machismo—the kind that made me want to beat up Denise's ex, the kind that made me size up other guys to see if I could take them. I preferred the company of women because I hated that behavior in men, but that doesn't mean I wasn't guilty of it myself.

B got additional time. My hope was his additional time would cause him to reflect on and consider his life choices. Who would I be if I didn't believe in contrition and reformation? If I doubted forgiveness? My fellow officers celebrated my bust, but when I went home that night, I drank myself to sleep all the same.

On days off, I'd sometimes go out for drinks with some of the officers from work, and they started to notice my high tolerance/dependence on alcohol. Two of them had an intervention with me, ultimately offering to help by taking me to late-night AA meetings after shift and waiting outside for me. All the while we were hoping none of us would be noticed and have to explain why we were there. There was stigma attached to seeking help for an addiction while working in law enforcement. One member just lost his sister to brain cancer, and he said helping me gave him a sense of purpose. Though I was grateful, and did try, there were nights the desire on the way home from work was just too strong.

Because of a promotion, I ended up working in the Control Unit of the Nebraska State Penitentiary, though it felt more like a demotion. It was ugly, hazardous work. The Control Unit was a prison-within-a-prison, a specialized unit that not every prison or even every state had. It housed the worst inmates in the state and sometimes from neighboring states. Forget bullies, forget lost wayward souls. These guys were the real deal, not just guys who'd killed someone, but cold-blooded murderers. These were guys who wouldn't think twice before murdering again or trying to escape and, in doing so, killing anyone who came across their path. These inmates were the prisoners other state prisons couldn't handle. So other states would arrange a trade with us, offloading their worst offenders and taking several more non-violent inmates saving us both space and money. (In a nutshell, this was a 3 to 1 swap, three good inmates for one of their violent inmates.)

In early 1998, I had to take a court document to S, one of the Control Unit inmates. He needed to sign the document. I opened the hatch in his door, and he appeared to be asleep, so I called his name. He rolled over, yawned, and stretched. I told him about the document, and though he was subdued, he knew what the document was and was expecting it. As I passed him the pen for his signature, the act of grogginess flipped off like a switch—he was alert and agile as a cat. He grabbed my thumb and bent it back. To save my thumb, I stood on my tiptoes, trying to get a better angle—but this destabilized me. S recognized my instability and used my imbalance to yank my entire arm through the hatch, trying to break my arm with all his might.

We couldn't open the door—it was a mechanical door that slid horizontally—opening it would have crushed my arm. Though I tried to pull my arm back, he now had his leg propped against the door, pulling my body against the door and pulling my arm into his cell. Two other staff members alternately stuck their hands and arms into the hatch along with mine first to try to yank my arm out of the hatch, and then to relieve the pressure on my arm when the weight of the inmate's body was keeping my arm firmly in place, pressed against the steel hatch frame in an attempt to break it. What S didn't realize, and to my relief, all those years of weightlifting gave me extra muscle tissue around my bones which likely what saved my bones from breaking.

Unfortunately, the extra muscle *did not* save me from the pain.

The pain tore through my entire body, and I was drenched in sweat from the adrenaline. I could smell the old stink of fear on me, though I wasn't thinking about the fear. The staff decided to get tear gas canisters to throw through the hatch—nothing else was working, and there was only so much pressure my arm could take before my bones broke. The problem was the cannisters were handy but not the gas masks. The staff didn't know how long it would take to retrieve one. They put wet towels over my face and told me to close my eyes and hold my breath. They sent in one cannister, but my arm was still held. S must have been holding his breath as well.

"Come on," I thought, "just pass out already."

But S yanked harder. I didn't want to speak to tell my staff it wasn't working, so I shook my head under the towel. I wouldn't be able to hold my own breath much longer. They sent in another tear gas cannister. Finally, S released my arm, and since I'd been pulling my weight backward, I flew back and landed flat on the concrete.

Within minutes, I was off to the hospital to be treated for cuts and bruises. There was bruising and a lot of pain, but I was otherwise okay. My condition could have been so much worse. I'd tried to follow the strict operational procedures of the prison, but we are not machines. I slipped up by handing him the pen directly, and it cost me.

S was also sent to the prison hospital in restraints, and heavily guarded, and when he returned, he told me, "Yeah, it could have been a lot worse. If I really wanted to, I could have bitten your fingers off. I just wanted to have some fun."

There it was again, that lack of feeling that gave me chills, that embodied the worst of us. I refused to believe, though, that this was what most of humanity could be. If time in the prison taught me anything, it was that pure evil is a rare thing, and meaningful redemption out of humility is possible for most.

I can't say one single event, no matter how good (like the drug bust) or how bad (like almost having my arm broken) changed my life. Maybe it was the long string of nights that built up to an inner horror of my own. On April 5, 1998, I finished my shift at the Control Unit that housed the worst inmates in the state. I stopped off at my little liquor store, and this time, instead of booze, I bought a 40-ounce bottle of beer. Nothing fancy. Once home, I loosened the collar of my uniform shirt, guzzled down the bottle of beer, and set the empty bottle on the kitchen counter. I looked at the bottle.

"That's the last time I'm ever going to drink again," I said out loud. And I knew in my heart it was true. I knew it as an absolute certainty. Here's the thing: In AA, they tell you never to project about your future sobriety—that's why it's "one day at a time." That philosophy was alright, but what I thought was, "If I don't have the first drink, I won't have a second."

I could make that commitment to myself. It sounded better to me.

Over twenty-four years later, that philosophy continues to work for me – I have remained sober since.

#

The change in me was immediate. Within three months, I was promoted to a caseworker position within the department, where I would learn so much by listening to the men who did their best to fight the alcoholism and drug addiction on their own. Working as a caseworker got me thinking about how far I'd come. I ended up working at two other institutions and was asked to work at the newly opened youth facility in Omaha, earning letters of accommodation from the institution.

Eventually, I became the Nebraska State Penitentiary Safety Director. I had keys to every lock in the place. Such responsibility was a sign of complete trust.

Finally, with the energy of sobriety and goodwill in my life as well as plenty of money saved up, I bought a home of my own. The house was a modest home in need of significant renovation but only in my mind. I was, subconsciously, repeating what my parents had done with their own houses.

Yet another occurrence would change my life forever.

Much of the work I was doing on my own or with the help of co-workers from corrections. I bought an old pickup truck to haul the debris out of my home and took the debris to the landfill. Eventually, I became a regular at the landfill and installed wood boards in the pickup's bed to haul bigger loads. Making runs to the landfill became second nature, and as my home project was nearing completion, it occurred to me that other people might need this service.

I put a small ad in the paper, offering to haul loads to the landfill. Soon, a steady stream of people called in need of my services. It wasn't long before I was hauling junk to the landfill whenever I wasn't working at corrections. Within a few months, I was ready to retire my pickup truck and buy a dump truck with the help of a small loan. Unfortunately, it was nearly impossible to get a bank to lend to a new business, even with my stellar credit. I tried several banks and all of them refused the loan.

The business growth was dead in the water, it seemed. One loan officer said, "Stay in corrections and work on your career there. Forget about a business venture—it's too risky." Another banker said he could give me a loan on an RV or a boat but not on refuse equipment for a new business. So, I went back to the drawing board and did my research. There were lenders specifically for the refuse industry, but the interest rate was more than I could afford to pay.

This all was silly. I had the customers. I knew the demand and what the community needs were. Yet I couldn't expand.

I did the one thing I didn't want to do: I called my father to see if he would loan me the money for the dump truck. He seemed mildly impressed at the work I was doing, though I know he did not like me working in corrections, and this new opportunity would be a way to leave my job, so he agreed to the loan. Within a week, though, he backed out without giving a good reason. I shouldn't have been surprised, but now I was back to Square One. I worked so much on fixing up my modest home, putting sweat equity into it, that I could use the house as loan collateral. I found a bank that would give me a line of credit with my house as collateral, and so I secured my dump truck. Now I needed to make sure I got enough work to pay it off, or I'd really be in a world of hurt.

I picked up any odd job or cleanup I could get my hands on until I finally landed a contract with a large drywall company needing someone to pick up their scraps after the workers hung the drywall, mostly in commercial buildings and apartments. I had no idea this type of service was needed, but Lincoln was in the middle of a seemingly endless building boom. The amount of waste leftover from these projects was eye-opening. The installers would cut the drywall to fit a room, and the trimmings were unusable. Into room after room of these big jobs I went, collecting the drywall scraps and taking them down to my truck, then going back for the next load—all after a full day's work at corrections. At least with the dump truck, I didn't have to make as many trips back and forth between the site and the landfill.

The drywall company liked my process of collecting the piles at the end of the day because I was out of the way of their workers, and in the evenings, I would clear the space, leaving it broom-swept and ready for the tapers to come the next day. It was the most honest day's work I'd ever done, and it was an endless string of days. My savings account grew—but my back wasn't happy with my prosperity.

That's when I got the idea to call my friend Jim.

Jim and I worked corrections together and had a great bond. He was in his mid-forties with a diverse background including a degree in comparative religions, several published books, and a former career as a vice president of a Nebraska credit union. He'd helped me make sense of so many things through his approach to life, which involved spirituality and simplicity. I could ask him about anything, including my divorce and my lousy living conditions. After that, I'd listen to him talk about ancient Greece or Rome, sometimes for hours. Whether it was advice or history, he always made me feel better. He was sure to have advice about my predicament.

I asked Jim to give me a hand one day after work, so he could see firsthand the operational requirements and get a sense of the work. I made sure not to complain to him but instead to let him draw his own conclusions. He agreed on a random day to help me after we both got off work. It didn't matter the day to me, because staying ahead of the tapers job was a seven-day-a-week job. The key was to never keep them waiting on the cleanup, or their timeframe was thrown off.

I picked Jim up in the dump truck and drove to the site, which was a future assisted living home several stories high. There was enough drywall scrap to cover a football field. All of it needed to be picked up by hand and put in my dump truck. Once that was done, the entire area would be swept, and the drywall would be hauled to the landfill. Having Jim there was a godsend. We made small piles of the scraps and then carried them out in unison. We swept up, working almost until midnight with the help of the temporary construction lighting. It wasn't just Jim's help that was so valuable to me, it was his company bringing the biggest relief because the job got so lonely.

As soon as we were done for the night, Jim sat back and heaved a sigh. "I see a couple of problems here, Charlie, one of which is your back is going to give out, leaving you without a business. But then, if you hire people to do this type of work, it will get expensive with the type of workman's comp you'd need, plus wages, and then you might not end up with any profit. While you're committed to this contract, you aren't building a book of businesses. Those who live by the big contract die by the big contract."

What he said made sense. If the drywall company were to fire me, I'd be forced to go back to odds and ends before I could build up a book of business.

"Look," Jim said, "you need equipment, specifically, dumpsters you can drop off all around the doors and windows, so the drywall scraps can be thrown directly into the dumpsters. When that area is cleaned, then you can move the dumpster. Work out a deal with the drywallers to throw the scraps directly into the dumpster rather than on the floor."

It all sounded great. Except. "I just put all the money I had into this dump truck. I can't afford dumpsters," I explained.

"Charlie, have faith!" Jim exclaimed, "You must envision the equipment you need; you need to pray for answers…and tell all your friends your intentions."

I drove Jim home, profoundly grateful for his insights but befuddled over how I'd be able to rustle up some dumpsters and trucks to haul them. He was right, though; I had nothing to lose in telling all my friends about my intentions related to expanding my little business. And he was also right about something else: Praying certainly never hurt anyone.

Going to work on Jim's suggestions brought hope into my life. I envisioned my future equipment and my company. I could see my name on the dumpsters. I started believing my visions of the future would happen—all while carrying loads of drywall to the dump truck. This was going to happen—or was I a boy whistling in the dark just before his hopes were dashed? I didn't believe so.

It wasn't long before I received a call from a man, I had done some work for. Bill heard I wanted to build my business but needed equipment. He knew I lacked funds but not the work ethic. Word traveled to him in this city of 275,000. He told me about a man he met in central Nebraska who owned a refuse business that sold out to a national company, and with that money, he started an equipment business, manufacturing his own brand of dumpsters. Bill said, "I told him what I know about you and the jobs you have done for me, Charlie. I told him you are a hard worker, and you do what you say you're going to do. Who can ask for more than that? I have his number. He told me to give it to you so you could give him a call."

I was astounded. "Bill, thank you, really," I said appreciatively. "I have to ask—how did you hear about what I need?"

"Charlie, Lincoln is a city that's really just a big town. Word travels fast, and we have only one Charlie from New York. I'd like to see you succeed."

That meant a lot to me. I didn't waste time in calling Jeffrey Cooper at Cooper Equipment Sales. When we connected, he was even more excited than I was to learn about my refuse business in Lincoln. He'd built a refuse business from scratch in Omaha, and his business was eventually bought out by a national company.

"The buyout was life-changing money," Jeffrey said, and invited me to come down to his manufacturing plant to discuss operations and tell him more about my business.

He talked like a New Yorker, without the accent. He had a fast-paced, can-do attitude showing me his wall of trucks that he'd built for different companies.

"What are your goals for this project, Charlie?"

I cleared my throat a bit and said, "I have to say, I have no working capital, but I do pay my bills on time. I have so much work in Lincoln, but I simply don't have the trucks and dumpsters to provide my customers."

Jeffrey smiled and said, "Well, that's why you're here today—I can help you with your equipment needs. Here's what I can do: I can give you credit for the dump truck you have. There's a local farmer I can sell it to, and maybe I can get all your money back or convert your truck to a roll-off and start you with some dumpsters. When we sell your dump truck body, you can buy the roll-off equipment. I will give you credit, and you can pay it down as you make money."

How could he have so much faith in me? How could he firmly believe I would have enough money to pay him?

"In the trash business, Charlie, it will be hard to fail with your work ethic."

That faith in me and my potential gave me a high better than any drug or pill. The farmer did buy my dump truck box, and then

Jeffrey turned my truck into a roll-off, and the containers were made, painted red, and lettered with my company name and phone number on the side. "U-Betcha Hauling Services Incorporated," each one proudly displayed.

"U-Betcha" was a phrase I'd picked up in Nebraska. Everyone said it, and it reflected the helpfulness and "no problem" nature of the Midwest. Customers and friends alike loved the name. That was it – my vision – the vision telling everyone what I wanted to do. My praying over it all had worked.

Next up, my business was in the Yellow Pages with a quarter-page ad. After that, my business growth was incredible—I had a steady revenue stream and a growing book of customers. Rather than relying on a single customer, and I could take on all the work I wanted, while the hydraulic lift took the work literally off my back.

As business continued to grow, I was able to buy more refuse trucks, and then I expanded to offer residential and commercial refuse services. Oh, and the banks that wouldn't loan me money before? They now were only too happy to lend me money at good interest rates because I had the business and all the tax returns to prove I was good for the money. Within a couple of years, I became financially independent. The kid who'd been beaten, occasionally homeless, and had been a rock-bottom addict was now a successful businessman.

With all the success, I never forgot all the people who worked to get me there, and I wasn't going to close the door behind me. I made a point to hire employees who had been down on their luck. I hired those recently released from prison or those who were in recovery from alcohol and drug abuse. Like my own angel Michael, I went to bat for the underdogs and gave them a second chance. I told all new hires we were a sober company, and I was sober. No drug or alcohol use was permitted. Most understood, and those who were struggling with their own addictions appreciated the supportive workplace environment.

As word grew along with my company, I was approached by men who were literally living on the streets and wanted to get their lives together. One young man lived in a self-storage unit, and at night he ran a power cord under the roll-up door and plugged it into the neighboring gas station to operate his space heater, run his radio and charge his phone. Hearing this, I hired him so he would no longer need to live like that. While he worked with us, he got off methamphetamines and eventually started night school, where he went on to get his degree in accounting. Eventually, he left my company for a job with the state as an accountant in their child support division. He went on to spread love and share the gift with all those he would help.

During this time, I still worked for corrections, but some of my co-workers there helped me on a part-time basis, picking up extra work as needed. Somehow, I had the energy to continue this for years. At least, until a Tuesday in September in 2001.

24. STAR TO THE RESCUE

Jenn initially had the idea to form a rescue back in Christmas of 2013, when we'd just gotten Sadie, half a year after getting Star. It had been so difficult to cut through the red tape and gain access to these animals. Rescues, though, could take dogs out of shelters and place them in homes far easier than a regular citizen could. After Browny's difficulties, this plan solidified and took shape.

"We're already halfway there, Charlie," she said. "The timing is right. We know so many of the ins and outs of doing this."

For months, she worked diligently at getting all the paperwork filled out, sent in, and approved. The Star Project, Inc., a non-profit organization, went live in 2015. S.T.A.R.: Saving Those at Risk.

Jenn's goal is to set up foster care for animals deemed at risk or those with special needs either because of abuse or neglect. She organizes a network of foster homes vetted to provide loving care until the animals can find their forever homes. She thinks of everything and covers the cost of all care while an animal is with The Star Project foster homes, using donations and volunteers, and also setting up educational materials and courses on canine compassion and responsible pet ownership. The non-profit's other work will be to promote no-kill as a nationwide philosophy while also lobbying to end BSLs.

"Now we can help other dogs like Star, like Sadie and Browny," she says happily.

Since Star is the namesake and also the dog, we can take everywhere we go, she is really our "spokesdog" for the organization. As part of the Humane Society of the United States Lobby Day, held at the Marriott Hotel in Downtown Lincoln, I give a talk about The Star Project and how Star's story inspired her mission. Star, of course, is with me, and while I tell her story, she sits at my side. The official event photos later posted, show she is looking up and beaming while I tell her story. Whenever I get to the rescue part, she adjusts her posture, and her smile gets even bigger—No Joke.

The talk is a success, and they invite me to give the talk again the following year.

Thus, my speaking engagements begin on the regular. A journalism professor at the university even invites me to come speak to his class. He has two conditions, though: I must bring Star and she must be free to roam around the classroom to meet the students and not be confined to a leash. This professor is speaking Star's language because she already believes she's human, and a leash is for dogs. (She lived the first year of her life roaming the streets of New York with Lech. This taught her not to wander off.)

Before long, Star has her own Wikipedia page, under "Star, the dog." This is incredible. Magazine features and news items, both radio and TV, are regular. Our project grows so much that in 2016, Star is placed on the front page of the *Omaha World-Herald*, along with a full page-and-a-half article. And she has another feature in the *Lincoln Journal Star*. In both cases, the response is tremendously in favor of Star, supporting her story and supporting the mission of The Star Project.

Now she is a *bone*-ified celebrity, we decide to bring her to other charity causes. She participates in Alzheimer's awareness walks to raise money and fund research for those who suffer from this currently incurable disease. Once again, the media covers her presence at the walk. One journalist refers to Star as the unluckiest and luckiest dog in the world.

Every time I take Star somewhere, people line up to greet her, to touch her or hug her as if she's a saint or icon with the power to heal. I get it. She has healing powers. She's been healing me, but there's something about her presence that serves as a gift to anyone who is in contact with her. So many emails detail how her story has moved people and set them on a path of healing (and animal advocacy!) People ask me to mail clippings of her hair so they can touch her.

"Star, do you know what all these people think of you?" I ask her.

She cocks her head and looks up at me with her one eye and seems to ask, "What do you think I'm here for?"

So many people reach out to tell me what a wonderful thing I've done for this dog, but I always say she's the one who's saved me. Even when I think of the ancillary effects, for example, before Star, my view of the world ended at the boundary of the United States but since her story has grown, I now have friends from across the globe. I use the Bing translator to have conversations with people on every continent.

I even had the privilege of telling Star's story to a radio program in the UK!

#

Through The Star Project, Inc., we wind up taking in foster dogs, but quickly realize some of these dogs have already found their forever home with us.

The first of these is, ironically, Big Charlie, a muscular eighty-five-pound Pit Bull. Big Charlie, despite his massive size, is under the impression he is a lap dog. In fact, he is our very first rescue with The Star Project. Once again, he is in his eleventh hour when our organization steps in. We do everything we can to find him a suitable home, but we soon see he is meant to be with us. Probably what seals the deal is movie night when he sits next to me and puts his paw in my hand, with his head on my lap.

Big Charlie turns out to be one of the needier pups, constantly craving human interaction. But he's so full of wonder. On car rides, he sits in the seat and gazes out the window, his eyes wide like a toddler's. One day, when we treat the big dogs to ice cream cones, we discover Big Charlie's complete devotion to ice cream, which he can eat without spilling or splattering a single drop. Early on in our family, Jenn tucks him into bed, and soon, he won't settle into bed until one of us tucks him in.

He truly is our gentle giant.

Next, we find Kylee, another Pit Bull mix. Her story is harder—we see her in a few different posts on social media, and we can't shake the image of her face, even in our sleep. She's still young, but she spent much of her early life tied to a pole in Brooklyn. At some point, she suffered an accident, though the shelter isn't clear if it was the result of a car hitting her or a human who beat her. Whatever the case, the result was her pelvis was broken, and she did not receive medical treatment.

"It's likely," the shelter tells us, "She won't be able to walk correctly, and probably never be able to run. She'll probably have issues later in life."

One of the photos posted of her on the adoption site shows her curled up in a ball, and we can see the outline of her ribcage. She is skin and bone. Alright, Jenn and I agree. We'll take her. As we did with Big Charlie, we arrange for Kylee to be transported to Nebraska, rather than for us pick her up. When she gets to our house, we're absolutely shocked at how skinny she is. Her face, though, is so sweet and Jenn and I both feel the immediate instinct to protect her. As we work with her during her foster stay, getting her to gain weight and helping her get over her fear of objects being raised overhead (an indication of how she might have gotten the broken pelvis), Jenn and I have an increasing sense we cannot let Kylee down.

"So, we're keeping her?" Jenn says.

"Done," I say resolutely.

She's tentative, but with Star's mellowness, Sadie's mothering, Browny's need to be loved, and Big Charlie's gentleness, Kylee, ever an old soul, thrives in her quiet way. She's happy off in a corner just resting or watching the other dogs at play. She is a watcher, though, and at Christmas, when we put up lights, she stares and marvels, as if she's an astronaut seeing entire galaxies up close.

Again, I'm reminded of how precious life is. If this is how I spend the rest of my life, then my life will truly have significance.

25. FOREVER CHANGES

I was going into work at the Nebraska State Penitentiary on Tuesday, September 11, 2001. My duty that morning was to count the narcotics and surgical knives at the prison hospital. Me, the recovering addict was now counting all the pills, liquid morphine and other powerful pain relievers. Since my final break with drugs and alcohol, I didn't take so much as an aspirin anymore—and it was a feat (and a job) I couldn't have done without my spiritual awakening at the monastery. (The short relapse I had on alcohol *firmly convinced* me that alcohol is also a drug.) I had a new set of laws to live by, both ethical and moral, and if I obeyed those laws, criminal law was something I'd never break.

At the front door of the hospital, under lock, I waited for Officer Wayman to admit me. Officer Wayman was a former United States Marine and was one of the most respectful and considerate people I have ever known. Beyond that, he was a class act.

Wayman said, "Mr. Cifarelli, good morning, Sir, are you ready to go to war?"

"What?" I said, "What are you talking about?"

I thought something bad was happening in the prison.

"Haven't you heard?" he asked.

"Heard what?"

14th & 2nd

"The Twin Towers and the Pentagon have been hit by terrorists."

Prisons back then kept cell phones and radios out of staff hands, because they were considered contraband. Our sole focus was to pay attention to inmates and not get distracted by outside events. Wayman, while making his rounds in the prison hospital, saw news of the attack on one of the prisoner's TV's. I had Officer Wayman lock the doors back up. The pill count would have to wait. I couldn't leave the institution, but I had to figure out where a TV might be. Training specialist Higgins had one in his training room. I ran to that part of the institution and flew into Higgins' office.

"Have you heard what the hell is going on?" I said, panting.

He gave me a blank stare.

"Dan, we need to turn the TV on," I implored.

Higgins wheeled it out of the closet, on its tall stand—the kind schools used to have. Then, he flipped it on. There were the two towers, both on fire. Neither of us spoke. How was this happening? In New York? Those towers?

It was maybe a few minutes before the first tower went down. We both gasped. The people who were trapped inside, the first responders who were inside—we knew instantly the loss of life we were seeing in real time.

The second tower fell.

The city I loved so much, the city that was such a part of my life, the city that would never leave me, now seemed to break apart before my eyes. There were no words. The news replayed the scene over and over again, also showing clips of the disasters of United Flight 93 in the Pennsylvania field, and the disaster at the Pentagon.

Those people in the Twin Towers and on the planes had no idea it would be their last day on earth. Those people thought they were going to a safe office sitting on a safe flight, because you're far safer in a plane than a car, that's what we're always told.

How many of those people did not like their jobs? All their plans, their hopes, everything they wanted to do with their lives, all of that was incinerated. I knew my life was never going to be the same, along with the rest of the world. No one is guaranteed anything, not even the next day. I was one of 500 employees in the Nebraska State Penitentiary, operating on three shifts. I answered to the associate warden, who answered only to the warden. There was talk of a bright future ahead for me in corrections, which, at one point, seemed like a natural path. But now I had my business, one I built, one I loved. In my business, I wasn't around death and regret and violence and atonement for violence.

I decided if I woke up the next day safe and whole, I was going to make a change.

That next day, the sun did come up, and I was safe and whole. I beelined into the associate warden's office.

"Come on in, Charles. What's going on today?" said the associate warden.

"Mr. Peart, I'll get to the point," I said, quickly.

"You always do, Charles."

"I will be resigning from the department."

"Why?"

"What happened yesterday woke me up," I said as I explained to him about my epiphany. I said, "I have decided that although I respect my job here, it is not what I want to do for the rest of my life. Time moves quickly, and I want to have an opportunity to do the things only business can provide. I'm turning in my two weeks' notice to you."

This was not the conversation he expected.

"Charles," he said, leaning back in his chair, "let me make some sense to you. You have worked very hard to be in the position you are in, and it would be a shame to throw all that away." He paused, looked at me and said, "Look, you don't know how the economy will do after these terrorist attacks, but you do know the job security you have here. It's already fall—the Nebraska winter will soon be approaching. You don't want to count on a business going into winter. I urge you not to make this hasty decision."

While my decision was abrupt, it was not made in haste. All afternoon and night, I prayed and reflected, and from there I knew deep in my gut leaving corrections was something I needed to do and something I was ready to do.

"Mr. Peart," I said, "although I made up my mind yesterday, I know in my heart I'm done here. If I'm not making a good decision, I can live with it. I trust my business and my work ethic will carry me forward. The department of corrections has given me a tremendous amount of knowledge I hope to use for the rest of my life."

I took a breath and awaited his response.

"Your mind is made up?"

"It sure is, sir."

Mr. Peart nodded and said, "I respect your decision. If you need anything from the department, let me know."

I thanked him and walked back to my duties, counting the sharps and pills and the days left before I was free from the department. I never looked back. I never was afraid. Graymoor had given me faith and trust, as well as security and peace.

As for Mr. Peart's concern, he needn't have worried. The housing boom in Lincoln was nonstop, and soon, I was picking up trash from sunrise to sunset, seven days a week, 363 days a year. Thanksgiving and Christmas were my only two days off.

#

U-Betcha was everywhere. We handled trash, demolition, fire damage, water damage, restoration, concrete removal—if customers had debris, we had trucks to haul it.

With the abundance of work, I didn't know how to say no or slow down, but I also wasn't interested in slowing. There was always more I could do, even though I had no idea how to run a company of that size and could only pause for a few seconds with the reflection that I should have been careful what I wished for. Just the number of phone calls I received and had to make to take orders and coordinate projects each day was staggering. All the responsibility was on my shoulders. This wasn't a gentle line of work. If a stop was missed, and especially if that home belonged to a CEO of some large corporation, they would light up my phone with enough choice words to make you think their stock just went down 20%. (People get quite angry when their trash isn't picked up, especially if the weather is hot or if it's after a weekend.)

The trucks experienced wear and tear, and if they broke down and needed repairs, a person might think I had a fleet of Ferraris when I got the repair bill. Plus, there were the endless compliance and regulatory laws for the trucking industry. I always had to stay up on making sure we were complying.

Certain patterns are hard to escape, and moderation, for me, is a foreign concept. But hey, working and making money were an addiction I could live with. Still, I was working a hundred hours a week. I was a human "doing" and not a human "being," with no desire to recognize that in myself.

Of course, there were perks: Though I was much better at managing my money, I figured, why not splurge? Retail establishments represented the giant candy store I had been deprived of as a kid.

I thought my parents would embrace my newfound success. I thought they would be relieved I'd made something of my life and find a new way to connect with me.

Such an embrace and reconciliation never happened.

If anything, the more my life improved, the more estranged my parents became. Also—my parents just got stranger.

"We're moving to Florida," my father said on a rare call. "We're selling the house."

"What are you doing with all your stuff? Are you taking it with you? Are you getting rid of it?" I wondered if there were any remnants of my childhood I might pick through when they packed up. "Do you need help?"

"We're putting the furniture in storage. It's a climate-controlled facility, so the antiques will be fine."

"Okay. What about—are there any photos maybe I could go through?" I asked.

"Oh, your mother took care of that," my father said, coolly.

My mother had hoarded all of the family photos, though for what, I'm not sure. There was no easy access to them at any point in my life.

"She took them out back to the barbecue pit and had a burning session."

"Of the photos?" I asked in disbelief.

"Yes."

"All of them?"
"Yes, Charles."

Could there really be almost nothing left of my childhood? There were no childhood drawings and I had only a couple of photos I managed to get my hands on years earlier. It was as if my past was erased. It certainly all felt like two lifetimes ago.

I knew in my heart they weren't my family, not really. Blood, yes, but that doesn't make a family. That didn't stop me from trying, for whatever reason. Was I trying to prove I was worthy of love, perhaps? Even though I didn't expect love from them, and I wasn't going to let their warped personalities define me, I couldn't shake trying to reach out like a son would.

Though they sold their house, they wound up renting another house on Long Island so they could come up from Florida to do…whatever it was they felt they needed to do on Long Island. I decided to drive out from Nebraska to see them. I left Lincoln at 3 a.m. in my brand-new black Cadillac Escalade, which had the new body style that had just come out, and I drove straight through, arriving at my parents' rental late in the evening.

My parents were surprisingly polite to me, though not effusive with their compliments. My mom made a passing comment that I looked good, at least. My father eyed my Rolex but said nothing about my car despite him being an avowed lover of all things Cadillac. My mom offered me a glass of water and I sat on the couch while they each took to their chairs, and we chatted about generalities like how other relatives were doing, or what they were up to. We also talked a little bit about my business.

I was reaching a point where I was getting offers for a buyout—just as my truck builder, Jeffrey, had said would happen. Though I didn't need the money, I would be hitting the jackpot and I could take some time off, finally. At some point while chatting, I dozed off, while sitting on the couch. I woke up to my mother, stooped over me and nudging my knee with her hand.

"Charles? Charles, wake up. I found you a hotel to stay at, it's just a few miles away."

"A hotel?" My mind was in a sleep fog, so it took a moment to process my mother wasn't letting me stay with them even though they had plenty of space in their rented house. Even after I had driven twenty-two hours to see them and even though there was less than a zero risk of me being under the influence and causing some trouble, I was now an outsider in my mother's house.

I was a casual acquaintance whose presence made her nervous.

The next day, I went over, and the two of them were just as toxic and horrifying to each other as they always had been, and I knew I didn't need that in my life. I told them I had other things to do. I went shopping, bought some clothes and hit the road back home to Nebraska.

#

Everyone in Lincoln knew me as "Charlie from New York." I was the guy who was all-work. I was the one-man city-who-never-slept. It was inevitable then, that if one of my acquaintances came upon another East Coaster, they would steer them in my direction. That's what happened in December of 2005 when I met Jenn from New Jersey. A friend of mine in the car business hired Jenn to work part-time in his office, and we were the only two people he knew from the East Coast, and he thought we would be a good match. He asked me to come by the office, so I did. I greeted Jenn and she was polite without being overly friendly. She did agree to a date, though.

While on the date, Jenn asked the kind of questions that weren't prying but were meant to dig deeper.

I tried to be vague. "Oh, I have had a few rough years," I said.

"Come on," she responded, "everyone has a few rough years,"

She got real with me. She knew I had a story, but she let me tell it. Once I did, she told me hers. One date became many more. I realized how there was a certain sensibility from home I had been missing. More than that, Jenn was brilliant. Her mind was so sharp, but she never used her intellect to talk over people or at them. She engaged deeply in conversation and had so much to offer, which brought out new ideas and reflections in me.

I was forty years old. She was twenty-six and beautiful. I might have tried to impress her, but right away, I could see she didn't think much of making shows. She reminded me of my ninth-grade health teacher, who once told me, "Try to be the real you and not the man of 1,000 faces." That advice rang like a bell in my head while I was talking with Jenn.

Jenn wasn't an extrovert. She was reserved, and raising her daughter, who was just four years old. She'd come through a series of dead-end jobs.

"Quit your job and focus on what you would like to do," I blurted out.

I wasn't trying to control her or patronize her or to act like the wise older guy who knew everything. Whenever I was with her, I couldn't do anything but keep it 100% real, about whatever was on my mind. I understood what she was doing, juggling, because it was in the best interest for her daughter.

"What would you like to do?" I asked her.

"I like the different aspects of business," she said, "and I like helping people."

She'd worked in human resources, and so we had long conversations during our nightly walks together. She picked my brain about starting a business, and then she started her own business in recruiting and found her niche. In the meantime, we found a life together, and I found happiness in helping to raise her daughter.

Jenn's presence in my life became my grounding influence. It was like dropping into technicolor Oz after living in sepia tones. She wasn't clingy or needy. She gave me the space to do what I needed, but she had a knack for knowing what I needed from her. In return, I gave her everything I could, in support and love, and I found myself nearly the best version of myself, at least as far as I understood myself to be at the time.

I still had a few more self-discoveries to make.

#

In 2007, I finally did sell U-Betcha to another company, made life-changing money, and now had all the freedom in the world. I signed a non-compete business contract for only three years, and then I had nothing but time on my hands.

I wouldn't be idle. I used the time to find ways to give back. In 2008, I got word that FDNY was leading an event in Little Sioux, Iowa, to clean up the site and erect a chapel in memory of the four boy scouts who were killed by a tornado. After 9/11, these firefighter heroes went around the country helping communities torn by tragic events. I showed up and did whatever I could do to help. Everything I did was motivated by the monks at Graymoor, especially Father Owen and Father Bernie. I remembered the love I found there. I shared that love by connecting and helping others after spending so much time focused on work. For three years, I nourished my soul.

#

Then, in 2010, my three years of non-compete ran out, and I was ready the day of with garbage trucks purchased and painted and lettered. The company that bought my business quickly found out and contacted me to offer me a position with them. U-Betcha now had another name and had grown considerably, running into a neighboring state.

"The potential is unlimited," they told me, "Plus, you'll have all the perks, along with an excellent compensation package."

"No way," Jenn said. "You can build a more significant business this time around. The people love you, and you're the right guy. Nebraskans—they love calling the New York guy to haul their trash. They may not be open to you handling their retirement accounts, but trash, yes. Go back to work for yourself; you've had a three-year rest. You're ready for round two."

"Yeah, but—" I appreciated everything she said, but I'd lost my confidence. I was like a prize fighter re-entering the ring after years away from the circuit. The purchasing company put enough doubt in me that I was starting to question my decision. What if I didn't do well? What if I blew all the money building the business back up and then it failed?

Jenn said, "What can I tell you, Charlie, you're going to make your own decisions."

I did. I picked the low-hanging fruit.

"It makes sense," I said, "I don't have to get something up and running. It's got its advantages." The job offered a safe salary with no investment on my end. The plan was failsafe and they purchased the garbage trucks I had just bought to go back into business allowing me to return that money to my accounts.

Jenn shrugged. She was right; though going to work for that big company made sense, ultimately, there were consequences, and I would pay another price for making a wrong decision. After working for myself so long, I wasn't happy always having to go by someone else's policy. It wasn't a bad experience, but I grew restless.

We forged ahead, though, and found joy and contentment in raising Jenn's daughter. Our common passion was animals, and we had an opportunity to get a dog rescued from a puppy mill. Before Star, there was Pete, a Jack Russell Terrier, and he turned out to be one in every sense of the word. He was smart, curious, active, a little bossy. There were some behavioral problems, though, as is the case with many dogs who come from puppy mills. There was plenty of activity for him in our home, with regular walks but also with all the squirrels hanging out in the trees in our yard. He spent hours barking at them.

During this period, I went to visit my Aunt Jenny, the wife of my father's brother, Joey, after she had surgery. She loved to tell stories and was one of the few who didn't hold to the adage, "all personal experience is a secret from the world," the way the rest of my family had.

She had an easy way in the comfort of her own kitchen with a pot of the strongest coffee I've ever experienced. After two cups, she was on a roll, and the two of us sat there, chatting about the family, about my uncle who died by suicide after hanging himself in the garage soon after he got a terminal cancer diagnosis. She was telling all the family stories.

"That bastard had a girlfriend on the side," she said angrily, "while I was busy trying to keep your cousin alive."

My cousin was born with a rare blood disorder and had hemophilia. Her condition was terminal her entire short life.

"Wow. I'm sorry, Aunt Jenny," I said sadly.

She took a sip of her fourth cup of coffee and then blurted out, "Charlie doesn't think you're his son!"

I nearly choked on my coffee and said, "What? Aunt Jenny, what are you saying?"

"Your mother had a lot of boyfriends before she met your father, and for him, that series of boyfriends was a continued threat. He assumed she was still seeing other men, especially when he was working long hours."

"You knew he was in prison?"

"Of course," she said, and then added, "and more than once."

"I didn't find out until I got my job in corrections!"

Aunt Jenny took another chug of her loaded up coffee. It was like a haymaker. I wondered if the coffee was coffee or if it was truth serum. It dawned on me that my aunt wasn't disputing the truth of this information.

"Wait, you don't think that do you, Aunt Jenny?" I asked incredulously.

She shrugged.

"Oh, come on. Look at me! I have his hairline! His nose!" I said in protest. I looked more like him now that I was older than I did when I was a kid.

"It didn't help you had that blonde hair when you were a boy."

I couldn't believe she believed this nonsense. Just as quickly as the floodgates opened, I could sense she worried she said too much, and she immediately changed the subject. All these years, she believed I wasn't my father's son, which meant she believed my mother had been unfaithful (when, of course, my father was most likely never faithful to my mother during their entire marriage).

It probably would not have mattered if I had turned into the spitting image of him in adulthood because the damage was already done. Had there ever been a moment when he loved me as his child? I couldn't imagine it. No wonder he had treated Christian and me as if we were from two different families. The closest I had felt to him was when he drove me to Graymoor. Maybe he thought that was the last time he would ever see me and allowed himself the most fleeting guilt and regret in his goodbye.

What do I even do with this information now, after all these years? Do I have sympathy for my father and his insecurities? Did he tell himself I wasn't his son, so he had an excuse to hate me?

I didn't say anything about this to Jenn when I got home, mostly because it was so ridiculous, but also, I didn't know what to do with this information.

26. HEAL

I've found my true partner in Jenn. Apart from being incredible at so many things, we share the love for animals, but also, she understands the real me like nobody else. The way Star doesn't demand attention—she recognized that in me as well. She understands sometimes I need to go off and do my thing, rescue my dogs, obsess over a project, and if I get too wound up, she gives me my space. It helps that Jenn is tremendously independent.

However, she will call me out when calling out is necessary.

Despite having Star, the foundation, all these dogs, and a great life, something in my life feels unsettled. There is a shadow inside me, buried deep. Maybe if we move back to New York, I suggest.

I say to Jenn, "I don't know, I love Nebraska, and this has been such a good home, but don't you feel ready for a change? Like maybe we need to get back to the East Coast?"

Jenn and I discuss this nightly. Once we finally decide that, okay, we'll look for a place in eastern Pennsylvania, because of the land and zoning related to the dogs. I throw myself into another house search. The only prerequisite I have in mind is I want a place in the woods with a long driveway and many cleared acres for the dogs to run. We end up finding a big colonial up a long driveway on a hill. It's a perfect spot to hide away from the world, but I feel like at least I'm close enough to Manhattan to drive in whenever I need my big city fix.

We say goodbye to our life in Nebraska, and I walk away from the job making me unhappy (that Jenn had warned me about taking because she knows me well). We move into our perfect new house, and nothing changes. My weight balloons to the highest it's ever been because all I want to do all day is eat junk food. I'm surly, I'm short-tempered, and without the stress of work to blame, I turn all my complaints to my family.

"Look, you need to figure out what's going on," Jenn warns me. "This house cannot be just another impulse buy you use for a temporary serotonin rush, because that will not last. It's time you get to the root of what is going on."

The root. Jenn is a person of few words, but when she does say something, it has meaning. I hear a lot in her short speech. The next few days are spent in a foul mood, and I start praying. I look at my dogs, living their lives in the present.

My past is not something I talk about, not really. In fact, I've spent so much time trying to live in the present that my past was something I'd largely blocked out. I couldn't figure out why my life didn't feel right, why, despite Star, Jenn, our kids and all the dogs and the rescue I couldn't seem to rescue myself. I casually mention to people I've been to hell and back, but I don't describe that hell. I don't talk about the years of abuse I had at home—it's all pushed down, out of sight, nearly out of mind, the old world of secrets at work.

I start reading a bunch of books. I read self-help books but also memoirs. I see people going to the edge and coming back from despair. In each book, the writer is confronting the darkest and ugliest parts of their histories. It's something I've never done. Perhaps that's why I spent all those years trying to win my parents' approval—I've glossed over the pain, ignoring it as much as possible. My brother dealt with it head-on early and got himself away from them. I was emotionally unable to do what he did. Instead, ignoring the pain was my way of fixing it.

Alright, then, I'm going to confront it once and for all, the whole thing. The Charlie everyone in my adult life knows is very different from the several Charlies I have been.

I give myself all the time I need. I descend into my basement as if I'm a caveman from the Paleolithic era, who descended underground to go through the rituals of death before they can be reborn into men. I'm not seeking some kind of hyper-masculine rebirth, here. No. I want to be reborn as a human. Not a calculator. Not a dealmaker. I don't want to be someone who lives split between an urgency to make money and an urgency to save dogs. I realize, too, that all the rescuing has been, in its own way, a means of filling that void. Rescuing dogs wasn't going to fulfill me until I stared into my internal void and wrestled it closed once and for all.

I have no idea what I'm doing. I use an old computer and hack away, no idea how to make a story. I just pour every one of my thoughts out, all of them as they come, stream-of-conscious, onto the pages. I pound out my feelings, my thoughts, my memories, my shames, my weaknesses, and, of course, the many horrors.

I barely eat. I have a pitcher of water, and the only time I leave is to replenish small amounts of food and some drink. I sleep on the couch down in the basement—this is true isolation. Occasionally, a dog wanders down, or Jenn walks down and peeks her head in to make sure I haven't turned into a full-blown Howard Hughes, but she doesn't interfere.

#

There it is a pile of pages that is my life. I've lived it, but it is hard to believe this all was mine. There have been so many different parts, each one so separate from the others.

What is left to do? I have to forgive myself for all of it. I will not carry this away in a hurt locker in my soul.

Besides, I'm exhausted.

And also—I make peace with my parents. It's not about reconciliation, because that's not what they deserve from me either. But I acknowledge what I need to acknowledge in order to let go of the hurt.

I don't buy the old saying, "Well, your parents did the best they could." No. No way. My parents did whatever they felt like doing. I may have fared far better if they had just dropped me in a basket on some random stoop at birth. My hands are a constant reminder of the abuse received, especially on cold, damp days. The constant pain that is now in my hands every time I hold a screwdriver or grip something it reminds of exactly where my father knocked them together. My pack includes all the people I have helped and can continue to help who are suffering from addiction or abuse.

I realize my parents also suffered and perpetuated the cycle of suffering onto me. My goal has been to stop the cycle and replace it all with compassion, tolerance, and understanding.

It's taken all these years, after the pursuit of money, the pursuit of things, gold watches, countless cars, to see none of those things filled the void in me. None of it filled that hole. I tried to put everything in it, but that hole was bottomless without another spiritual intervention.

What I hope is reflected in these pages is the idea that we need to take care of one another. We all need to reach out and recognize we're sharing this planet, and it's not as big as we think it is. In these pages are all the people who took care of me, so I was able to take care of others, sure, but especially Star.

Being transactional had become another addiction. Working was another addiction. It was a shadow life, as much as being addicted to drugs had me living a shadow life. It was only when I put my pain out there, acknowledging it in one go, that I could see the damage done. Looking back over the last twenty-five years since I set foot in the monastery, I'm able to say with complete certainty that I'm a miracle. People like me generally do not survive, and if they do, they often wind up in prisons due to one different choice among an assortment of bad options. I was given grace by God so I may do better things. This faith helped me survive. And it opened me up to allowing love to come into my life, real and meaningful love.

After 25 years and an awakening, I contact Graymoor to thank them again for all they gave me. I speak with their communications director, Cynthia.

"Charles, would you like to come up to tell our men here about your story?" Cynthia looked up the stories of me online and shared with the brothers of Graymoor the news of Star and the miracle of her rescue. "It was your rescue, as well," Cynthia tells me.

Sadly, Father Owen, the man who opened me up to great love, passed away in 2012, the same year Star was shot and miraculously survived.

Star and I drive up to the mountain of hope, and the brothers arrange for me to meet with the men there and also to have lunch with the board of directors and tell my story to them as well. I tell them the CliffsNotes version of the whole story, and how much it means to come full circle twenty-five years after my father dropped me off for my spiritual awakening.

I've come so far—forgiving and reconciling with my feelings about my father. My heart is full. After this, I'm going to reach out and talk to my father, see what might possibly be reconciled between us now that I'm fifty-three.

Star and I go home, and a few days later, I get a text from my mother: "Charles, call me when you get a chance."

When I call, she answers with a casual tone, saying, "Hello, Charles, I wanted to let you know that your father unexpectedly died in the hospital early this morning."

A pause.

"How?!?" I ask, and then say, "From what?!?"

"I don't know yet," she replies, "but I'm asking for an investigation into it."

"He's dead? So—what is next?" I ask, in disbelief.

"Oh, nothing," my mother says coolly, "There's not going to be a service or obituary or anything like that."

No service? Is that it? I think to myself.

"I just wanted you to know. Goodbye, Charles," my mother says as she hangs up the phone.

I check my phone. The whole call has lasted under a minute. A few days after my swelling of magnanimity for my father at

Graymoor, my mother calls to say he's dead, and that's that. As if she was telling me the weather. Was it cruelty on my mother's part? A complete lack of emotion? Had she wreaked as much havoc on him as he did on her?

It felt like an ending, but not the one I'd prepped myself for. What I have, though, is my last meaningful interaction with my father, which took place in 1999.

I'd come to Long Island from Nebraska to see my old friends and to see my old house in Merrick. I dropped in for a very brief visit. When it was time for me to leave, my father walked outside to talk with me—a remarkable occurrence in itself. The gulf between us physically was immense—I was in the best physical shape of my life, while his hair had gone completely white. He now looked frail and fragile. I was polite and reserved with my guard up, but it seemed like my duty to have even a fragment of a relationship with my parents back then.

My father looked at me and complexion softened. "I'm sorry, Charles, for hitting you when you were growing up. I'm really sorry." He was choked up as he spoke, but as soon as he finished, he quickly composed himself.

I listened to him in silence. What do I say to this? What did he want, absolution? I wasn't going to roll over and let him off for the horrors he'd put me through. I was tempted to say, "I'm glad you feel this way, you deserve to suffer as you made me suffer."

Was I happy he was saying this? Did it matter at this point? What could I possibly say in return?

"Okay," I said. "Goodbye, Dad."

I left it at that. It was all I was capable of giving to the man who would forever be a mystery to me.

EPILOGUE

I know Star can't live forever. It doesn't occur to me, though, eight years after getting her, that her being gone from my life could imminently happen. But that's the reminder I get one Saturday morning when I see she's having trouble. She is spotting a lot with urine. I think maybe it's a simple urinary tract infection, but then I see her hind leg has swollen.

I start to feel around with my fingers and find a small mass in her belly area. She has no interest in eating or drinking and she can barely walk. These symptoms come on almost overnight.

In a panic I rush her to an emergency vet who will see Star on short notice, all while our nation is in the middle of a pandemic, which complicates life further.

I keep thinking, "Not my Star, not now. Not yet. I'm not ready."

I cry like a naïve child at the thought of her not making it the week or the month. I cry and I pray, and I allow myself to remain in denial. Despite everything I've been through, it's the scare of my life.

The vet targets her bladder and does an ultrasound. He does not find any masses or stones but concludes there's a mass outside her stomach. I take her on Monday to her normal vet, and she aspirates the mass. I wait the whole week, not knowing the prognosis—they use the "C" word regularly. On Thursday, I get the news it isn't cancer—it's an inflammatory response to something else going on in her body. Her lymph node is *that* swollen.

I take her to Philadelphia, where there are specialists who look her over, but can't find out what the real problem is. There's the thickened bladder, which isn't good. They can't decide whether or not to remove the mass from her tummy.

"Charlie," Star's vet tells me, "We're at eight-plus years since she was shot in the head. Every day is a miracle."

Her words shake me to my core. The doctors are preparing me, and I'm not even thinking about saying goodbye.

Worried I have to make our final memories together, once Star is on an anti-inflammatory and is treated for a UTI, I decide I want to take her back to New York City for perhaps one final time. I carry her to my car and lay her in the back seat and drive her to the East Village. I find a parking spot a few feet away from the Kentucky Fried Chicken at 14th & 2nd where Star used to hang out with Lech.

Almost immediately, a guy comes up to me and says, "Hey, that's Star! I follow her on Facebook!" The neighborhood is tight and follows all the news, and Star is a big deal there. I still can't believe it, though. They take photos of her, with her, all of us in masks, all of us finding new ways to communicate and be together in these crazy times.

Star lights up immediately and even starts walking. She recognizes her old haunts, and something within her comes alive here. After moving around for ten minutes, I buy Star some food and water and she eats and drinks as if she's back to her old self. We then drive down to Freedom Tower to pay our respects to the fallen, honoring the day marking a pivotal change for the nation and for my life.

My city girl has a highly emotional day – she is happy on the one hand, yet deeply reflective and subdued on the other.

The next day, she's not cured by any means, but she gets around the house, eating and drinking and being closer to her usual self. Within a couple of days, her edema has almost disappeared. Are you kidding me? She really is a miracle dog.

14ᵗʰ & 2ⁿᵈ

I don't know how long this miracle will last, but right now, every day is precious. Like Star, I try to live in the moment, not worrying about present or past. In fact, in the past year or so, I've gotten my weight under control because food no longer controls my life. All of Star's calm has passed onto me. Releasing my hurt has allowed me to let go of my final addiction. I no longer have to eat my feelings. At a recent appointment, my doctor told me he was quite pleased with my progress. He said I was as fit as a man in his twenties. My twenties: A decade so horrible for me I buried large stretches of my experience. Here's to another go-around.

Some days it's still tough, but I can look in the mirror. I can look in my own eyes, pause, and say, "I know that guy. He's a good guy, he's alright. He's had his problems, but he's alright."

I have to slow down to know who that guy is because I can go so quickly in this life and not really take the time to identify who I am. I'm not sure people truly know how much Star has helped me. She saved me. She is constantly saving me from myself. Star isn't needy, but she's content, and her contentment makes me be content. It makes me be okay. Through my time with Star, I finally find myself able let go of all the "stuff" I always felt like I needed. "Things" are no longer important. Life isn't about transactions.

More than anything, it occurred to me one day that Star gave me back my childhood. The horrible one I had was another lifetime. It's not buried—it's disconnected. It happened to me, but it's not who I am. For the first time, because of Star, I was acting like a silly kid and his dog. The carefree life Ringo and I should have had: A life of sunning ourselves in the backyard, or roaming the neighborhood, or having friends over for barbecues, was stolen away by abuse and insanity, but because of Star, I learned the absolute freeing joy of play. The total delight of not just focusing on the moment but being fully in the present and finding the pleasure of the moment.

I take her for a drive to pick up some parts for a shelving unit I want to put in the basement, and she sits in her usual spot, perched in her dog bed on the back seat, watching out the windows. I look back at her, and there's her signature smile, ear-to-ear. She turns her smile on to me, the dazzling light of it. That's what I see—her smile, not her wounds. It is then I realize I've been smiling just as widely as she has.

"We're okay right now, Star," I say reassuringly.

One day at a time.

It's never felt truer in my life.

End Note

There are no coincidences. The fact that Star miraculously and inexplicably survived her shooting at 14th & 2nd is no accident. Nor is the fact that I later rescued her. 14th & 2nd is much more than a Manhattan intersection – it is a crossroads in my life more than once. When I drove taxi, I used to love taking fares to 14th & 2nd because it was where I could buy pills at the open drug market located there and feed an addiction that would propel me to the gates of Graymoor and put me on the road to redemption – a road that started and, in many ways, ended at 14th & 2nd.

ABOUT THE AUTHOR

Charlie Cifarelli is businessman from Long Island, New York. After rising through the ranks as a corrections officer in several maximum-security prisons in the Midwest, he tapped into his entrepreneurial spirit starting his own successful business. Charlie is also co-founder of a non-profit organization focused on animal advocacy. Charlie speaks at various business and social awareness functions and has been featured in newspapers and magazines such as the *Omaha World Herald, East Village Times* and *Dogster Magazine*. Charlie has appeared on both radio and television including WPIX in New York and NETV in Nebraska. Charlie enjoys spending time with his family, which includes his seven rescued dogs. Any inquiries may be directed to charlie@thestarprojectinc.org.

Made in the USA
Monee, IL
14 January 2023

25301458R00167